Darwin and Facial Expression

DARWIN
and
FACIAL EXPRESSION

A CENTURY OF RESEARCH IN REVIEW

Edited by

PAUL EKMAN

Laboratory for the Study of Human
Interaction and Conflict
University of California, San Francisco
San Francisco, California

1973

ACADEMIC PRESS New York and London
A Subsidiary of Harcourt Brace Jovanovich, Publishers

ACADEMIC PRESS, INC.
111 Fifth Avenue, New York, New York 10003

United Kingdom Edition published by
ACADEMIC PRESS, INC. (LONDON) LTD.
24/28 Oval Road, London NW1

Library of Congress Cataloging in Publication Data

Ekman, Paul.
      Darwin and facial expression.

      Includes bibliographies.
      1.   Facial expression.   2.   Darwin, Charles
Robert, 1809-1882.   The expression of the emotions
in man and animals.   I.   Title. [DNLM: 1.   Behavior.
2.   Behavior, Animal.   3.   Emotions.   4.   Facial
expression.   5.   Nonverbal communication. BF511
E36d 1973]
BF531.E35 1973   152.4′2   72-12196
ISBN 0–12–236750–2

Contents

List of Contributors   vii

Preface   ix

Acknowledgments   xi

1. **Introduction**

    Paul Ekman   1

2. **Facial Expression of Emotion in Nonhuman Primates**

    Suzanne Chevalier-Skolnikoff   11

    Introduction   11
    Darwin's Findings   12
    The Current State of Knowledge on Facial Expressions in Nonhuman Primates   14
    The Nervous System: Its Evolution and Its Role in the Production of
      Facial Expression   50
    The Muscular Anatomy: The Evolution of Facial Muscles and Facial
      Expressions   58
    Conclusions   83
    References   83

3. **Facial Expressions of Infants and Children**

    William R. Charlesworth and Mary Anne Kreutzer   91

    Introduction   91
    Darwin's Contributions to Our Understanding of Infant and Children
      Expressions   93
    Darwin's Observations of Infants   95
    Darwin's Observations of Children   100
    Darwin's Conclusions   101
    Post-Darwinian Studies of Infants' Facial Expressions   102
    The Infant's Recognition of Expressions   119
    Concluding Remarks on Infant Expressions   124
    Post-Darwinian Studies of Children's Facial Expressions   126
    Remarks on Methodology and Substantive Gaps in Studying Children's
      Expressions   137

The Child's Recognition of Expressions   139
General Remarks on Recognition of Expression   146
Absence and Presence of Opportunities to Learn Facial Expressions   148
General Remarks on Absence and Presence of Opportunity   159
Conclusions   160
References   162

4.   Cross-Cultural Studies of Facial Expression

Paul Ekman   169

Introduction   169
Darwin's View and His Evidence on Universality   171
Theorists of the Culture-Specific View   174
How to Study Facial Expression across Cultures   187
The Evidence   191
Attempts to Prove the Culture-Specific Hypothesis   193
Attempts to Demonstrate Universality   204
Conclusion   218
References   220

5.   Darwin and the Representative Expression of Reality

Lewis Petrinovich   223

Natural Philosophy Prior to Darwin   224
Darwin's Writings   225
Darwin's Major Contributions   231
The Essential Breakthrough in "The Origin of Species"   233
Probabilistic Functionalism   242
Representative Design   245
Ethology   248
"The Expression of the Emotions"   251
References   254

6.   Conclusion   257
Paul Ekman

Epilogue   261
Paul Ekman

Author Index   265
Subject Index   271

List of Contributors

Numbers in parentheses indicate the pages on which authors' contributions begin.

William R. Charlesworth (91), Institute of Child Development, University of Minnesota, Minneapolis, Minnesota

Suzanne Chevalier-Skolnikoff (11), Langley Porter Neuropsychiatric Institute, University of California, San Francisco, California, and Department of Anthropology, Stanford University, Stanford, California.

Paul Ekman (169), Laboratory for the Study of Human Interaction and Conflict, University of California, San Francisco, California

Mary Anne Kreutzer (91), Institute of Child Development, University of Minnesota, Minneapolis, Minnesota

Lewis Petrinovich (223), Department of Psychology, University of California, Riverside, California

Preface

A century ago Charles Darwin published his work on *The Expression of the Emotions in Man and Animals,* thirteen years after his revolutionary *The Origin of Species* and one year after the *Descent of Man.* The book was a bestseller in its time. "On the day of publication 5267 copies were sold—a remarkable tribute to Darwin's reputation, to his skill in amassing and marshalling relevant facts, and to the book's extraordinary interest as the first serious attempt to apply evolutionary principles to the subject [Huxley, 1965, p. 102]." Darwin claimed that we cannot understand human emotional expression without understanding the emotional expressions of animals, for, he argued, our emotional expressions are in large part determined by our evolution. Not only are there similarities between man and certain other animals in the appearance of some emotional expressions, but the principles which explain why a particular emotional expression occurs with a particular emotion apply across species. To explain and support his theory, Darwin described emotional expressions in infants and children, in adults from various cultures, in the mentally ill, and in animals.

Darwin and Facial Expression celebrates the centennial of the publication of Darwin's work on emotional expression. Darwin's central concepts and key sources of information are reconsidered in light of the work of the last hundred years. There is a chapter each on animals (the nonhuman primates), on infants and children, and on people in various cultures. Each of these chapters gives Darwin's ideas on the topic and then presents a critical integration of current knowledge about facial expressions of emotion. It is a tribute to Darwin that each of these chapters concludes that many of Darwin's observations, and a large part of his theoretical explanations and forecasts, are substantiated by current knowledge.

These chapters consider emotional expressions in the face only, and not body movements, because most of Darwin's discussion was of the face, not the body, and his theory seems most applicable to the face (cf. Chapter 4, pages 180-181, 184-185). There is no chapter on facial expression in the mentally ill, although Darwin did consider this matter, because there has been no follow-up research.

A more general chapter describes Darwin's conceptual and methodological contributions, tracing his influence through the history of psychology. The concluding chapter integrates and summarizes how Darwin's ideas have fared in light of current knowledge about facial expression.

Consistent with the nature of Darwin's contribution, this centennial volume is intended to be relevant across disciplines, for persons interested in emotional expressions in psychology, anthropology, zoology, and ethology. For the book to be useful to those from such separate disciplines, it has been necessary to avoid or explain technical terms known only within one discipline. And, because not only the scientist but the layman as well was interested in Darwin's book on emotional expression when it was first published, our intention in preparing this book was that it be interesting and understandable to the layman and the college undergraduate, as well as to the scientist.

Paul Ekman

REFERENCES

Darwin, C. *The expression of the emotions in man and animals.* London: John Murray, 1872. (current ed.) Chicago: University of Chicago Press, 1965.

Darwin, C. *The origin of species.* (6th ed.) New York: The Modern Library, 1872.

Darwin, C. *The descent of man.* (2nd ed.) New York: D. Appleton, 1889.

Huxley, J., & Kettlewell, H. B. D. *Charles Darwin and his world.* New York: The Viking Press, 1965.

Acknowledgments

I am grateful to Wade Seaford, who first suggested the idea of celebrating the centennial of the publication of Darwin's *The Expression of the Emotions in Man and Animals.* I thank Silvan S. Tomkins for his encouragement in the planning of this book, and also for his encouragement and inspiration in my own research studies. I am grateful also to Patsy Garlan for her editorial help and criticisms, and to Nina Honbo for her help in compiling this book.

My work in preparing this book was supported by a Research Scientist Award, 5-K02-MH06092, and a research grant, MH 11976, both from the National Institute of Mental Health.

Paul Ekman

Introduction

Paul Ekman

University of California, San Francisco

It is paradoxical that 100 years should have elapsed between the publication of Darwin's book and a book such as this. Serious attention has not been focused previously upon the value of Darwin's work, *The Expression of the Emotions in Man and Animals.*[1] Never before has current knowledge on facial expression been drawn together to reveal the importance of Darwin's contribution, the accuracy of his observations, the pertinence today of the questions he raised, and the durability of much of his theory about emotional expression. The failure of Darwin's work on emotional expression to have the influence it so well deserved is paradoxical—and not because the value of his work is just apparent now. (After all, the history of science is filled with examples of men whose work was ignored in their time, only to be rediscovered later.) The paradox lies in the fact that Darwin was a famous scientist at the time he published *The Expression of the Emotions.* His work on evolution, which revolutionized thinking for scientist and layman alike, had been published 13 years earlier. Far from being ignored when it was published, the book on expression was a best seller. Also, the topic of emotional expression was not obscure, but intrinsically popular.

---

[1]Although the volume, *Expression of the Emotions in Man,* edited by P. H. Knapp (1963) paid tribute to Darwin's book on emotional expression in its title, it actually had little to do with either Darwin or facial expression. Only 3 out of 18 chapters made reference to Darwin, and only two chapters dealt with facial expression.

Yet this book had little influence on the scientific community over the following 90 years.

The lack of influence is easily shown. In his recent excellent appraisal of all of Darwin's work, Ghiselin (1969) commented:

> That *The Expression of the Emotions* has not been well understood is clear from the fact that it was a historical dead end. Nobody took up the train of reasoning and developed it, although the work was widely read, and although it did become an element in various controversies . . . there is little evidence that the real merits of the work have come to be appreciated [pp.187–188].

In this book, Charlesworth and Kreutzer point out in ''Facial Expressions of Infants and Children'' (Chapter 3) that less than a third of the studies they reviewed indicated that the author was directly or indirectly influenced by Darwin. Chevalier–Skolnikoff, in ''Facial Expressions of Emotion in Nonhuman Primates'' (Chapter 2), indicates that, there was no progress in the study of facial expression of primates from Darwin's time until the 1960s. In the work I reviewed in ''Cross–Cultural Studies of Facial Expression'' (Chapter 4), the majority of the systematic studies of facial expression showed little influence from Darwin.

Five issues are relevant in explaining why *The Expression of the Emotions* had so little influence. Ghiselin (1969) suggested, ''One reason why Darwin's psychology has not been understood is his tendency to express himself in anthropomorphic terms [p.188].'' Darwin did not hesitate to use terms based on man's experience in describing the behavior of animals. He said, for example,

> Dogs also exhibit their *affection* by *desiring* to rub against their masters . . . I have also seen dogs licking cats with whom they were *friends*. This habit probably originated in the females carefully licking their puppies—the dearest object of their *love*—for the sake of cleansing them [1965, p. 118; Italics added].[2]

In discussing Darwin's anthropomorphism, Petrinovich (Chapter 5 of this book) agrees with Ghiselin's interpretation that this was partly a stylistic device that Darwin used to communicate more readily with his reader. Partly, also, Darwin's anthropomorphism may be interpreted as an outgrowth of his belief in the continuity of the species. If man has evolved from animals, many of the phenomena observable in man must exist in at least some animals as well—hence some justification for talking about emotion in animals. While Darwin's belief in the continuity of the species may have led to his anthropomorphism,for which he was condemned by some, his theory on the continuity of the species was responsible for the development of

---

[2]All of the page references for our quotations from Darwin's *The Expression of the Emotions in Man and Animals* are from the 1965 University of Chicago Press edition.

animal and comparative psychology.[3] It is only if the species are continuous and man not wholly different from other animals that it makes sense to have a *psychology* of animal behavior, for psychologists to compare species, and for such studies to be relevant to a psychology of man.

Chevalier-Skolnikoff (Chapter 2, p. 8) points out that contemporary scientists studying animal behavior object to characterizing animals as having emotions. The use of such terms is said to interfere with the real need for careful description of animal *behavior* itself. Such scientific work, conducted free of anthropomorphic terms by those who would or do condemn Darwin for anthropomorphism, has led to findings which in a sense vindicate Darwin. Rather than finding that nonhuman primates do not engage in behavior which can be characterized as emotional, the evidence now shows that Darwin's use of anthropomorphic terms may have been a correct forecast. In reviewing the evidence, Chevalier-Skolnikoff says

> Through the examination of behavioral sequences and the interpretation of how the behavior functions, primatologists are fairly confident that the interpretation of the emotional nature of facial behavior in nonhuman primates is correct. . . (Chapter 2, p. 23].

The second reason for the lack of influence of Darwin's book was his reliance on anecdotal rather than systematic data. While the rationale and legitimacy of Darwin's anthropomorphism is subject to some dispute, at least in light of evidence now current, there is little question about the fallibility of anecdotal information. It is dubious data for various reasons: The amount of behavior observed is typically small; it is often reported without contextual information; the observer has no check against his own biases; and usually description and interpretation are mixed without distinction. Chevalier-Skolnikoff (pp. 15–20) contrasts Darwin's use of anecdotes with the systematically gathered information about behavior in current studies of nonhuman primates. Petrinovich (p. 236) explains how animal psychologists rejected the anecdotal method in favor of laboratory studies, where systematic observation and experimental manipulation was possible.

Darwin was aware of the problems inherent in anecdotal data (cf. my discussion of this in connection with his cross-cultural studies, Chapter 4, (pp.172–173). For example, he placed more confidence in a report if it described the full context in which the behavior occurred. But Darwin was limited primarily to information gathered by others, since he was confined by illness to his own home for most of the last 42 years of his life—the period during which he wrote all of his major works. It is interesting to note that

---

[3]Boring, 1950, and Petrinovich, Chapter 5 of this book, give Darwin credit for the development of these fields.

the one source of information which he was able to gather himself, observations on children by diaries he kept of his own children's behavior, has been almost completely substaniated in later work (Charlesworth & Kreutzer, Chapter 3).

While he often dealt with faulty data, Darwin's great strength was in using so many different sources of data, in testing his theory by its ability to explain widely divergent phenomena. Few scientists concerned with emotional expression since Darwin have similarly evaluated their theories by obtaining information about the behavior of children, animals, members of different cultures, the mentally ill, and the blind.

The third reason why Darwin's work on emotional expression had so little influence was his emphasis on the innate basis of at least some emotional expressions. As both Chevalier-Skolnikoff and Charlesworth and Kreutzer point out, while Darwin allowed that learning influences facial expression, his emphasis was on the innate basis, and it was mostly about this that he wrote. Darwin did not systematically explain the ways in which learning influences facial expression and the complex interplay between learning and innate factors.

Darwin's emphasis upon innate determinants is probably the most crucial reason for the rejection of his work, at least by psychologists. Petrinovich (p. 240) explains how in 1914 Watson, the founder of behaviorism, rejected the notion that inheritance played any part in variations in behavioral characteristics across individuals and attributed these solely to environmental effects. Watson claimed that to understand man, to understand why one man differs from another, we need only consider what is learned; and that this is the only proper focus for psychology. Behaviorism ruled the day; genetic and other biological determinants of behavior were not the subject of much experimentation or theory. Instead, learning, and then also perception and cognition, became central topics for research in psychology. The popularity of the behaviorist view was due in part to the power of the questions asked and the methodologies offered to generate replicable research. In part, the popularity of Watson's view may reflect the fact that it was harmonious with the democratic *Zeitgeist*—the hope that all men could be made equal if their environments were equally benevolent. On this point Chiselin (1969) commented,

> Watson flatly rejected the idea that inheritance plays any role in determining behavior patterns, evidently because of his cultural predisposition toward human equality. Although it is easy to sympathize with such democratic zeal, its concealment of the truth has not been without its deleterious effects. . . . Rejecting inheritance for metaphysical reasons served only to hinder the progress of psychology. And it is sobering to observe that democratic societies are every bit as prone to the kind of dogmatism that caused the Soviet Union to reject Mendelian inheritance and

to embrace Lysenkoism because the latter, like the Watsonian notion, fitted in better with the prevailing creed [pp.191–192].

Even a behavioristic view as orthodox as Watson's need not have required abandoning the notion that there is a genetic basis for facial expression, but only an emphasis on the influence of learning—that in various ways learning modifies built-in, genetically determined emotional expressions. But matters did not rest at that. Instead, the pendulum swung away from Darwin to the opposite pole. The popularity of cultural relativism, combined perhaps with the influence of behaviorism, led anthropologists concerned with emotional expression to claim that there was no innate contribution to facial expression, that there are no constants across cultures in any aspect of human facial expression. (See my discussion of LaBarre and Birdwhistell, Chapter 4, p. 179–187.)

An index of just how far the pendulum did swing is that much of the work of the last 10 years has taken as its aim the reestablishment of the proposition that there are some universal facial expressions, and that this is due to *some* innate or genetic contribution to facial expression. This is the conclusion of each of the authors who review a body of research evidence in this book: on animals (Chevalier-Skolnikoff, Chapter 2); on infants and children (Charlesworth & Kreutzer, Chapter 3); and on members of different cultures (Ekman, Chapter 4). Each author maintains that only certain aspects of facial expression are genetically determined and argues for the influence of nongenetic determinants as well. The authors agree that there is a major genetic contribution in the morphology of facial expression—the particular patterns of facial muscular movement associated with particular emotions.

The fourth reason why Darwin's book had little influence was his adoption of Lamarck's theory that learned characteristics could be inherited. Chevalier-Skolnikoff (Chapter 2) discusses this matter, explaining how Darwin also used his principle of natural selection to account for the evolution of emotional expressions. This principle, which has stood the test of time, was rejected in Darwin's day, while the alternative mechanism proposed by Lamarck and accepted in Darwin's day is now disproved. Darwin's placing greater emphasis on Lamarck's theory than on his own principle of natural selection is really not intrinsic to the theory he propounds. While he did claim that expressions learned by an animal later become inherited, the evolution of facial expressions does not require such Lamarckian reasoning. Darwin also provided natural selection as the basis for the evolution of emotional expression: "Animals who had a genetically based tendency to substitute facial displays (e.g., threats) for more dangerous actions (e.g., fighting) probably had a higher survival ratio, thus passing this propensity on to their descendants (Chevalier-Skolnikoff, Chapter 2, page 32)." Ghiselin (1969) commented on this issue, "Those who criticize *The Expression of the Emotions* on the grounds that it presupposes inherited habit overlook the fact that Darwin invokes natural selection as a more effective mechanism [p. 209]."

The last reason we will consider for the book's failure to achieve the influence it deserved is Darwin's adherence to the deductive method, which lessened his impact on those who now work mostly in his tradition. Petrinovich (Chapter 5) points out that the "most direct line of Darwinian influence on the study of complex behavior has been through the branch of Zoology called ethology." According to Petrinovich, ethologists believe it is necessary to observe carefully the behavior of the organism in its natural environment, and they emphasize the instinctive bases of behavior. "The approach of the ethologists is toward the molar, functional, and dynamic view which characterizes Darwinism . . . (Petrinovich, Chapter 5)." While most ethologists make reference to Darwin, they do not give his work on emotional expression very great emphasis. Ghiselin (1969) explains this as follows:

> Turning to the ethologists, or zoologically oriented students of animal behavior, one has little difficulty in seeing why they have failed to give Darwin the credit he deserves. Instead of going back to fundamentals, as did the founder of the science, and constructing theoretical models to be tested by means of the hypothetico-deductive approach, they have largely relied on more primitive forms of induction. What theoretical systems they have elaborated contain little reference to evolutionary theory. In conformity with the European tradition, they have tended to employ the sort of typological comparison that still prevails among many morphologists. They have simply gathered facts, put similar behavior patterns together, and superimposed a historical rationalization. Thus Lorenz states: "It is an inviolable law of inductive natural science that it has to *begin* with pure observation, totally devoid of any preconceived theory and even working hypothesis." A more pernicious fallacy could scarcely be enunciated. Darwin, in all of his work, including that on behavior, proceeded with a diametrically opposite methodological assumption. Small wonder that he has not received the recognition he deserves [p. 212].

Petrinovich, in his appraisal of Darwin, emphasizes his use of the deductive method as one of his most important contributions. He provides several telling quotes from Darwin on his manner of approaching phenomena, such as "No one could be a good observer unless he was an active theorizer."

Let us now discuss the sources of information Darwin used to "ascertain, independently of common opinion, how far particular movements of the features and gestures are really expressive of certain states of the mind . . . [1965, p. 13]." A major source was the "expression of the several passions in some of the commoner animals . . . [1965, p. 17]." He said this was of paramount importance for determining the generality of his explanations of the origin of emotional expressions. Chevalier-Skolnikoff, in Chapter 2, summarizes Darwin's findings, then presents a comprehensive account of the current state of knowledge on facial expression in nonhuman primates. She reports research on the description of facial expression, on the function of facial expression, and on the various determinants of facial expression. Her chapter makes two crucially important additional contributions to our knowledge about facial expression. Chevalier-Skolnikoff discusses at some length, and in considerable detail, how the evolution of the nervous system is related to the variations in facial expressions across different species. She explains how differences in the brain may be responsible for human facial expressions being more subject to voluntary or habitual control than are those of other animals. She shows how similarities in other parts of the brain may be responsible for the similarities in facial expression across species as well as for the universality of facial expression in human beings. Chevalier-Skolnikoff also provides a thorough, detailed, discussion of the evolution of the facial musculature. She points out that among Darwin's major contributions to the study of facial expression were his emphasis on the facial musculature as a determinant of expression and his understanding of the intimate relationship between form and function. Her explanation of the evolution of the facial musculature and the differences across species is thus within Darwin's tradition, and expands our knowledge of how facial expression in different species is related to differences in musculature.

Darwin's second source was infants and children, whom he observed because he felt they showed emotions with extraordinary force. In Chapter 3, Charlesworth and Kreutzer recapitulate Darwin's findings on infants, then critically review research since Darwin on facial expressions in infants and children. They consider specific behaviors such as crying, smiling and laughing, and more global emotional states such as surprise, fear and anger. Charlesworth and Kreutzer also present an important survey of studies on wild or feral children, institutionalized children and blind children, which they interpret with regard to the issue of whether there is an innate contribution to facial expressions of emotion. Finally, their chapter provides a thorough discussion of the methodological problems encountered in studying facial expression in infants and children, and draws attention to many questions that have not yet been systematically addressed.

A third source of information for Darwin was the facial behavior of persons in differing cultures. He wished ''to ascertain whether the same expressions and gestures prevail, as has often been asserted without much evidence, with all the races of mankind, especially with those who have associated but little with Europeans [1965, p. 15].'' Darwin considered this information important, because he held that if the same expressions signified the same emotions across various cultures, we could infer that they were innate. In Chapter 4, I have reviewed Darwin's methods of studying facial expression across cultures and his reasoning about the innate basis for any universals that may be discovered. The views of the three major theorists who have contested Darwin's theory and findings—LaBarre, Klineberg, and Birdwhistell—are critically evaluated. In this part of the chapter, two theoretical issues are introduced that are crucial to interpreting the contradictory impressions obtained by observers of emotion expression. Distinctions between facial expressions of emotion, facial simulations of emotion, and facial gestures (or *emblems*), are elaborated. The concept of *display rules* is introduced to explain socially learned, culturally variable rules regarding the control and management of facial expressions. Critical analysis is made of all the systematic, quantitative experiments intended to prove that facial expressions are culture specific, and ways are discussed for avoiding methodological pitfalls. Finally, all of the evidence supporting universal facial expressions is reported and integrated, including new evidence not previously published.

Another source of information for Darwin was the mentally ill, whom he thought should be studied "as they are liable to the strongest passions, and give uncontrolled vent to them [1965, p.13]." There is no chapter on this topic, because, strangely, there has not been any systematic follow-up in this area of research. While there is little reason to doubt Darwin's view that the facial expressions of the mentally ill would be fruitful to study, almost no one has done so. How the mentally ill interpret facial expressions has been studied, but this is not relevant here. Our own laboratory is now studying facial expressions in depressed psychiatric patients, but unfortunately that information is not ready for publication.

Darwin mentions another source of information—painting and sculpture—which he was disappointed to find was not of much use to him. He thought this was because "in works of art, beauty is the chief object; and strongly contracted facial muscles destroy beauty [1965, p.14]." Gombrich (1972), who has been concerned with the study of action and expression in Western art, writes that no one has studied the history of facial expression in art. Certainly if Darwin were alive today, the very reasoning which suggested the possible utility of art and sculpture might cause him to look at photographs and motion picture film. To my knowledge there has been no thorough study of facial expressions of emotions shown in the cinema of different nations, or in commercial or amateur still photographs, or in family albums, although such a study might be interesting and relevant.

The last source Darwin discussed was a series of photographs supplied to him by the French anatomist Duchenne (1862), who electrically stimulated the facial muscles of a man whose skin was not sensitive. Darwin showed these photographs to people and asked them what the man was feeling.

Darwin used these data to verify some of his thinking about the emotional meaning of particular facial muscular contractions. While no one else, to my knowledge, has electrically stimulated the face to obtain pictures of facial expression, the use of observers' judgments of the emotion shown in facial photographs has been widely used and is discussed in Chapter 4.

While Darwin did not list studies of blind children as a separate source of information in his introduction, he did describe such studies later in his book and cited their importance, because the blind have no opportunity to learn facial expression visually. As mentioned earlier, Charlesworth and Kreutzer review this topic in their chapter, also considering feral and institutionalized children who may similarly lack all of the visual stimulation available to the normal sighted child.

In closing this introduction, I might mention that Darwin closed his introduction by presenting what was then known about the anatomy of human facial musculature. He continually referred to this description in later chapters when he proposed the muscular movements that depicted each of the emotions. Since Darwin, there has been little interest until recently in further description of facial musculature from the point of view of its relationship to expression. Huber's work (1931) and the recent work of the Swedish anatomist Hjortsjö (1970) are exceptions. In recent years there has been a bit more interest in describing in a systematic way the muscular movements that are associated with each of the emotions. Building largely on the work of Duchenne, one of Darwin's sources, and on the work of Darwin himself, Tomkins, Friesen, and I have developed a systematic procedure for measuring and classifying the movements of the facial musculature and determining which emotion is being shown on the face (Ekman, Friesen, & Tomkins, 1971; Ekman, 1972). A few other authors have developed somewhat similar methods for describing the movements of the face (Blurton Jones, 1972; Grant, 1969; Leventhal & Sharp, 1965), but they have not attempted to link their descriptions to emotions.[3]

REFERENCES

Birdwhistell, R. L. The kinesic level in the investigation of emotions. In P. H. Knapp (Ed.), *Expression of the emotions in man.* New York: International Universities Press, 1963.
Birdwhistell, R. L. *Kinesics and content.* Philadelphia: Univ. of Pennsylvania Press, 1970.
Blurton Jones, N. G. Criteria used in describing facial expressions. In N. G. Blurton Jones (Ed.), *Ethological studies of child behavior.* London: Cambridge Univ. Press, 1972.
Boring, E. G. *A history of experimental psychology.* New York: Appleton 1950.

[3]See Ekman, Friesen, and Ellsworth (1972, Chap. 16) for a discussion of these various ways of measuring facial behavior.

Darwin, C. *The expression of the emotions in man and animals.* London: John Murray, 1872. Reprinted Chicago: Univ. of Chicago Press, 1965.

Duchenne, B. *Mécanisme de la physionomie humaine ou analyse electrophysiologique de l'expression des passions.* Paris: Baillière, 1862.

Ekman, P. Universals and cultural differences in facial expressions of emotion. In J. Cole (Ed.), *Nebraska symposium on motivation, 1971.* Lincoln, Nebraska: Univ. of Nebraska Press, 1972.

Ekman, P., Friesen, W. V., & Tomkins, S. S. Facial Affect Scoring Technique: A first validity study. *Semiotica,* 1971, **3**(1), 37–58.

Ghiselin, M. T. *The triumph of the Darwinian method.* Berkeley: Univ. of California Press, 1969.

Gombrich, E. H. Action and expression in Western art. In R. A. Hinde (Ed.), *Nonverbal communication.* London: Cambridge Univ. Press, 1972.

Grant, N. G. Human facial expression. *Man,* 1969, **4,** 525–536.

Hjortsjö, C. H. *Man's face and mimic language.* Lund, Sweden: Studentlitteratur, 1970.

Huber, E. *Evolution of facial musculature and facial expression.* Baltimore: Johns Hopkins Univ. Press, 1931.

Knapp, P. H. (Ed.), *Expression of the emotions in man.* New York: International Universities Press, 1963.

LaBarre, W. The cultural basis of emotions and gestures. *Journal of Personality,* 1947, **16,** 49–68.

Leventhal, H., & Sharp, E. Facial expressions as indicators of distress. In S. S. Tomkins & C. E. Izard (Eds.), *Affect, cognition and personality, empirical studies.* New York: Springer, 1965.

2

Facial Expression of Emotion in Nonhuman Primates

Suzanne Chevalier-Skolnikoff
University of California, San Francisco
Stanford University

INTRODUCTION

What are the origins of expressive movements in man? Have his facial expressions evolved from those of his animal ancestors? Are expressions innate or are they learned? What are the purposes or functions of facial expressions? To what extent are particular movements of the features expressive of certain states of the mind? Can the emotions being experienced be recognized from the expressions displayed? These are the kinds of questions asked about facial expression by Charles Darwin in 1872 in his publication, *The Expression of the Emotions in Man and Animals.*

In his treatise on the expression of emotion, Charles Darwin examined the facial expression of animals, and particularly the primates,[1] in order to discover the origins of expressive movements in man. He chose this comparative approach because of his belief in the principle of evolution. Assuming an evolutionary origin of man, it logically followed that man's closest living relatives, the primates, might actually be quite similar to man's ancestors, and could provide clues to the origins and development of human facial behavior. In an attempt to discover how human expressions evolved, Darwin investigated the nature, functions and origins of primate facial expressions. In his work, he collected and organized practically all of the available evidence, including comparative descriptions from direct observations of animals, as well as anatomical, neurological and physiological evidence.

[1]Throughout this paper, the term "primates" refers to the nonhuman primates.

From Darwin's time until the late 1920s there was virtually no progress in the study of the facial expressions of primates. The initiation of field and zoo studies by Sir Solly Zuckerman, the British zoologist and statesman, in 1929 and 1934, and by the American psychologist C. Ray Carpenter in 1934 considerably advanced the field of primate behavior for the first time since Darwin, though there was little emphasis on facial expression. The period between the late 1930s and late 1950s represents another hiatus in primate studies. In the late 1950s, with the field studies of Stuart Altmann in 1956 on rhesus monkeys, and Sherwood L. Washburn and Irven DeVore and Ronald Hall in 1958 on baboons, a new era of investigation in the behavior of nonhuman primates began. Recent studies focusing specifically on facial expression began in 1962 with Robert Hinde and Thelma Rowell's investigation of a colony of captive rhesus monkeys. Since then, the field of study has accelerated rapidly, and at present there are conservatively estimating, more than 600 publications relevant to communication in nonhuman primates, and well over twice that many concerned with primate social behavior in general. Altmann's 1968 article is the most extensive bibliographical review of communication in nonhuman primates.

Darwin's work of 1872 still provides the point of departure for research on facial expression in nonhuman primates. However, today, 100 years later, a great deal of additional supportive and occasionally conflicting evidence is available to answer Darwin's questions, and we find that some of his questions must be rephrased.

DARWIN'S FINDINGS

The findings presented by Darwin on facial expression in primates can best be examined under three categories:[2] (1) descriptive, i.e., what the expressions look like; (2) functional, the utility of the expressions to the animals; and (3) causal, the determinants and origins of the expressions.

Descriptions

Darwin's descriptions were based on his own observations, as well as on descriptions from the literature and from other observers, particularly zookeepers. Since not all expressions of every species considered were systematically compared, his descriptions represent a miscellaneous collection of data. The facial musculature was often considered in the description. Darwin noted that there is considerable variability in the expression of emotion in the different species and genera of nonhuman primates. His

---

[2] See Nissen, 1958, for a discussion on how to classify behavior.

principle descriptive finding was that some expressions made by nonhuman primates are similar to those of man.

Functions

Darwin investigated the functions of facial expressions both in terms of the general utility of expression in the life of the animals, and in terms of the functions of particular expressions in particular species.

He concluded that in animals, as in man, facial expressions communicate how the animal feels. Darwin considered the expression of emotions essential to the welfare of group-living species, for through facial expressions and vocalizations, animals are attracted to one another, stay together, reproduce, and regulate social interactions. This conclusion was an important one in 1872, for it contradicted the accepted theory of the time, viz., that since men and animals were qualitatively distinct, the former being divinely endowed with a soul and with reason and the latter only with instincts, man alone could, by volition, express such emotions as love or affection.

With respect to particular expressions, Darwin deduced that certain expressions are associated with particular affect, or feeling, states. These are the states of pleasure, joy or affection; pain; anger; and astonishment or terror. This conclusion was based primarily on Darwin's observations of the interactions of captive animals with their keepers.

Causes or Determinants

After an inductive investigation in which he appraised almost all the available data, Darwin concluded that the determinants of most emotive expressions can be understood in terms of three principles: (a) the principle of serviceable associated habits, (b) the principle of antithesis, and (c) the principle of the direct action of the nervous system.

The first principle is that *consciously* performed behaviors, originally necessary to survival (such as fleeing from or attacking an enemy), become *unconsciously* associated with certain states of the mind (e.g., fear or anger), and through "habit" come to be unconsciously performed when these states of mind are aroused, even if the original action (e.g., fleeing or attacking) is unnecessary (as when a male monkey, approaching a female to copulate, feels fearful and makes a fear expression). Darwin elaborated on the mechanism whereby this might have occurred, and pointed out that habit or practice is important to the development of many behaviors in man. He attributed this to the theory expounded by his contemporaries that nervous routes become more efficient with use due to changes that use produces in the nerve cells. These changes in the nerve cells are then inherited, and in this way acquired habits become inherited. Darwin called these inherited acquired habits, or innate tendencies to perform particular actions, "instincts." He noted that some practice is often necessary before an individual can carry out an instinctive behavior effectively, despite its innate basis.

The second principle is that under opposite states of mind (e.g., fear rather than anger) actions opposite in form will be performed involuntarily (e.g., cringing from rather than lunging toward). As in the case of serviceable associated habits, the mechanism for the development of these behaviors is association through habit, and subsequent inheritance.

The third principle is that the excited nervous system acts directly and involuntarily upon the body. Thus a stimulus (e.g., one monkey hitting another monkey on the hand) generates a nerve force that in turn becomes transmitted in certain particular directions, depending on the connection of the nerve cells and upon habit, and thus produces particular bodily reactions (e.g., withdrawal of the hand, fear expression on the face, cringing away of the whole body, as well as the "glandular" reactions of urination and defecation).

Darwin speculated that these three mechanisms work together in determining expressions of emotion, and that it is not generally possible to tell to what extent each mechanism contributes to producing a particular behavior.

THE CURRENT STATE OF KNOWLEDGE ON FACIAL EXPRESSIONS IN NONHUMAN PRIMATES

Descriptions

Recent descriptions are generally consistent with Darwin's descriptions of facial expressions in monkeys and apes. However, as a result of more rigorous observation procedures and new methodological techniques, contemporary descriptions are more detailed than were Darwin's and have eliminated earlier inaccuracies. This refinement in descriptive technique is essentially the natural consequence of further research.

Though Darwin himself was working toward objective data collection, and though he had commented in his introduction on the inaccuracy of memory and the unreliability of anecdotal material, many of his actual descriptions were second hand[3] and anecdotal. Despite his effort to validate the reliability of his sources, some appear to have been more reliable than others. For example, Dr. Duchenne, a contemporary of Darwin's who inves-

---

[3]This lack of first-hand observations was due, at least in part, to Darwin's ill health, which began to plague him around 1840 and eventually rendered him essentially an invalid. He was forced to lead a reclusive life, and was only able to work 4 hours a day [Ghiselin, 1969].

tigated the anatomy and physiology of the human face by electrical stimulation, surely should have been a reliable source. An anonymous woman who sold a macaque monkey to the Zoological Society, and Mr. Sutton, the zookeeper, were evidently poorer informants. Both report that this macaque wept copiously when grieved, a highly unlikely occurrence since there has been no evidence of weeping in monkeys reported in any of the recent primate literature.

A new methodological approach for the study of animal behavior was developed between the 1930s and 1950s.[4] The aims of this new approach were to eliminate errors and to objectify data collection. The procedures incorporated the following guidelines:

(a) An unbiased approach free from anthropocentric preconceptions.

It is ironic that though Darwin's contribution to the study of facial expressions was in great part due to his anthropomorphic[5] approach, recent prog- in the field is due chiefly to the elimination of the anthropocentric bias! The reason for this seeming inconsistency is that an anthropocentric viewpoint can be of great value in *formulating questions,* particularly about such animals as the monkeys and apes, which are closely related to man and share much of man's biology and psychology, but it must be avoided in attempting to *answer questions.* Darwin's great contribution was that he formulated many of the key questions about facial expression and emotion; present-day investigators are still primarily trying to answer Darwin's questions (Ghiselin, 1969).

(b) Rigorous appraisal of second-hand data, with the elimination of anecdotal reports by unreliable and untrained observers.

(c) Description of behavior in objective terms (for example, the term "bared-teeth" is preferable to "smile" or "grin" in describing a particular expression).

(d) Immediate or simultaneous data collection, since, as Darwin noted, the recording of past events is often inaccurate.

(e) Preliminary studies which are inductive, with observation leading to the formulation of hypotheses.

This approach is generally followed by the ethologists and anthropologists, but is not universally accepted by all scientists. For example, the psychologists who study animal behavior generally follow a deductive approach, starting with hypotheses and designing experiments to prove or disprove them.

[4]See, for example, Carpenter (1934); Darling (1937); Schnierla 1950); Marler (1961, 1965); and Marler and Hamilton (1968), for discussions on methods.

[5]Ghiselin (1969) points out that the initial anthropomorphic impression that one has from reading Darwin is in great part due to Darwin's choice of words for literary effect, rather than to basic anthropomorphic interpretations.

The deductive approach has certainly met with some success. However, preliminary inductive observations give the investigator an opportunity to become familiar with the general behavior of the animals he is studying, thereby providing him with a background for making more probable hypotheses and for correctly interpreting his experimental results.

(f) Initial studies which attempt only to *describe* the behavior.
(g) Observation of animals under natural conditions where the adaptive functions of their behavior can be understood.
(h) Subsequent studies in the laboratory where more detailed observations can be recorded and hypotheses tested by experimentation.
(i) Focus of these later studies on the functions and causes of the behaviors already described.

Because investigators have incorporated these methods into their research, most of the work since the mid-1930s has yielded consistent descriptive data. In addition, these methods have facilitated the collection of systematic data suitable for comparative studies. However, a number of new, possibly unsolvable problems have emerged. As Schnierla (1950) has pointed out, the behavior of animals is so complex that one can never record and describe everything that even a single animal does, much less everything that occurs during an interaction involving several animals. For example, during a 6-second interaction recorded on film in a study on communication in *Macaca speciosa*—recently renamed *M. arctoides* (Chevalier-Skolnikoff, 1971, in press)—the following sequence was observed:

> Stanford, 4/16/68, about 2 P.M. *(description from notes and film).*
> "Mom," the most subordinate adult female in the group is sitting next to "Gar," the dominant male, "Girl," a subadult female, and "Boy," a subadult male. Mom looks about (nervously) as the dominant male forcefully restrains and grooms her five-week-old infant. She looks directly at Girl, the most subordinate animal in the vicinity, but Girl is looking the other way and does not receive the look. Mom shoves her nose directly into Girl's face, but Girl ignores her and continues to look the other way. Mom retrieves her infant and again looks directly at Girl, grasps her chin, and turns her face. As Mom starts to deliver an open-mouthed stare toward Girl (redirected aggression directed toward the most subordinate animal present), Girl with head oriented toward Mom again averts her gaze and avoids receiving the threat. Mom nips Girl on the shoulder, and Girl draws away. Boy (who often supports Girl in dominance interactions) has been sitting behind Mom and now nips Mom on the head. Girl (now supported by Boy) turns toward Mom with an open-mouthed stare, and both animals rush at each other with attack faces. Just as the two animals are about to make contact, Mom leaps back and off the shelf with a shriek.

This description is actually very sketchy, but it does show how complex an interaction often is. The interaction involved the behavior of five animals. Communicative behavior occurred in three sensory modes: tactile, visual and vocal. Visual behavior included eye behavior (direct looks, avoidance), facial expressions, and body postures. Particular clusters of behavior occurred simultaneously. For example, the "attack faces" included such simultaneous behavior as staring eyes, open mouths, ears flicking forward, hair erected over the neck and shoulders, forward body posture and movement, and lifting of one arm, as if getting ready to slap. Furthermore, the behavior followed a particular *sequential* integration as well, the animals adjusting their behavior to each other as the sequence progressed; e.g., Mom would not have reached out to turn Girl's face if Girl had initially looked at her and received her threat. Because of the impossibility of recording everything, data recording must be selective. Such selection results in an interpretative rather than a completely objective record. This is even the case with film or videotape records, since the choice of when to film is itself selective. Furthermore, the total context, which includes smells and activities occurring on the hidden side of the animal, is often missed in a film record.

Another problem has emerged in the attempt to define and identify a behavioral unit. Since the behavior of an animal is an ongoing process, it is often difficult to tell whether a bit of behavior is one unit or "act" or a series of acts. Altmann (1965) has suggested that the problem can be objectively solved by breaking behavior up into functional units, separating acts as the animals do, judging from the reactions of animals of the same species in social groups. However, much behavior, including facial expression, occurs as a continuum with gradual transitions from one expression to another, making it impossible to make objective divisions. Some investigators consider behavioral units to be long, functional sequences, such as a "fight" (Bertrand, 1969), while others divide behavioral sequences into short units that are components of the long sequences, such as "bite," "hit," etc. (Altmann, 1962).

Extensive and vehement conflicts have arisen over what constitutes a "unit" of behavior. Miller, Galanter, and Pribram (1960) suggest that, in terms of its neurological mediation, behavior is organized hierarchically into large molar units which are made up of a number of smaller molecular units. For example, if one monkey is attacked by another monkey, the attacked animal's escape response may, on the molecular level, involve a series of reflexes that are organized on the higher, molar level as an escape-run away from the aggressor. Since the reflexes and the well-organized escape are both involved in the response, one cannot argue that one level of description would be "better" or more accurate than the other. On the contrary, the complete description must include all levels. The hierarchical organization of the nervous system and its relationship to behavior will be elaborated later in this chapter.

Apart from the development of methods for collecting accurate data, there was little advance in descriptive studies of facial expression in nonhuman primates from 1872 until the early 1960s, and, in fact, with the possible exception of Koht's 1935 study on the chimpanzee, Darwin's work continued to be the most extensive work on the subject. In 1962, investigations were published reporting the systematic development of "ethograms," or catalogues of behavior in rhesus macaques (Altmann, 1962; Hinde & Rowell, 1962; Rowell & Hinde, 1962) and in baboons (DeVore, 1962). This systematic approach was the first significant advance over Darwin's study of 1872.

Since the 1960s, a number of investigators (van Hooff, 1962, 1967, 1971; Shirek-Ellefson, 1967; Chevalier-Skolnikoff, 1971, in press) have gathered much more detailed descriptions of facial behavior than those of previous studies through the development and use of behavioral checklists. Each facial expression consists of what van Hooff (1962) calls "expressive elements." Expressive elements are anatomical features (such as the ears, eyes, or mouth) in a particular position (i.e., forward, wide open, closed). The use of checklists of facial elements to describe facial expressions, such as van Hooff's (1967), facilitates systematic collection and comparison of data. Furthermore, the recent development of frame-by-frame analysis of motion-picture film and videotape (employed by van Hooff, 1967, and Chevalier-Skolnikoff, 1971, in press) has also augmented the accuracy and detail of descriptions of facial expressions, particularly when they involve movement. To permit comparison, descriptions of the same facial expression by Darwin (1872) and van Hooff (1967) are presented below.

From Darwin, 1872

Expression of *Cynopithecus niger* or Celebes macaque (now generally called *Macaca niger*) "when they are pleased by being caressed." (See Figure 1.)

> ... the *Cynopithecus niger* draw back their ears and utter a slight jabbering noise ... With the cynopithecus, the corners of the mouth are at the same time drawn backwards and upwards so that the teeth are exposed ... The crest of long hairs on the forehead is depressed, and apparently the whole skin of the head drawn backwards. The eyebrows are thus raised a little, and the eyes assume a staring appearance. The lower eyelids also become slightly wrinkled; but this wrinkling is not conspicuous, owing to the permanent transverse furrows on the face [p.133].

From van Hooff, 1967

A summary description based primarily on observations of a number of Old World monkey species, "the teeth-chattering face."

> [The expression] is ... characterized by a rapid opening and closing of the mouth ... The teeth meet when the mouth is fully closed. The lips, on the other hand, do not meet, since they are fully vertically retracted.

The expression elements:

The eyelids may be fully apart or in the normal position.
The eyebrows and the upper head skin may be retracted.
The ears may be retracted as well.
The mouth is opening and closing rapidly and the teeth chatter audibly.
The mouth corners are retracted.
The lips are vertically retracted, thus baring the teeth.
The body posture may contain backward as well as forward tendencies. It may
  be slightly hunched or the broad side of the body may be presented [pp. 41–42].

(a)   (b)

FIG. 1. Facial expressions in *Cynopithecus niger* (from Darwin, 1872). (a) *Cynopithecus niger* in a placid condition. (b) *Cynopithecus niger*, when pleased by being caressed.

One can see that while Darwin's description was accurate and detailed (and also had greater literary merit), a description written in terms of expressive elements is more useful for comparative studies.

Though the face[6] has been considered to assume the most important role

---

[6]Miller and his colleagues have shown in a series of experiments that the face does transmit information. They have noted that the eyes appear to play a particularly prominent role in this transmission. In a series of experiments using a "cooperative conditioning" method that they developed, monkeys were taught, or conditioned, to avoid a particular auditory stimulus by pressing a lever that would turn the sound off. If the monkeys failed to press the lever, they received a shock. The trained animals were then tested in pairs in a situation in which one animal heard the sound stimulus but had no lever to press, while the second animal could not hear the sound stimulus but could see a videotape of the face of the first monkey and did have a lever to press. If the second animal could receive some cue from the first animal that the auditory stimulus was on and pressed the lever accordingly, both animals avoided receiving a shock. The animals learned to avoid the shock 89% of the time. Frame-by-frame analysis of the videotapes of facial expressions of the first animals revealed that after they heard the auditory stimulus, prominent changes could be seen about the eyes, featuring definite widening and a peculiar glazed or unfocused quality; tightening of the facial musculature, especially about the mouth, also occurred (Miller, 1971).

in visual communication (Darwin, 1872; Izard, 1971[7]; Marler, 1965; van Hooff, 1962; van Lawick-Goodall, 1968), both Darwin and the majority of contemporary investigators have noted that the whole body is often involved in sending signals, and nonvisual communications are often given simultaneously as well. For this reason, most contemporary studies on facial expression also include information (now usually collected systematically) on simultaneous behavior occurring in other body parts, such as body posture, locomotion, manual gestures, hair erection, voiding of excrement, and vocalizations (e.g., Andrew, 1962, 1964, 1965; Marler, 1965; van Hooff, 1967; van Lawick-Goodall, 1968). The analysis of constellations of behavior from different body parts and different sensory modes reveals that some groupings of elements usually occur together, while others have the capacity to vary independently (Marler, 1965). In cases of invariable constellations the various elements communicate redundant information. Redundancies (for example, an open mouth and roaring vocalization) would help to insure that the message (a threat) would be received. Variations in groups of elements make possible the communication of subtle gradations of information.

Behavior occurs in sequential constellations as well as simultaneous ones. Since the significance of a behavior may depend upon behaviors occurring either before it or after it in a sequence (Altmann, 1965; Marler, 1965), descriptive studies should ideally examine behavior in its sequential context.

The significance of constellations of behavior brings the investigator to the problem of the functions of the signals, and points out the close relationship between form and function. The form (what a behavior looks like) and functions of signals are related because, as we shall see later, they have been selected together during evolution. Therefore, examining them separately is somewhat artificial.

Functions

All the recent investigators of facial expressions either implicitly or explicitly agree with Darwin that the functions of these expressions are communicative, and that such communications regulate social behavior. For example, Richard Andrew (1963a) states "Facial expression has evolved, like other displays, to communicate information about the probable future

[7]Izard (1971) reports an experiment with rhesus monkeys *(Macaca mulatta)* whose facial nerves had been sectioned to render them incapable of making facial expressions. When these animals were placed in social groups with each other and with normal controls, they attacked more than twice as often as the normal animals, and mounted (a behavior that resembles the male copulatory position, but signifies dominance in nonsexual social contexts) more than six times as often. This report suggests that animals unable to make normal facial threat expressions are forced to resort to whole body communications, which function less well in communicating *threats* and often result in actual *attack*.

behavior of the displaying animal [p. 1034]." Peter Marler (1965) writes "By far the greatest part of the whole system of communication seems to be devoted to the organization of social behavior of the group, to dominance and subordination, the maintenance of peace and cohesion of the group, reproduction, and care of the young [p. 584]."

In animal studies, communication[8] is generally defined as behavior in one animal, the sender, which evokes a response in another animal, the receiver (Altmann, 1967; Marler, 1965; van Lawick-Goodall, 1968). The conclusion that facial expressions in nonhuman primates are communicative is based on the analysis of sequences of behavior which reveal that these expressions do evoke responses in other animals. The question of whether the behavior is intentional or not is generally evaded, since no method has been devised as yet to tell what an animal is thinking. This is, nevertheless, an important question, and it will be broached again later on pages 26 and 38, and in the discussions of the nervous system.

Contemporary investigators have attempted to study the functions of particular facial expressions by examining such variables as (a) the age and sex categories of the senders and receivers; (b) the contexts in which the behaviors occur, such as feeding, aggression within the troop, play; and (c) the responses of the receiver, such as fleeing, threatening, approaching (Shirek-Ellefson, 1967; van Hooff, 1962, 1967). For example, if a particular open-mouth expression consistently and exclusively occurs between young animals of either sex as they approach each other during play sequences and results in the receiver approaching the sender and continuing to make play responses, one can conclude that the expression functions to promote cohesive (the receiver approaches the sender), friendly (no aggression results), playful (play results) behavior. Ideally, functional interpretations should be objectified by time-sampled, quantitative collection of sequences of behavior followed by statistical analysis of the data. However, studies on facial behavior in nonhuman primates have hardly reached this stage of sophistication, and most functional interpretations are based on the observers' subjective interpretations of sequences of behavior (e.g., Andrew, 1963b, 1963c, 1965; Hall & DeVore, 1965; Hinde & Rowell, 1962; Jay, 1965; Kaufman & Rosenblum, 1966; Simonds, 1963; van Hooff, 1962, 1967; van Lawick-Goodall, 1968). Though most of these observations are unquantified, the interpretation of social functions based on the responses of animals to other primates of the same species living with them in social groups—many of them in the wild—is a great advance in the study of primate behavior. Comparing the functional interpretations derived by observ-

---

[8]Some investigators of communication in man (e.g., Ekman & Friesen, 1969) include the concept of conscious intent or volition in their definitions.

ing the *interactions* of animals in social groups with Darwin's interpretations, derived for the most part from observations of the *reactions* of primates to human observers and catetakers, shows that the modern methods result in far more detailed interpretations. Furthermore, recent interpretations of particular expressions are not all consistent with Darwin's (though most of them are!), and they indicate that some of Darwin's interpretations were incorrect. For example, Darwin did not consider any of the bared-teeth expressions to represent fear (see Figure 19e and discussion on p. 80), and he considered the rapid jaw and lip movements (lip smack) to represent laughter rather than affection (see Figures 19h and i). In addition, the accuracy of these recent unquantified studies has been supported by the few quantitative investigations of communicative behavior (van Hooff, 1971, and Shirek-Ellefson, 1967, on facial displays; Winter, Ploog, & Latta, 1966, on vocal behavior).

Johan van Hooff, the Dutch ethologist, has made a study of the communicative behavior of chimpanzees in the chimpanzee consortium of the Aeromedical Research Laboratory in New Mexico. The consortium is a laboratory arrangement consisting of a 7-acre outdoor area with attached sleeping rooms that house a social group of 25 chimpanzees. In order to determine the functions of the various behavioral elements observed during the study, van Hooff (1971) examined the behavioral sequences of *individual*[9] animals during social interactions. He found that certain elements tended to precede or follow each other more frequently than others. Furthermore, some elements tended to form sequential clusters, since a number of particular behaviors regularly occurred together in sequences. These behavioral clusters were related to other clusters, and the relationships could be represented hierarchically as in Figure 2, which resembles the model of a family tree. The appearance of naturally occurring hierarchical clusters of behavior enabled van Hooff to make relatively objective functional interpretations. In Figure 2, the behaviors (at the top) "relaxed open-mouth," "gnaw-wrestle," "grasp poke," "pull limb," "gymnastics," "gnaw," "hand-wrestle," "gallop," and "mount" form a natural unit in terms of the frequency with which one follows the other. This natural unit has been interpreted by Van Hooff as *play*. Other natural units have been interpreted as *aggressive, affinitive, excitement,* and *submissive*. Examination of the hierarchical structure of chimpanzee behavior, represented in Figure 2, shows that play and aggression form a large cluster (one of the two main branches in the figure). This large play-aggression cluster has been distinguished from other

---

[9]Note that this study differs from Altmann's (1965) study below (p.39) in that van Hooff is examining the behavioral sequences performed by individual animals, while Altmann examined interactive sequences occurring between two animals.

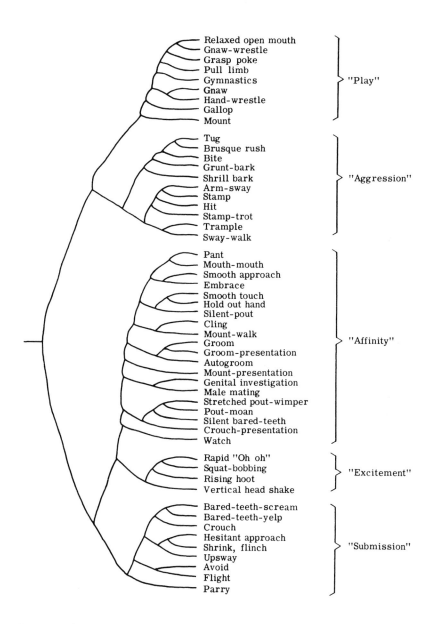

FIG. 2. Results of the cluster analysis of chimpanzee behavior. (The behavioral elements are placed in a hierarchical structure, based on the frequencies with which one follows another in social interactions.) (From van Hooff, 1971.)

behaviors, since the behaviors in these two clusters follow each other more frequently than they follow other behaviors in other clusters. Likewise, within the main clusters, such as the large *aggressive* cluster, subclusters are often revealed. For example. the "tug," "brusque rush," "bite," "grunt bark," and "shrill bark," subcluster represents *attack* behavior while the "arm-sway," "stamp," "hit" and "stamp–trot" subcluster represents *bluff* behavior.

Field studies of various primate species have revealed that social groups or "troops" are generally made up of several adults of each sex and their young. They generally number around 15 to 80 individuals, depending on the species. Individuals rarely change groups, and a troop usually maintains the same membership (except for births or deaths) for months or sometimes years. Consequently all animals within a troop know each other well. Groups are structured in such a way that each animal holds a particular position in the troop in terms of its ability to assert its will or to dominate others. This aspect of social organization is called the dominance hierarchy. Once dominance relationships are established, each animal in a troop knows its relationship to every other animal. Since the behavior of an animal is related to its dominance, its behavior can be predicted, and such predictable social ordering keeps conflict at a minimum. Thus if one animal, "Hairy," is eating and another animal, "Stripe," approaches, it can be predicted whether Hairy will ignore, threaten, or flee from Stripe, depending upon the relative dominance of the two animals.[10]

Qualitative studies by Simonds (1963), Hinde and Rowell (1962), van Hooff (1962), 1967), and Chevalier-Skolnikoff (1971, in press), as well as Shirek-Ellefson's (1967) quantitative study on the correlations between the relative dominance status of two interacting animals and the facial expressions they display, reveal that not only is the gross behavior of the animal (e.g., threatening or fleeing) related to the dominance status, but so is the particular kind of facial expression the animal makes. For example, should Hairy threaten, the kind of threat display he manifests will depend on whether he is dominant or subordinate to Stripe. If he is a crab-eating macaque (called *Macaca irus* by Shirek-Ellefson, 1967, but now called *M. fascicularis*) he will give an "open-mouth stare" threat if he is dominant (Figure 3a), and a "bared-teeth stare" threat (Figure 3b) if he is subordinate (Shirek-Ellefson, 1967). In some species (e.g., stumptail monkeys, *Macaca arctoides*, Chevalier-Skolnikoff, 1971, in press), as many as four different kinds of threat expressions are used according to the relative dominance status of the animals involved.

---

[10]Other variables, such as the presence of other group members, are also involved; thus under certain circumstances a subordinate animal may threaten a dominant one.

FIG. 3. Dominant and subordinate threats in *Macaca fascicularis* (from Shirek-Ellefson, 1967). (a) Top. "Open-mouthed stare"; a dominant threat (called "open-mouth threat" by Shirek-Ellefson). (b) Bottom. "Bared-teeth stare"; a subordinate threat (called "scream threat" by Shirek-Ellefson.

Further examination reveals that continua of expressions occur between different affect or emotional states. Thus one can observe expressions representing gradations on a scale from fear to anger, with various degrees or "blends" of fear-anger in between. Similarly, continua can be observed between fear and affection, where affection is interpreted from correlations of particular facial expressions with approach and proximity behaviors, such as embracing, huddling and grooming.

It appears that facial expressions like the above communicate emotional states. Even with today's knowledge of the activities of the brain, it still is not possible to know what an animal is thinking. However, through the examination of behavioral sequences and interpretation of how the behavior functions, primatologists are fairly confident that the interpretation of the emotional nature of facial behavior in nonhuman primates is correct. Investigators feel particularly confident of their interpretation of the behavior of the monkeys and apes because of these primates' close evolutionary relationship and biological similarity to man. Such interpretations are, as we will see, supported by similarities in the forms and activities of the brains of human and nonhuman primates, for the parts of the brain which mediate emotional responses in man also mediate facial expressions in the nonhuman primates.

Facial expressions also convey degrees of emotional intensity. For example, a dominant stumptail monkey *(Macaca arctoides)* will give a "stare" threat, or a "stare" threat with ears flicking forward and raising and lowering of the eyebrows, or an "open-mouth" threat, or a "round-mouth" threat as he becomes increasingly angry (Chevalier-Skolnikoff, 1971, in press). By abstracting such continua, one can chart the facial expressions of primates, as Leyhousen (1956) has charted those of cats, according to intensity and emotion, as in Figure 4 for the emotions fear and anger.

Such gradations in intensity and shifts in affect state can occur through time as the situation and the motivations of the animals shift. Within a few seconds a sender often displays a number of gradually or abruptly changing expressions. As the emotional displays of the sender shift, corresponding shifts occur in the behavior of the receivers. These observations show that nonhuman primates are capable of expressing extremely subtle variations in affect.

The discovery that primates are capable of displaying gradations of threat behavior, as, for example, on an anger-fear continuum suggests that there may be less species variability than Darwin imagined. His observations of "bared-teeth" threats in some species and "pout" threats in others may actually represent different kinds of expressions on an anger-fear continuum, and both kinds of threats may actually be present in the repertoire of each species. Similarly, some of Darwin's functional interpretations should

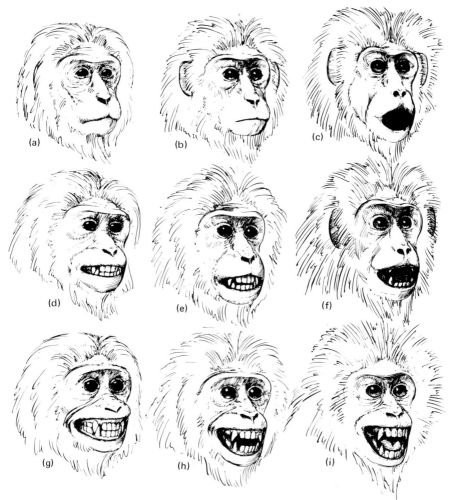

FIG. 4. Facial expressions of *Macaca arctoides* according to intensity and emotion. (Note that on the anger axis [top row, left to right] as the monkey becomes increasingly angry, the stare intensifies, the ears are brought forward, the hair is raised over the head and neck, the lips are tightened and contracted, and the mouth is opened. On the fear axis [left column, top to bottom] as the animal's fear increases, the gaze is averted, the ears are drawn back against the head, where they do not show, and the lips are retracted horizontally and vertically, baring the teeth.)

Reading left to right, and from top to bottom, the expressions are:
(a) Neutral face.
(b) "Stare"; mild, confident threat.
(c) "Round-mouthed stare"; intense, confident threat.
(d) Slight "grimace"; slight fear.
(e) *No name;* a mild fear-anger blend.
(f) "Open-mouthed stare"; moderately confident, intense threat.
(g) Extreme "grimace"; extreme fear.
(h) Mild "bared-teeth stare"; extreme fear, blended with anger.
(i) "Bared-teeth stare"; intense fear-anger blend.

probably be modified, since some of the expressions he describes under one functional category in all likelihood represent blends. For example, the bared-teeth anger expression of the Celebes macaque (Cynopithecus niger) which Darwin says is practically indistinguishable from a "pleasure" expression, may well be an anger–fear blend. Unfortunately, the recent studies on facial expressions in primates have not focused on all the same species Darwin described, so that such speculations cannot yet be verified.

Contemporary investigators agree that primate facial expressions primarily convey emotional states (Marler, 1965; Lancaster, 1968), and they do not appear to convey environmental information, such as the location of food or the appearance of a particular kind of danger. In man, facial expressions also primarily convey emotion, while the communication of complex environmental information is considered one of the critical characteristics of human language (Bastian, 1965; Lancaster, 1968). In some primate species vocalizations appear to convey environmental information. Vervet monkeys (Cercopithecus aetheops) have calls that are specific to particular predators, and the animals make different responses to these different kinds of alarm calls (Struhsaker, 1967). However, it is possible that such calls are actually expressing different degrees of emotionality in response to the different predators. In most monkey and ape species,[11] a few gestures and some tactile behavior also appear to convey essentially affect-free information, as when a mother touches her infant's back as a signal for it to cling to her.

While facial expressions are affect displays, they can evidently carry more specific meaning in particular situations. For example, repeated observations may reveal that if the dominant male in a particular monkey species chases a subordinate male and the subordinate male "grimaces" (a fear expression), the dominant male will stop chasing and leave. In such a context, grimacing results in the receiver leaving the sender, and the expression can be thought of as a distance-increasing device. However, it may also be observed that if the dominant male makes a grimace as he approaches the subordinate male, the subordinate male will approach and embrace the dominant. In this context, the grimace functions as cohesive behavior. Thus the precise function of a signal is context-bound, and its precise "meaning" applies only to a particular situation (Shirek-Ellefson, 1967). This functional context-dependency of emotional expression is an extremely important concept, for it is only in conjunction with context that affect expressions can coordinate social interactions.

[11]Chimpanzees in the wild use a particularly large number of these affect-free gestures (van Lawick-Goodall, 1968). Under experimental laboratory conditions chimpanzees have been taught a gestural language—American Sign Language (Gardner & Gardner, 1969, 1971)—and an artificial language involving the manipulation of pieces of colored plastic representing words (Premack, 1970a, b). In both cases the instructed animals did learn to express environmental information.

Through facial displays, the nonhuman primates express their emotions. Such emotional expression functions to control social relationships.

The Determinants of Facial Expression

Facial expressions are determined by an array of interacting factors. Though these include modified versions of Darwin's three principles, our knowledge of causal factors has grown enormously, especially during the last 20 years, and contemporary notions of the determinants of facial expression differ considerably from those of Darwin.

One of the main advances in the investigation of behavioral determinants has been a reorganization and reclassification of data to permit systematic exploration of causal factors. This trend was initiated by the psychologists Lehrman (1953, 1961) and Beach (1947, 1955, 1958), and has recently been incorporated into primate studies by Harlow (1963), Altmann (1968), Washburn and Hamburg (1968), and Hall (1968). As Beach (1947) pointed out,

> Every behavioral act constitutes a response to external and internal stimuli. In order to evoke overt reactions the stimuli must be transformed into nervous energy which is transmitted from peripheral receptors to various integrative mechanisms of the central nervous system; and these mechanisms in turn excite others whose activity elicits the muscular or glandular changes that constitute the behavior which we observe [p.297].

Accordingly, it becomes evident that stimuli, the nervous system and its activity (neurophysiology), and hormones are all involved as the immediate determinants of a particular behavior. Furthermore, as Beach adds, previous experience and genetic potential are additional determining factors. Adaptive evolutionary pressures, which largely determine the gene-

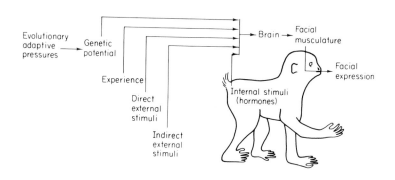

FIG. 5. Diagrammatic representation of the determinants of facial expressions.

tics, are also, as Darwin recognized, determining factors. Thus every behavioral act is determined by multiple factors that can be classified under the preceding categories (stimuli, hormones, experience, etc.). Consequently, one cannot accurately call a behavior "determined by inheritance" (or by the genes, or any other single factor), since multiple systems of the animal and multiple aspects of the environment are involved in producing *all* behaviors.

Evolutionary Adaptation and the Origins of Facial Expression

Darwin's first two principles, the principle of serviceable associated habits and the principle of antithesis, both involve evolutionary behavioral adaptation. His basic premise, that noncommunicative behavior has been modified to serve communicative functions, is central to the contemporary theories of origin presented by the ethologists Richard Andrew (1962, 1963a, 1963b, 1964, 1965) and Robert Hinde (1966). Hinde calls this evolutionary process "ritualization." Ritualized behavior, which has been studied most thoroughly in fish and birds, has been classified as deriving from four sources:

(1) "intention movements," or serviceable associated habits, as Darwin called them (Tinbergen, 1952; Hinde, 1966);

(2) "redirected activities" (Tinbergen, 1959; Hinde, 1966);

(3) "antithesis" (Darwin, 1872); and

(4) "displacement activities" (Tinbergen, 1952; Hinde, 1966).

(1) Many of the facial expressions of primates appear to have evolved as Darwin suggested, from intention movements—the incomplete or preparatory phases of initially noncommunicative activities. These activities include attack, locomotion toward and away, protective responses, and movements associated with respiration and vision (Darwin, 1872; Hinde, 1966; Andrew, 1962, 1964; Huber, 1933). The threat postures of most primates, for example, contain elements derived from attack (mouth open and ready for biting) and locomotion toward (body musculature tense and ready to advance), while the submissive postures contain elements derived from protective responses (retraction of lips and ears) and locomotion away from the sender. Such intention movements could have developed ontogenetically—that is, during the lifetime of the individual, rather than phylogenetically through evolution. Thus, an individual monkey might through experience develop the habit of opening the mouth as if ready to bite whenever it felt angry at another animal. However, the regularity with which many expressions and postures occur within a species does indicate an evolutionary derivation.

(2) ''Redirected'' activities are derived from intention movements, but are directed toward animals other than the animal that elicited the display. Often a monkey intermediate in the dominance hierarchy, if threatened by a superior, will direct a threat toward an inferior animal who was uninvolved in the initial encounter, rather than return a threat to the more dominant monkey.

(3) Unlike intention movements, which indicate ''positive'' motivational information, ''reversed'' signals (or ''antithetic signals,'' as Darwin called them in his principle of antithesis) have evidently evolved because they signal the direct opposite of other signals (Darwin, 1872; Marler, 1961). Accordingly, gaze aversion, a common signal of mild submission, is a striking reversal of the stare, which is a component of all threat displays. Similarly, in some monkeys, e.g., the stumptail macaque, *Macaca arctoides* (Chevalier-Skolnikoff, 1971, in press), the play expression is almost identical to one of the threat expressions except that the eyelids are lowered and the gaze is averted, thereby signaling that the apparently threatening or attacking face is really a play face (see Figures 19c and k).

As in the case of intention movements, it is not clear whether such antithetic expressions are evolutionarily or ontogenetically derived. In a study of the ontogenetic development of communication in stumptail monkeys, the play expression was found to develop gradually, and in small infants the eyelids were not lowered (Chevalier-Skolnikoff, 1971, in press). While these observations suggest that ontogenetic experience may be an important factor in the development of this play expression, the gradual ontogenetic change could actually be due to maturation, and independent of any particular kinds of social experience.

(4) Displacement activities are behaviors that normally occur in one context, but appear in a different context which involves conflicting behavioral tendencies, and in which they appear to be functionally irrelevant. For example, scratching—a behavior that obviously functions to remove irritants from the skin—may occur in a tense situation in which one animal is ambivalent about whether to attack or flee from a second animal. In such a situation, scratching is obviously irrelevant. Though such behaviors do occur in primate repertoires, few if any facial expressions appear to be derived from displacement activities.

While Darwin's concept of ritualization is still accepted today, the mechanisms he proposed to explain its functioning are no longer considered entirely valid. The main objection to Darwin's proposal is its Lamarckian basis. In 1859, when Darwin published the *Origin of Species,* he emphasized natural selection in discussing evolutionary processes, although he also incorporated the inheritance of acquired or learned characteristics into his theory. The theory of natural selection met with severe criticism, however,

while the theory of inheritance of acquired characteristics, a theory generally accepted in scientific circles at that time, was favorably received. Subsequently Darwin deemphasized the natural selection aspect of his evolutionary theory, and in 1869 published a speculative paper on "pangenesis,"
elaborating on how acquired characteristics might be inherited. In 1872,
when *The Expression of the Emotions in Man and Animals* went to print,
Darwin was still emphasizing the Lamarckian mechanism of inheritance
of acquired traits, and natural selection was presented as merely a subsidiary
force. Today we know that only the genes are inherited, and these are
not affected by individual experience. Natural selection, the process by
which those individuals better fit to survive in a particular environment
live to produce more offspring, is still accepted today and is considered
the main evolutionary force.

With the rejection of Lamarckian inheritance and the acceptance of natural selection as the primary evolutionary force, it is no longer necessary to assume that the prototypic, action-oriented behaviors (e.g., attack) from which
facial displays (e.g., threat expression) evolved were necessarily *consciously*
or voluntarily performed. In fact, since the neocortex, the part of the brain
which is specialized to mediate voluntary, conscious behavior is the last
part of the brain to have evolved, and the general trend in vertebrate evolution
has been from simple stereotyped behavior to complex behavior involving
learned responses (see discussion of the nervous system, pp. 43–46), it is
highly unlikely that most of the prototypic behavior patterns were voluntary.
Rather, through natural selection, the animals who had a genetically based
tendency to substitute facial displays (e.g., threats) for more dangerous actions
(e.g., fighting) probably had a higher survival ratio, thus passing this propensity on to their descendants.

In his discussion of vocalizations in animals, Darwin speculated on the
relationships between sound function and the structure of sound signals.[12]
He did not, however, speculate on such relationships in visual signals.
A number of contemporary investigators have examined the adaptive value
of visual communication, as compared with such other sensory modalities
as hearing or touch, to primates under particular environmental situations.
Marler (1965) notes that visual communication enables all recipients to
locate the signaler in space; that is, if you can see a facial expression
you can locate the animal who is making it. Consequently, this mode of
communication can be dangerous for small animals that have a great number
of predators from which they must hide. Therefore, visual communication
would be less likely to have developed than a communicative mode which

----

[12]Contemporary views on such relationships are presented in Marler, 1965, 1968; Busnel,
1963; and Collias, 1960.

is effective when the animals are hidden. The fact that Moynihan (1967) notes a correlation between size and variety of facial expression in New World monkeys may be related to the vulnerability of small species. However, it could also be related to the fact that expressions are harder to see on small faces than on large ones. Moynihan finds that among New World monkeys the night monkey, *Aotus trivirgatus,* has no visual displays except for gross postures or body movements, and most communication is vocal, olfactory, and tactile. This emphasis on nonvisual modalities is an adaptation to nocturnal life; viz., it is difficult to see in the dark. Similarly, the nocturnal prosimians make great use of olfactory communication (Marler, 1965).

Among Old World monkeys the more terrestrial forms, such as the macaques (Rowell & Hinde, 1962; Hinde & Rowell, 1962), and the savanna (plains) species, such as the baboons (Hall & DeVore, 1965) and patas monkeys, *Erythrocebus patas* (Hall, 1968), capitalize on visual communication, which can be received well in open grasslands, and have relatively limited vocal repertoires, which might attract predators. The most extreme example of such ecological adaptation is that of the patas monkey, which has adapted to predators by responding to danger with silently fleeing at speeds up to 35 miles an hour and hiding in the tall savanna grasses. Hiding animals freeze and will not vocalize even if discovered and picked up, as Hall was occasionally able to do when he located them in the grass! Though baboons are less vocal than forest-living species, such as the guenon, *Cercopithecus mitis* (Gartlan & Brain, 1968), Hall found patas monkeys to vocalize about 1/40th as frequently as baboons, and often no vocalizations were heard for days at a time.

Marler (1965) also emphasizes the adaptive relationships between social organization and modality of signals employed. Among most Old World monkeys and apes, animals live in tightly knit social groups and signals for close-range communication are most commonly in demand. Visual signals are suitable for these communications, and the close proximity of group members makes their use feasible.

Many species are adorned with facial markings, hair, etc., which accentuate differences between species and between expressions. These species-specific markings permit the receiver to identify the sender readily as being of the same or a different species. Such markings are particularly common among species that inhabit different ecological niches within the same forests. The markings are probably of particular importance in identifying the species of potential mates (see Figure 6).

In some primate species there has been selection for particular facial markings, especially in the form of hair patterns and skin color, which accentuate particular facial expressions. Thus some species possess ruffs

FIG. 6. Species-specific facial adornments in four cercopithecus species. (Such facial markings accentuate differences between closely related species, permitting animals receiving communications to identify senders readily as being of the same or different species.)

(a) Hamlyn's guenon, *Cercopithecus hamlyni* (San Diego Zoo Photo).

(b) L'Hoest's guenon, *Cercopithecus l'hoesti* (San Diego Zoo Photo).

(c) Moustached guenon, *Cercopithecus cephus* (San Diego Zoo Photo).

(d) Spotnose guenon, *Cercopithecus nictitans*.

FIG. 7. Mangaby *(Cercocebus torquata)* mother hugging her juvenile offspring and threatening the photographer. (Note how the white skin above the eyes accentuates her threat and gives her the appearance of having two enormous white eyes.)

of long hair around their necks and shoulders which are erected during threats, making the animals seem larger and more ferocious. In other species, such as the mangaby pictured in Figure 7, the upper eyelids are of a contrasting color (white) and are lowered in threat, displaying what from the distance looks like great white eyes.

Genetic Potential

The first work on genetics, published by the monk Gregor Mendel in a single paper in 1865, did not attract the attention of his contemporaries. The whole field of genetics was completely unknown to Darwin, and did not gain importance until its rediscovery in 1900. However, Darwin was aware of the importance of heredity, which plays a central role in his evolutionary theory, although, as mentioned above, the Lamarckian theory he espoused is no longer accepted.

Although today we understand a great deal about genetics and its role in the evolution of behavior, there has been no study of the genetic basis of any signaling pattern in a nonhuman primate (Altmann, 1968).

There are, nevertheless, enough data available to make some postulations regarding the role of the genes in determining facial expressions. While Darwin probably exaggerated the variability in facial expression between species, considerable species variability does exist. This variability is apparent in van Hooff's (1967) descriptions of facial displays, and in fact an experienced observer can distinguish many species by descriptions of their facial expressions alone. For example, the expression which van Hooff calls the "silent bared-teeth face" (called a grimace or grin by many other investigators), when shown by the rhesus macaque (Macaca mulatta) has the following characteristics: mouth more or less closed; mouth corners horizontally retracted; and lips vertically retracted, thus baring the teeth and, with strong retraction, showing part of the gums. However, when the "silent bared-teeth face" is shown by the gelada baboon, Theropithecus gelada, the upper lip is turned inside out, up over the nose, thereby producing a bright white (teeth) and pink (inner lip) muzzle display. The differences in this expression are found in all individuals of these two particular species. Such species-specific differences are undoubtedly determined by species differences in genetic makeup.

Although there is variability among species, closely related species tend to have similar facial behaviors, as one might expect on the premise that closely related species are more likely to have similar genetic makeup than distantly related species. It was on this premise that Darwin examined facial expressions of primates in conjunction with his investigation of the evolution of human facial expression. There are exceptions, however. For example, Aotus, the New World night monkey, is very different behaviorally from its most closely related diurnal relatives in that it exhibits few, if any, facial expressions (Moynihan, 1967). This difference can be explained in terms of its evolutionary adaptation to a very different kind of life in a very different kind of ecological setting. This adaptation has evidently resulted in a genetic makeup which differs considerably from that of related species, and determines Aotus' deviant behavior.

Experience

The effect of experience upon facial behavior was repeatedly considered by Darwin, but because of his belief in Lamarckian inheritance of acquired characters, his lines between inheritance and experience were often hazy. With the rediscovery of Mendelian genetics and the rejection of the theory of Lamarckian inheritance, it has become evident that experience affects only the individual and is not inheritable.

Observations of the development of facial expressions in infant stumptail monkeys *(Macaca arctoides)* raised with their mothers in a social group have shown that newborn infants make few expressions and that the number of expressions increases as the infants grow older. Furthermore, the early manifestations of many expressions differ from the facial expressions of adults, and expressions often acquire their adult forms gradually (Chevalier-Skolnikoff, 1971, in press). Observations of the developmental sequence, however, cannot reveal what variables affect the development of the expressions, as experimental studies can.

The experimental work of Harlow and his colleagues (Harlow, 1961, 1963; Harlow & Harlow, 1962, 1969; Harlow, Dodsworth, & Harlow, 1965; Harlow, Harlow, & Hansen, 1963; Harlow & Zimmerman, 1959; and Mason, 1960, 1961, 1963, 1965) has demonstrated that early social deprivation results in severe affect disturbances. Rhesus monkey infants raised in social isolation, either in bare wire cages or with artificial mothers, do not manifest normal play behavior, sexual behavior or maternal behavior. Play and maternal behaviors do not generally occur at all, and sexual behavior is incomplete, the animals showing sexual interest and motivation but being unable to complete a sexual act. The experience gained by a monkey growing up in a normal social group is essential to the development and manifestation of normal emotional behavior patterns.

However, few studies have focused on the effects of deprivation on the manifestation of facial expression specifically, and the facial expressions of socially deprived animals have not been systematically described.

Miller, Caul, and Mirsky (1967) conducted an experiment in which 3- and 4-year-old isolation-raised rhesus monkeys and same-aged normal monkeys were trained to avoid a certain stimulus and were then put into the "cooperative conditioning" situation (see footnote 6, page 19). The isolation-raised animals did transmit fear, but evidently not as well as normal monkeys, suggesting that no particular socialization experiences are *essential* to the manifestation of fear, but that they may enhance the communicative effectiveness of the expression.

Sackett (1965) reports that in nine months of perhaps 50 hours of weekly testing of the responses of isolation-raised infant rhesus monkeys to colored slides, some of which were of monkeys making affect expressions, he observed only three threats, while in normals, threats would have occurred much more frequently (personal communication). None of these threats were made by small infants, and the few threats observed in the older infants may have been influenced by experience acquired during testing (personal communication). These data suggest that certain kinds of experience may be essential to the manifestation of threats. However, if particular "socializing" experiences are essential to the development of threats, they may affect the *motivation* for threatening rather than the production of the motor pattern. Thus unsocialized rhesus monkey infants may never feel aggressive, but might be capable of producing a threat expression should an aggressive emotional state ever be felt.

William Mason (1965), who has performed many of the deprivation experiments and has had a great deal of contact with isolation-raised macaques, holds that many communicative behaviors, such as facial expressions, appear in relation to particular affect states in the absence of social experience, but that their connection with specific eliciting stimuli, their contextual relevance, and their effectiveness in controlling and coordinating social behavior are heavily dependent upon social experience.

Mason's speculation indicates, as Ekman (1972) has also suggested for human beings, that *the way in which an emotion is expressed* is relatively invariable within a species, but *the conditions that will elicit an emotion* and its accompanying expression are variable and highly subject to experiential influences. In other words, if a monkey feels playful, his particular expression will resemble the playful expression of any monkey of his species. However, what conditions, if any, will make him feel playful depend upon his past experiences and how he was raised. Furthermore, Ekman emphasizes that the human individual may inhibit the expression of the emotions he feels or produce other expressions that are considered culturally more appropriate to the situation than the expression of his actual feelings. Such alterations could be voluntary or unconscious. It is possible that a monkey also may feel playful or angry, but choose not to express the feeling. There are at present no data to *prove* that monkeys have voluntary control over their expressions of emotion. However, the presence in the monkey brain of relatively large frontal lobes—the part of the brain which in man is specialized to mediate voluntary behavior—suggests that monkeys may also be capable of voluntarily controlling their facial expressions. Observations of the behavior of primates also *suggests* voluntary control. For example, one often sees one monkey "sneak" up to another animal with a "blank" or neutral expression on his face and then playfully attack the second monkey.

Observation of individual variation in facial expression in primates suggests that experience may have some slight effect on the way in which an emotion is expressed, though experimental studies are necessary to verify that these differences are experientially rather than genetically determined. For example, van Lawick-Goodall (1968) observed that one particular male chimpanzee frequently went around with his lips pressed together and the corners of his mouth drawn back in a "mock smile," even in situations which could not be interpreted as friendly or playful.

Miller (1971) reports evidence indicating that animals that know each other best communicate best. He placed a mother rhesus monkey, the mother's 18-month-old son, who had been raised in social contact with his mother only, and a strange young wild-born and -raised animal in the "cooperative conditioning" situation described earlier. The mother's communications to her son were 90% successful; the son's communications to his mother were 90% successful; the stranger's communications to the mother were 50% successful; and the stranger's communications to the son were 30% successful. So it appears that personal experience between particular animals enhances communicative ability. These findings also indicate that there are individual variations in expressive behavior. Consequently, animals that have grown up together in wild troops would be expected to communicate more effectively than recently artificially composed groups of monkeys.

A number of field and laboratory studies (Sade, 1965, 1966, 1967; Imanishi, 1957; Kaufman & Rosenblum, 1967, 1969; Kawai, 1958; Kawamura, 1963, 1965) show that macaque monkeys, particularly females, generally attain the same dominance status as their mothers. This seems to occur through learning. As the infant grows up under the protection of its mother in a social group, the mother is able to protect it from her subordinates but not from animals more dominant than she is. Since the precise expression that an animal will display in a given situation often depends on his dominance status, the learning involved in dominance acquisition also has its effects on the production of facial expressions.

It has also been found that while dominance status relates to the mother's status and tends to be learned early, it never becomes absolutely fixed, and experiences can affect it at any time. In an experiment performed by Miller, Murphy, and Mirsky (1955), it was found that the dominance hierarchy of a group of adult rhesus monkeys could be artificially altered. One monkey (a subordinate) was chosen as a conditioning stimulus. The other group members were exposed to the stimulus animal and were given an electric shock in an apparatus constructed for this purpose, whenever they were permitted to see the stimulus monkey, until they learned to avoid the shock by pulling a lever. After the group members had become conditioned to avoid the stimulus monkey, they were returned to the group and it was found that the stimulus animal had risen in dominance.

Stuart Altmann (1965) in an analysis of sequential behavior in free-ranging rhesus monkeys that had been imported from India and were living on Santiago Island, off the coast of Puerto Rico, found (as did van Hooff, 1971, above) that the sequential behavior of monkeys is far from random. The likelihood that one particular behavior performed by one group member will follow another particular behavior by the same monkey or by another group member can be expressed in terms of probabilities. So, while one cannot predict with certainty whether behavior "B" will follow behavior "A," one can say whether such a sequence would be likely or unlikely. In this way the regularity of behavioral sequences can be estimated.

Altmann also found that the accuracy of his predictions of what behavior would occur increased as the string of antecedent events increased. These results are, in a sense, a measure of the social memory of the animals, and of the extent to which previous experience determines ongoing behavior. Altmann speculates that in theory this process of looking farther and farther back into the history of the interaction process could be continued until no further reduction in the uncertainty of behavioral predictions could be obtained.

So far, our discussion has focused on the effects of experience on the *manifestation* of facial expression. The effects of experience on the *recognition* of facial expressions is another problem that was broached by Darwin. Though there are still few data on this subject, it was found by Sackett (1966) that isolation-raised infant rhesus monkeys 60 to 80 days of age reacted appropriately (they withdrew) to colored slides of other monkeys threatening. However, between birth and 9 months of age, they did not show any consistently appropriate reactions to pictures of other monkeys displaying fearful expressions or sexual behavior. It would appear that the socialization experience is not essential for a monkey to recognize some facial expressions (e.g., threat expressions), but it may be for him to recognize others (e.g., fear expressions).

The experimental study by Miller, Caul, and Mirsky (1967) described above (on the ability of 4- and 5-year-old isolation-raised and normal rhesus monkeys placed in a "cooperative conditioning" situation to communicate fear) supports the speculation that isolation-raised animals do not *recognize* fear expressions (though, as reported above, they can *communicate* fear). The isolation-raised animals did not respond to the fear expressions of normals or other isolates, while the normal monkeys did.

Though we have learned a great deal about the effects of experience on primate social behavior in general, an area in which there were no data at all in Darwin's time, we still know little about the effects of experience on facial expression specifically. The few experimental findings that are available do not paint a clear, consistent picture of the effects of experience on expression. Darwin speculated that while the recognition of expression might be highly dependent upon learning, its manifestation was not. Miller, Caul, and Mirsky's (1967) findings on fear expressions, and Mason's (1965) statement above suggest, in agreement with Darwin, that the relationship between particular expressions and particular emotional states is not dependent upon a normal socializing experience. However, Sackett's study on the expression of threats in isolation-raised monkeys and van Lawick-Goodall's reports on individual variation in facial expression suggest that experience may have some effect. It appears further, in agreement with Darwin, that socially naïve animals do not recognize some expressions (e.g., fear). However, contrary to Darwin's speculation, socially naïve animals evidently do recognize other expressions (e.g., threats). The evidence from deprivation experiments does strongly indicate that the appropriate contextual use of and reaction to facial behavior and its role in coordination of social interactions are highly dependent upon a normal socialization experience.

External Stimuli

Facial expressions are influenced by external events or stimuli. The most influential direct stimuli are from other animals within the social group—their activities, and particularly their emotional displays. The appearance or behavior of animals of the same or a different species in other social groups and of predators are also common direct stimuli. A number of qualities of the stimulus animal, such as its age, sex, and dominance status influence the response that an animal will make. As shown by Altmann (1965) in his study of sequential behavior (above), most expressive behavior in the higher primates occurs in response to a number of stimulus conditions and is not stimulus-specific. So, while direct stimuli influence the nature of resulting behavior, they do not elicit stereotyped, invariable responses.

Facial expressions are also influenced by an array of environmental factors apart from direct social stimuli. These "indirect stimuli" are such factors as whether it is day or night, warm or cold, rainy or dry, forest or grassland, and such situations as the proximity or activities of other animals either of the same or a different species that are not directly involved in eliciting the interaction. They are important determinants, for in an otherwise equivalent situation they can greatly influence whether a particular behavior will occur or not. For example, Rowell (1966), in a study of forest-living baboons living in Queen Elizabeth National Park, Uganda, found that while baboons moving in open country are relatively quiet, animals traveling through thick cover with poor visibility kept up a continuous chorus of grunts. These grunts were audible only for a short distance and evidently served as contact noises which enabled the group to stay together.

Andrew (1962, 1963a–c, 1964) suggests that the amount of change in stimulation, or "stimulus contrast," is the factor that determines which expressions occur. For example, a sudden change in the external environment, such as the appearance of a predator, will elicit a particular expression, and the kind of expression elicited depends upon the degree of environmental change. He speculates that moderate stimulus contrast will result in expressions which serve to bring the major sense organs to bear on the stimulus—these are the "alert" expressions—and that sudden intense stimulus contrast will evoke protective responses. However, van Hooff (1967) and Moynihan (1964) both point out that while the theory that expressions are evoked by stimulus contrast is undoubtedly a valid concept in a very general sense, the different primate signal patterns are certainly not caused solely by a series of stimuli differing only in strength. Certain stimuli tend to provoke *particular* qualitatively and functionally distinct adaptive patterns such as maternal behavior, sexual behavior, etc. Furthermore, the effect of the stimulus is just one of the factors determining facial expressions; experience, endocrine balance, etc., are also contributing causes.

Hormones

Another determinant of facial expressions in nonhuman primates is hormone balance. A number of studies on primates have shown that hormones can affect behavior. For example, females show more sexual behavior when they are in oestrus, or sexually receptive. In female monkeys, the amount of estrogen, the female sex hormone, varies rhythmically according to the female's menstrual cycle. Estrogen levels are highest at the time of ovulation, when the newly mature egg is ejected and available for fertilization, and they become lowest during menstruation. The female's sexual behavior fluctuates rhythmically as her estrogen hormone levels vary, and these behavioral changes are caused by the hormonal fluctuations (Michael & Herbert, 1963; Goy & Eisele, 1964). A female who is ovulating has a higher probability[13] of displaying sexual behavior than does a female who is at a different point in her menstrual cycle. Accordingly, the probability of a male's mounting also depends upon the hormonal condition of the female.

Michael and Herbert (1963) have also discovered in a series of laboratory experiments on rhesus monkeys, *Macaca mulatta,* that grooming, the activity so common among monkeys in which one animal picks through the fur of a partner, often removing foreign material, also fluctuates according to the female estrus cycle. Females groom least when their estrogen levels are high, but males groom most when their female partner's estrogen levels are high. Ovariotomy, an operation which removes the ovary, the source of estrogen production, eliminates these grooming cycles, so it appears that hormonal levels can affect the behavior of senders and indirectly of receivers as well.

With respect to facial expression, macaques often lip smack during grooming and during sexual encounters. The higher frequencies of male

---

[13]The absence of estrogen results in lower frequencies of copulation, but does not completely abolish it (Goy & Eisele, 1964).

grooming and sexual behavior correlated with high estrogen levels in the female might well result in higher frequencies of male lip smacking at this time in the female's cycle. Similar fluctuations in frequencies of certain facial expressions in females might be directly determined by hormone variations as well.

In a study of the free-ranging rhesus monkey colony on Santiago Island, Wilson (1968) found that the frequencies of aggressive acts of males, judged from the number of wounds and deaths, was correlated with the mating season, the time of year when testosterone levels in males are probably highest (Sade, 1964; Conaway & Sade, 1965; Vandenbergh, 1965). He also found that six males castrated after puberty, and thus lacking testosterone in their systems, gradually fell in dominance rank several years after castration. These observations indicate that testosterone contributes to the manifestation of aggression, and consequently to the display of facial threat expressions in this species. Rose, Holaday, and Bernstein (1971) have also found experimental evidence that testosterone contributes to the manifestation of aggressive behavior in laboratory groups of rhesus monkeys.

Rosenblum (1961) found that male and female rhesus monkey infants differ in the frequency of their facial threat expressions. Subsequent work by Young, Goy, and Phoenix (1964) has shown that these sex differences are determined by an interaction between hormones and the brain. In a prenatal period during which the various organ systems of the fetus are developing, the male sex hormone, testosterone, produced by the testes of the male fetus, reorganizes the developing neural tissues. Neural tissue thus affected will in postnatal life mediate masculine behavior patterns. The neural tissue of the female is not normally subjected to testosterone and therefore retains the original feminine organization and after birth mediates female behavior patterns.

Thus it becomes evident that hormones can have permanent effects on the behavior of an individual, as revealed by the work of Young, Goy, and Phoenix, and they can also have transient effects, as demonstrated by Michael and Herbert, by Wilson, and by Rose, Holaday, and Bernstein.

The Nervous System

The neurological processes of the animal enable him to assimilate external and internal stimuli (e.g., hormones) and to organize and perform adaptive responses which are mediated by the muscular anatomy. The central nervous system is the organization center of the animal, and his behavior, including his facial expressions, are dependent upon the action of this system.

In 1872, Darwin was highly aware of the general functions of the nervous system, but he knew little about how it actually worked. Though our neurological knowledge has grown enormously since Darwin's time (particularly since the late 1930s), we are only beginning to have some idea of how it processes such complex behavior as facial expression.

The central nervous system of an advanced mammal, such as a monkey or a man, is made up of a series of nerve centers. The spinal cord and the most posterior part of the brain control the simplest behaviors, the reflexes. The midbrain and the basal areas of the forebrain, such as the hypothalamus, mediate stereotyped behaviors concerned with vital functions of the organism, such as sexual and emotional behavior. The cerebral cortex, the outermost layer of the forebrain, receives complex environmental stimuli (e.g., what the animal sees, hears, smells, and feels) and mediates voluntary, planned behavior and complex, learned behavior (see Figure 8).

Modern research on the neurological basis of emotion essentially began with a theory of emotion presented by Papez in 1937 (see Pribram, 1967, for a review of the theories of emotion). Papez proposed that the concept of "emotion" implies (a) a way of acting and (b) a way of feeling. Since it had been found previously (Bard, 1929) that an animal with the cortex totally removed can display facial expressions associated with emotional states, Papez speculated that structures below the cortex—specifically the hypothalamus—could independently cause an animal to make facial expressions. He proposed that motor impulses must be sent *down* the nervous

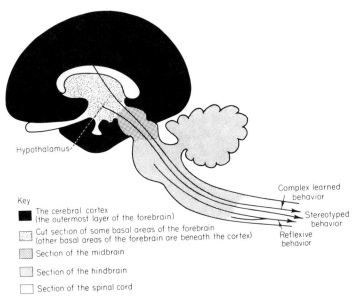

Hypothalamus

Complex learned behavior

Key

■ The cerebral cortex
(the outermost layer of the forebrain)

▨ Cut section of some basal areas of the forebrain
(other basal areas of the forebrain are beneath the cortex)

▨ Section of the midbrain

▧ Section of the hindbrain

□ Section of the spinal cord

Stereotyped behavior

Reflexive behavior

FIG. 8. Schematic diagram of a sagittal section of the brain, illustrating the hierarchical organization of the nervous system of an advanced mammal.

system in order to cause the behavior, since the higher centers had been removed. He further speculated that in the intact animal the activity of the hypothalamus (causing emotional behavior) is held in check and modulated by the cerebral cortex, and that the subjective feeling of emotion is also dependent upon the cortex. This implied that normally impulses from the cortex traveled *downward,* thereby modulating the activity of the hypothalamus, and that the hypothalamus, in its turn, sent motor impulses *down* the nervous system, activating the behavior, and sent impulses *up* the nervous system to the cortex, where they resulted in emotional consciousness (see Figure 9).

Thus, in the higher primates, the cerebral cortex receives the complex environmental stimuli to which emotional expression is often a reaction, and the cortex probably exerts some voluntary control over the manifestation of facial expression. However, the *emotional* responses are mediated by subcortical structures. It is because of this hypothalamic mediation of facial expression that these emotional responses are relatively stereotyped in form. The stereotypy of facial expression and its causal basis are of great theoretical importance, for it is because of the stereotyped quality of facial expression that emotional behavior has often been called "instinctive" or "innate." This question of the "innateness" of facial expression will be discussed later.

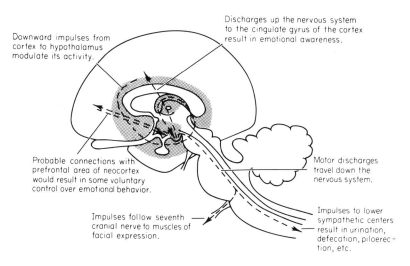

FIG. 9. Schematic diagram of a sagittal section of the brain, illustrating the major pathways of the limbic system (the major structures are stippled). (After Papez, 1937; Netter, 1962; MacLean, 1962; and Wallace Laboratories, 1965.)

Papez's theory of emotion is still somewhat controversial. However, it has for the most part been confirmed and extended by the more modern studies. Some of these propose additional structures as part of the limbic system.

Because the developments in the field of neurophysiology are among the most striking advances in the field of facial expression since Darwin, for those readers who are interested in pursuing the subject in greater detail, the nervous system, its evolution, and its relationship to emotional behavior will be further discussed in a later section of this chapter.

The Muscular Anatomy

One of Darwin's major contributions to the study of facial expression was his emphasis on facial musculature as a determinant of expression. Facial expression is dependent upon the anatomy of the face, and particularly upon the facial muscles.

Because of the intimate relationship between form and function, the two must be considered together. During evolutionary development, the functions of the muscles determined their form. During individual development also, form and function are interdependent and inseparable; the well-exercised muscle is larger than the poorly exercised, and the form of a muscle and the bony structures to which it is attached will determine its functional potentials. This relationship between form and function was well understood by Darwin. Although there has been a considerable advance in knowledge of both the comparative anatomy and the behavior of the face, few have attempted, since Darwin, to bring these two areas of research together. I will therefore briefly summarize here the general evolutionary trends, and for those readers who are interested, I will attempt a more detailed synthesis of the material on facial musculature and expression in a later section of the chapter.

The most primitive primates, the prosimians, have not developed the high visual capacities typical of the monkeys and apes. One of the reasons high visual acuity has not developed among the prosimians is that most prosimian species are nocturnal. Prosimians rely primarily on smell, sound, and touch for information about their environment. Consequently, prosimians make few facial expressions. In prosimians, facial movements function primarily to bring the nose and ears into action and for eating and attack (biting).

In the Old World monkeys, a dramatic shift toward visual functioning has occurred. This shift is part of the adaptation of monkeys to a diurnal, arboreal (tree-living) way of life. For animals who must leap rapidly through the trees, keen vision is essential. A corresponding shift in facial anatomy is the reduction of the musculature of other structures previously involved in olfactory, auditory, and tactile reception (e.g., the wet nose, ear musculature, and facial whiskers). There is a concomitant increase in the size and number of muscles of the midfacial region, resulting in mobile lip and cheek areas. These muscle groups probably developed primarily as a feeding mechanism, but they may have been selected for their expressive value also. One might imagine that the ability to express emotional states would be of great value to the group-living monkeys. (Many prosimian species lead relatively solitary lives, coming together only to mate.) Old World monkeys make more facial expressions than prosimians. There are, however, a number of prosimian and Old World monkey expressions which are similar in both form and function and are undoubtedly homologous—that is, they have the same evolutionary origins (see Figure 10).

The apes follow the trends evident in the Old World monkeys: There is a further reduction in ear musculature and a further increase in the musculature of the midfacial region. The selective pressures responsible for the continued increase in the midfacial musculature in the apes is unclear, for there is evidently little or no increase in the number of emotional expressions produced (see Figure 10), and most ape and Old World monkey expressions are clearly homologous (see Figures 19 and 21). However, apes appear to be capable of more mobility of the lips than is reflected in their emotional expressions. This increased mobility of the lips may function primarily in feeding.

In man, one sees a general continuation of the trends seen in the monkeys and apes, except that while there is increased muscle differentiation (more discrete muscles) in the midfacial region, there is a *reduction* in the size of these muscles. This reduction in size is probably a response to tool use, which has removed the selection pressures for strong teeth, jaws, and lips. (For more than two million years man and his ancestors have had tools to use instead of teeth for food getting, as, for example, for killing animals; food preparation, such as cracking the shells of nuts; and for defense.) The increased muscle differentiation about the muzzle may be an adaptation for fine muscle control necessary for speech. Human beings are capable of making a large number of facial expressions (as can be seen by watching a child making faces in a mirror!). However, facial expressions are evidently associated with only a small number of emotional states—about the same number as have been reported for the apes (see Figure 10). Some of the ape and human expressions are similar, and are probably homologous (see Figures 21 and 23). It is not yet known why man uses so many different expressions to express only a few emotions; it may be that the different expressions convey subtle differences in emotional states.

If today one attempts to make a phylogenetic examination of facial expression by comparing the expressions of the living primates, as in Figure 10, one finds what Darwin would have expected. One sees a kind of family

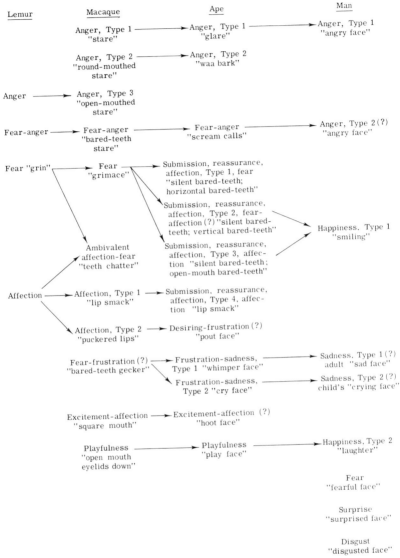

FIG. 10. Probable evolutionary development of some facial expressions in primates.

tree of expressive behavior, with certain branches dying out and others showing continuity.

During the past 100 years, the collection of additional data has clarified the evolution of the facial musculature and facial expressions. Recent studies have strikingly confirmed most of Darwin's findings, and there has been little theoretical advance in these areas since Darwin.

On Darwin's Conclusion That Facial Expressions Are "Innate" or Inherited

From the preceding discussion of the determinants of affect expressions, it becomes evident that a facial expression cannot be characterized as inherited or "innate." Actually only the genes are inherited, and complex interactions between the organism and its environment are *always* involved in the production of any behavior, including facial expression. Darwin (1872) was definitely aware that environment could influence behavior that he classified as "innate." For example, he wrote that

When there exists an inherited or instinctive tendency to the performance of an action, or an inherited taste for certain kinds of food, some degree of habit in the individual is often or generally requisite. We find this in the paces of the horse, and to a certain extent in the pointing of dogs; although some young dogs point excellently the first time they are taken out, yet they often associate the proper inherited attitude with a wrong odour, and even with eyesight [p.30].

Nevertheless, the impression that Darwin considers expression to be determined by inheritance alone rings strongly throughout *The Expression of the Emotions*.

The fact that the repertoires of facial expressions of various primate species differ does indicate that the different genetic makeups of these species are determinants of these differences. Under no circumstance could a gelada baboon learn to use a macaque repertoire of facial expressions, since his genetic makeup has not endowed him with such a potential. On the other hand, the expressions and emotions are always influenced by the individual experiences of each particular animal. A dominant animal, who has attained his high social position through his socialization experience may never make a subordinate threat, though he has the genetic potential to do so. Therefore one must ask *which particular inborn and which experiential factors are determinants of facial expression, and by what mechanisms they produce the behavior*, rather than whether a behavior is "innate" or learned. In this chapter, a number of the specific determinants of facial expressions have been distinguished and some of the mechanisms by which they function have been examined. These include certain hormones, parts of the nervous system, the muscular anatomy of the face, and particular stimuli which elicit facial expressions, as well as genetic and experiential factors. Here, with regard to Darwin's assumption of the "innateness" of facial expression, special attention should again be directed to the nervous system and the manner in which it functions in the production of facial expression. Darwin considered facial expressions of emotion "innate" or determined by heredity rather than learned because of the stereotyped nature of these behaviors and because of their universality throughout the races of man. The stereotypy and universality of facial expressions of emotion are due to their mediation by the basal area of the forebrain, which produces stereotyped behavior, rather than to environmental immunity.

THE NERVOUS SYSTEM: ITS EVOLUTION AND ITS ROLE IN THE PRODUCTION OF FACIAL EXPRESSION

The mechanics of the nervous system as an integrative center and its role in the production of facial expressions of emotion can perhaps be most easily understood by tracing its evolutionary development.

The nervous systems of vertebrate ancestral forms, which were probably similar to the primitive fishlike creatures, Amphioxus, evidently consisted of paired, segmentally arranged *peripheral* nerves that led from the skin to a *central nervous system.* The central nervous system was made up of a *spinal cord,* with a slight enlargement at the anterior end corresponding to the vertebrate brain (Storer & Usinger, 1957). Stimuli, such as chemical changes in the water or something touching the animal, generated nervous impulses that passed from the skin or mouth along a peripheral *sensory* nerve for that segment to the spinal cord. Within the spinal cord, the impulses were relayed to *motor* nerves, which activated the segmental muscles, thereby causing the animal to move (see Figure 11). The behavior of these primitive animals was essentially *reflexive* or automatic. Certain stimuli caused the animal to approach and feed; others caused it to retreat.

With the evolution of the vertebrates (e.g., fish), the central nervous system became more complex. A definite brain developed at the anterior end,

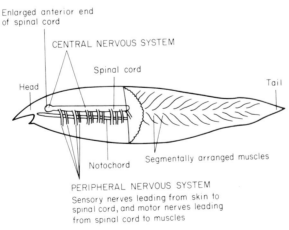

FIG. 11. Schematic diagram of the nervous system of a hypothetical vertebrate ancestor. (Simplified from Romer's 1970, and Storer & Usinger's 1957 descriptions of Amphioxus.)

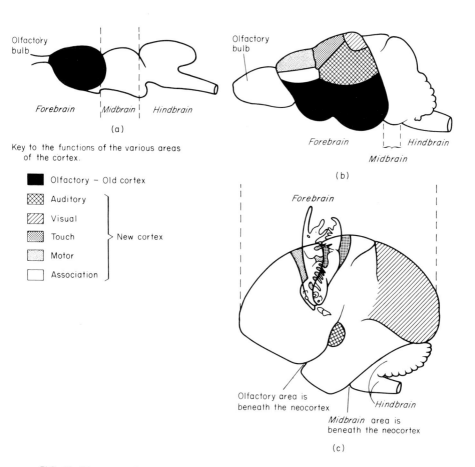

FIG. 12. Diagrammatic representations of the evolution of the cerebral cortex.
(a) Primitive vertebrate stage (fish or amphibian).
(b) Primitive mammal stage (insectivore). (Redrawn from Romer, 1970.)
(c) Advanced mammals stage (monkey). After Clark, 1959; Rose & Woolsey, 1949; and Woolsey, 1965. (Note that the miniature drawings of the monkeys in the touch and motor areas of the cortex roughly show which body parts are related to each part of the brain.)

consisting of lower (hind and midbrain) and higher (forebrain) centers (see Figure 12a). The most posterior part of the hindbrain processed reflexive behavior similar to that of Amphioxus. The more anterior parts of the lower brain centers mediated the vital functions of the organism such as sleep, feeding, reproduction, and primitive emotional responses. These behaviors—feeding, reproduction, etc.—in the more primitive vertebrates were stereotyped, species-specific behaviors. The forebrain was specialized for the reception of olfactory stimuli and for the general arousal of the organism.

As olfactory stimuli entered the olfactory area of the forebrain, impulses were sent down to the lower brain centers, which activated the animal. This primitive arousal mechanism was the precursor of the *limbic system,* which is the seat of emotional activity in higher vertebrates. Its original function was to arouse the organism to action should the environment change, enabling the animal to escape danger or to obtain food. As the brain evolved, the olfactory arousal system gradually enlarged so that it came to be activated by stimuli in all sensory modes (Aronson, 1970).

During the early mammalian evolution especially, the forebrain enlarged, developing sensory centers in the outermost layer, the *cortex,* for registering other sensory stimuli such as light, sound, and touch, which had previously been more simply processed in the lower brain (see Figures 12b and c). In the more primitive mammals, including the prosimians among the primates, the brain is still most highly specialized for handling smell stimuli. However, in the Old World monkeys, apes, and man, the areas for processing stimuli in other sensory modes (particularly the visual) are very highly developed (Clark, 1959), as are additional specialized areas called *association areas.* Association areas function in integrating sensory stimuli from two or more sensory areas of the brain, such as the visual and auditory, thus enabling the animal to modify its behavior according to the more complex information it is now able to obtain. Association areas also provide a mechanism for storing information, which makes it possible for the animal to profit from past experience and to learn. Perhaps most important, the association areas enable the animal to ''make choices'' based on sensory input and stored information. Finally, a further specialized area developed in the cortex for mediating voluntary motor responses, or willfully executed behavior (Romer, 1970; Dethier & Stellar, 1964). Behavior mediated by the motor cortex includes variable, learned motor skills, unlike the stereotyped behavior mediated by the lower brain centers.

As the forebrain enlarged, the new cortex mushroomed out laterally from the old olfactory cortex, which also functioned as an arousal mechanism. This left the old cortex forming a ring or border around the brain stem (comprised of the midbrain and hindbrain). For this reason the old cortex has received the name ''limbic'' (meaning *border*) cortex (see Figure 13). It is, evidently, the limbic cortex which receives the impulses that Papez speculated pass up the nervous system to the cortex and result in emotional consciousness.

In addition to special sensory, association, and motor centers in the cortex, there developed an area deep within the forebrain, the *hypothalamus* (see Figure 8), which took over many of the vital functions previously mediated by the lower brain centers, including sleep, feeding, drinking, reproductive, and emotional behavior (Noback & Moskowitz, 1962). There is some con-

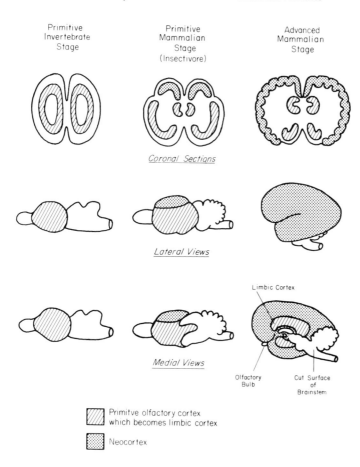

FIG. 13. Schematic diagrams of the growth of the neocortex. (As the neocortex mushroomed out dorsally and ventrally, the older, olfactory cortex assumed a medial position surrounding the brainstem.) (After Romer, 1970; Clark, 1959; and MacLean, 1954.)

troversy as to whether the hypothalamus is the primary structure responsible for mediating expression or whether it is more like a relay station for expression initiated by other limbic structures. Most of the theories are quite hypothetical still, for the actual chemical–physiological mechanisms are not yet understood.

In summary, we have a developmental pattern as follows. In the vertebrates, impulses pass in a reflex arc along sensory nerve fibers to the spinal cord and back along motor nerves to the muscles, causing automatic, unconsciously motivated, reflexive behavior. In the primitive vertebrates, reflexive behavior is combined with a limited number of stereotyped response patterns. Finally, in the higher vertebrates, there are elaborate voluntary motor responses based upon the integration of complex external stimuli in all sensory modes, as well as past experience and internal stimuli (see Figure 14, which diagrams the pathways followed by nerve impulses as a facial expression is produced by a monkey).

The processes responsible for producing complex behavior in higher mammals are integrated hierarchically by a vertical organization of the brain roughly parallel to this evolutionary development. That is to say, impulses pass up and down from the lower reflex centers of the spinal cord and hindbrain to the lower centers of the forebrain (e.g., the hypothalamus), which mediate stereotyped behavior, to the complex integrating centers of the cortex with their various specialized functions. It should be stressed that sensory reception, associational integration, and motor response are processes occurring continuously through time in the normal waking animal, and constant adjustments and feedback loops of the nervous system, passing up and down the many levels and across the many specialized areas of the brain, enable the organism to readjust its activities continually.

In an advanced mammal, the hindbrain, midbrain, and basal areas of the forebrain are capable of handling some simple learning processes such as "conditioning," thereby modifying the behavior mediated by these structures to the extent that the behaviors will occur in some situations and not in others. These brain centers cannot, however, deal with complex learning processes which might significantly modify the form of the behavior; nor can they exert voluntary control over the behavior. As already emphasized, facial expressions of emotion are mediated by subcortical structures, and are, as is characteristic of behaviors mediated by basal brain structures, relatively stereotyped in form. It is the cerebral cortex that receives complex environmental stimuli and mediates both voluntary, planned behavior and complex, learned behavior involving new motor patterns. The cerebral cortex often accomplishes these functions by simultaneously repressing the more stereotyped activities of the lower brain centers. Thus, while purely emotional responses are mediated by subcortical structures and are consequently relatively stereotyped in form, the cerebral cortex can exert some control over the form and manifestation of facial expression. It is because of the potential of the cerebral cortex to override the functions of the lower brain structures that cultural traditions such as "display rules" (see Ekman, this volume, and Ekman, 1972) can exert their effects on facial expressions in man. The extent to which the cerebral cortex can affect facial expression in nonhuman primates has not yet been determined.

The preceding sketch of the evolution of the nervous system has outlined the development of the structures of the brain pertinent to emotional behavior

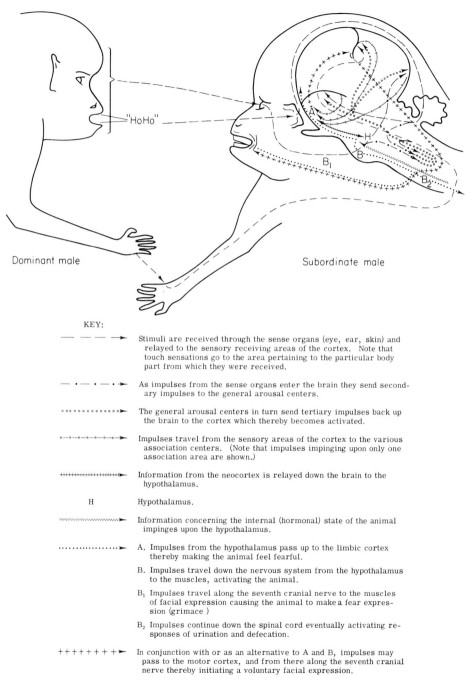

Dominant male   Subordinate male

KEY:

— — — →   Stimuli are received through the sense organs (eye, ear, skin) and relayed to the sensory receiving areas of the cortex. Note that touch sensations go to the area pertaining to the particular body part from which they were received.

— • — • — • →   As impulses from the sense organs enter the brain they send secondary impulses to the general arousal centers.

∘∘∘∘∘∘∘∘∘∘∘∘∘►   The general arousal centers in turn send tertiary impulses back up the brain to the cortex which thereby becomes activated.

∘—∘—∘—∘—∘—∘—∘→   Impulses travel from the sensory areas of the cortex to the various association centers. (Note that impulses impinging upon only one association area are shown.)

++++++++++++++++►   Information from the neocortex is relayed down the brain to the hypothalamus.

H   Hypothalamus.

wwwwwwww►   Information concerning the internal (hormonal) state of the animal impinges upon the hypothalamus.

••••••••••►   A. Impulses from the hypothalamus pass up to the limbic cortex thereby making the animal feel fearful.

B. Impulses travel down the nervous system from the hypothalamus to the muscles, activating the animal.

B_1 Impulses travel along the seventh cranial nerve to the muscles of facial expression causing the animal to make a fear expression (grimace)

B_2 Impulses continue down the spinal cord eventually activating responses of urination and defecation.

+ + + + + + + +►   In conjunction with or as an alternative to A and B, impulses may pass to the motor cortex, and from there along the seventh cranial nerve thereby initiating a voluntary facial expression.

FIG. 14. Schematic diagram of the pathways followed by nerve impulses in a subordinate monkey as he interacts with a dominant monkey. (See text for further explanation.)

as well as the development of the mechanisms through which the brain mediates behavior. Papez's (1937) theory of emotion (presented on page 44) clearly described the roles of the cortex and the hypothalamus in determining emotional responses in higher mammals. Papez's theory implies that while invertebrates and lower vertebrates (fish, amphibians, and reptiles), which essentially lack a cortex, can make emotional responses (such as an attack), only the higher vertebrates, which possess a well-developed cortex, can experience conscious emotional feelings and control their emotional expression.

Recent experimental studies have essentially confirmed Papez's theory of emotion. The experiments of Bryan Robinson (1967), in which 5880 areas in the forebrains of unanesthetized rhesus monkeys were electrically stimulated by inserting electrodes into their brains, revealed that the sites eliciting vocal behavior, which, like facial expression, is primarily an emotional response, are primarily within the limbic system.[14] Similarly, in a series of stimulation experiments, Paul MacLean (1962) found that limbic stimulation elicits sexual behavior in squirrel monkeys *(Saimiri sciureus).*

Jose Delgado's (1969) stimulation experiments support Papez's hypothesis that motor displays of facial expression occur through downward discharges of nervous impulses and that such downward discharges elicit only the motor displays without the accompanying subjective emotions. Delgado found that stimulation of the lower brain centers of macaques and chimpanzees left free in their social groups resulted in what he calls ''false rage.'' This is purely a motor response which, though it looks like anger, is not acted upon by other animals in the group and cannot be conditioned; thus the animal, being unaware of what it is doing, cannot be taught to make or avoid such responses.

A number of studies have emphasized the role of the cortex in the expression of emotion. MacLean and Delgado (1953) found that the stimulation of the cortex occasionally elicited very complex behavioral patterns, particularly aggression. This finding was in contrast to observations that stimulation of lower brain structures often elicited very simple fragments of behavior, and it supported the vertical and hierarchical theories of cerebral organization: that impulses pass up and down the brain, and that the higher forebrain structures have control over the functions of lower structures and mediate more complex behavior. Furthermore, the stimulation experiments of Delgado (1963) and Rosvold, Mirsky, and Pribram (1954) showed that neither brain stimulation nor surgical ablations generally produce standard effects. On the contrary, the effects are dependent upon such factors as the animal's position in the dominance hierarchy, the past experiences of

---

[14]*"Limbic system" refers to both the limbic lobe of the cortex and the deeper structures of the brain, such as the hypothalamus, which Papez and others proposed were involved in the manifestation of emotional behavior.*

the individual, the social setting, and the other animals with whom the animal might interact. For example, Delgado (1969) found that when a particular macaque monkey was placed in a social group in which she was dominant she would, upon electrical stimulation of a particular brain site, display threat expressions; when this animal was stimulated in the presence of animals more dominant than she, no threats were given. Similarly, Delgado (1967) found that stimulation of a particular brain center would elicit aggression from a particular monkey if he were placed with one group of subordinates, but would not elicit aggression if he were placed with another subordinate animal with whom he was particularly friendly. So, even in the electrically stimulated animal, the behavior elicited is often modulated by experience and incoming stimuli through processes that occur in the great association areas of the cerebral cortex.

MacLean (1962) emphasizes the anatomical findings that nerve tracts connect the limbic system to the prefrontal cortex in squirrel monkeys *(Saimiri sciureus)*. This cortical region is the large association area that has generally been found to pertain to voluntary behaviors involved in anticipation and planning. Such connections suggest that even in these New World primates, there may be considerable voluntary control over emotional behavior.

In summary, the behavior of a monkey depends upon his assessing what is going on around him—as, for example, the dominant male in his group threatening him—through the reception of the relevant sensory stimuli. Thus, a threat expression from the dominant male is received through the eyes, threat vocalization through the ears, and a blow on the arm through sensory receptors in the skin of the arm. The stimuli set off nerve impulses that enter the brain and are relayed, according to the sensory mode, to the appropriate parts of the cortex. The information concerning the dominant male's expression is relayed to the visual area of the cortex, that concerning the vocalization to the auditory area, and that concerning being hit is relayed to the area of the sensory cortex which pertains specifically to the arm—for, in the case of tactile stimuli, segregation occurs according to the body part from which the stimuli are received (see Figure 12c). As these impulses pass up the nervous system to the sensory areas of the cortex, secondary impulses are relayed to the general arousal centers lower in the brain. From the arousal centers, impulses are relayed back up the brain to the sensory areas of the cortex, activating these areas. The sensory information (regarding the expression, vocalization, and blow from the dominant monkey) is then relayed to the association cortex, which has become extremely elaborate in the higher mammals, and particularly in the higher primates, in which large portions of the cortex are devoted to associative activity. Within the association cortex, experiential information is processed. (For example, the information that when our subordinate monkey was threatened the last time by the dominant male, he was then bitten.) Subsequently information concerning sensory stimuli and experiential factors is probably relayed down the brain to the hypothalamus and other subcortical structures, where it is further processed, as is hormonal information concerning the internal state of the animal. The animal is now ready to make a response. Should he make an emotional response (such as a fear grimace), impulses will be sent from the hypothalamus *up* to the limbic cortex, making him feel fearful, and impulses will be sent *down* the brain to the motor nerves and to the facial muscles, making him grimace and also making him perform other autonomic (unconscious) behaviors, such as urination and defecation.

Should the monkey make a voluntary response, impulses will pass from the association areas to the appropriate area of the motor cortex and then *down* the brain to the motor nerves. It is likely that the behavior displayed is often the result of both emotional involuntary and voluntary activity. For example, the fearful animal might urinate and defecate, but mask the fear grimace with a blank expression (see Figure 14).

Even from this very superficial discussion of the role of the nervous system in the display of emotion, one can appreciate its intricacies and complexity. In Darwin's day very little was known about the nervous system. Darwin commented on reflex behavior and on "habit." But he conceived of the development of "habit" as a process that occurs in the peripheral nervous system rather than in the central nervous system. Furthermore, Darwin had little idea of the integrative properties of the nervous system, and of the way in which experiential variables and incoming stimuli are processed and motor responses carried out.

THE MUSCULAR ANATOMY: THE EVOLUTION OF
FACIAL MUSCLES AND FACIAL EXPRESSIONS

As was pointed out in the previous section on muscular anatomy, among Darwin's major contributions to the study of facial expression were his emphasis on facial musculature as a determinant of expression and his understanding of the intimate relationships between form and function. There have been a number of studies made on the anatomy of the primate face since Darwin's time (e.g., Huber, 1930, 1931, 1933; Gregory, 1929; Szebenyi, 1969). The most comprehensive work, that of Huber, is still to be verified. Furthermore, there has been no comprehensive systematic study interrelating the evolution of the muscles with that of the facial behavior of these animals. Because of this lack, a brief survey, collating the available data on these two subjects is presented here.

The muscles of facial expression in primates are derived from the superficial muscles of the neck region of more primitive vertebrates (see Figure 15). In present-day amphibians and reptiles these superficial muscles are still essentially limited to the neck region. Consequently, these animals are capable only of opening and closing the eyes, nose, and mouth (actions performed by deeper groups of muscles). Besides their limited excursion into the area of the face, the muscles of amphibians and reptiles are not connected to the skin. Thus the facial skin of these animals is immobile and they are essentially devoid of facial expression (Huber, 1930, 1931, 1933; van Hooff, 1967).

FIG. 15. Schematic diagram of the superficial *platysma* and the deeper *sphincter colli profundus* muscle groups as they split off from the primitive *sphincter colli* muscles of the neck and grew into the facial region in a hypothetical primitive mammal. (Adapted from Huber, 1931.)

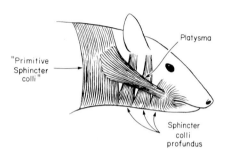

"Primitive Sphincter colli"

Platysma

Sphincter colli profundus

In mammals the primitive neck muscles gave rise to two muscle layers: a superficial longitudinal layer, the *platysma,* and a deeper transverse layer, the *sphincter colli profundus,* which have come to extend well into the facial region (see Figure 15). These muscles developed extensive connections with the skin and became increasingly complex, differentiating to perform specialized actions (see Figure 16a and b). As the neck muscles moved into the facial region, they pulled the seventh cranial nerve, by which they had been previously innervated, along with them (Huber, 1931). The derivation of all the muscles of facial expression from the same primitive sphincter muscles of the neck explains why all these muscles are innervated by the same nerve (see Figure 16c).

The development of large superficial muscular sheets—with extensive connections to a vascularized skin (a skin that contains blood vessels), sweat glands, and hair—over the bodies of mammals may have evolved as insulation for these warm-blooded animals (Gregory, 1929). Huber (1930) and van Hooff (1962) suggest that the appearance of extensive facial musculature in mammals is closely connected with the new functional developments: extensive chewing of food and suckling of the young. Without the facial muscles that form the cheeks and lips, extensive chewing and suckling would not be possible. Indeed, among the primitive mammals, such as the duck-billed platypus, which lacks extensive superficial facial musculature including lips and cheeks (Huber, 1930), the milk is ejected from the mammary glands and the infants lap up the exuded milk with their tongues (Burrell, 1927).

Andrew (1963a, 1964) notes that among the primates, facial mobility

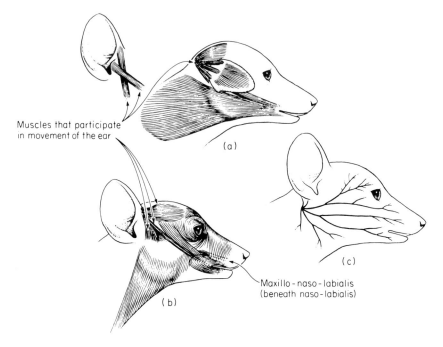

Muscles that participate in movement of the ear

(a)

(b)

(c)

Maxillo - naso - labialis
(beneath naso - labialis)

FIG. 16. Diagrams of the musculature of facial expression and its innervation in the lemur.
(a) Differentiation of the *platysma* muscle group. (After Huber, 1931.)
(b) Differentiation of the *sphincter colli profundus* muscle group. (The *platysma* muscle group has been dissected away.) (After Huber, 1931; and Hill, 1953.)
(c) The pathways of the seventh cranial nerve, the facial nerve, which innervates the muscles of facial expression. (Note that the nerve branches out from the neck region, the site of phylogenetic origin of the muscles which it innervates.) (Redrawn from Huber, 1931.)

is most prominent in groups that live in large permanent societies, such as the Old World monkeys, New World monkeys, and some lemurs. He speculates that it was because of the adaptive value of communication for group-living mammals[15] that both the expressions and the specialized musculature have evolved. Some modern authors, such as Buettner-Janusch (1966) and Andrew (1964), like Darwin, also consider that facial expressions may have evolved as adaptations for making particular kinds of vocalizations, as protective responses, and as intention movements.

The lemurs, the macaques, the chimpanzee and gorilla, and man have been chosen for examination because they are among the best studied, and because they approximate a series of evolutionary stages within the primates. However, it must be stressed that the living primates do not pre-

---

[15] Among other mammals, the species in which facial expressions are most highly developed also tend to be the most social species. In addition, van Hooff (1962) notes that the species that have highly developed facial expressions also have highly developed vision, which enables them to use the expressions for social communication.

cisely represent past evolutionary stages, since all species have been continually evolving.

The facial musculature of the Madagascar lemur (Lemur variegatus), a prosimian and a relatively primitive primate, is not well differentiated. It is nevertheless specialized for the reception of sound, smell, and touch stimuli. These special receptors are highly adaptive for an animal that inhabits an essentially nocturnal arboreal ecological niche. As an adaptation for sound reception, relatively large groups of muscles have developed around the ears, making them highly mobile (see Figures 16a and b). As an adaptation for receiving smell and touch stimuli, muscles have differentiated about the snout, which control the movement of its sensitive wet tip, the rhinarium (Huber, 1931; Hill, 1953; Napier & Napier, 1967).

Andrew (1963c, 1964), who has extensively though unsystematically studied the evolution of primate facial expressions, describes five facial expressions in lemurs, three of which involve movement of facial muscles about the mouth (see Table 1).

The fact that a vocalization invariably accompanies three of the facial expressions in these primitive primates (see Table 1) supports the hypothesis that the evolution of primate musculature was at least in part an adaptation for making particular kinds of vocalizations. Though lemurs are evidently capable of some muscular mouth movements, the presence of the rhinarium and philtrum, the wet parts of the nose that extends from above the nostrils to the margins of the lips, prevent the muscles of the lips from completely encircling the mouth. In addition, the upper lip is firmly anchored in the midline to the underlying upper jaw by a frenulum. These structures prevent the degree of mouth movement possible in the higher primates, which lack a rhinarium, philtrum, and frenulum (Clark, 1959; Hill, 1953; Napier & Napier, 1967). (See Figures 17a and b.)

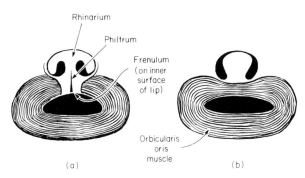

FIG. 17. Diagram of the evolutionary development of the orbicularis oris muscle of the mouth. (Adapted from Clark, 1959; and Hill, 1953.)
(a) The more primitive condition in the tree shrew, the most primitive living primate.
(b) The condition in a more advanced primate, such as the macaque, in which the muscle has come to encircle the mouth.

TABLE 1

Some Facial Expressions of Lemurs[a]

Context and emotion	Name of expression	Eyes	Ears	Mouth	Vocalization
Confident threat (anger).		Direct gaze.		Jaws open; lips contracted, covering the teeth in some species.	Invariably accompanied by "bark" or "cough."
Subordinate threat (fear-anger).				Alternation of jaws open and lips contracted, covering the teeth (above), and lips retracted horizontally, producing a "grin" (below).	Invariably accompanied by "yips."
Extreme sub-mission (fear).	"Grin."	Gaze aver-sion.		Lips retracted horizontally, producing a "grin."	Invariably accompanied by "shrieks."
Greeting (affection).				Repeated tongue protru-sion. (When the animals come close together, tactile licking takes pre-cedence over visual expression.)	
Solicitation for grooming.		Eyes half closed.	Drawn back.		

[a] The table presents only partial descriptions of the expressions to convey a general impression of their appearance and to permit comparisons between species. The descriptions are abstracted from Andrew's (1963c, 1964) descriptions of some of the facial expressions of several lemur species.

The facial musculature of the macaques reflects a reduction in sound, touch, and smell reception and an increase in muscle differentiation about the mouth, resulting in increased oral mobility in facial expressiveness, in feeding, and possibly in vocalizing. This shift to visual functions (facial expressions) is part of the general adaptation of monkeys to diurnal (daytime) life in the trees, as well as to a complex social life. The shift away from the acoustic function is reflected in both a reduction in the number, size, and activity of the extrinsic ear musculature (the muscles external to the ear, which produce ear movement) and a reduction in the relative size of the ear. (Compare Figures 16a and b with Figures 18a and b.) Though there has been a reduction in ear musculature and mobility, the muscle of the forehead *(frontalis)* is well developed, and among many of the macaques simultaneous retraction of the scalp, forehead, and ears is, as Darwin emphasized, a prominent feature of the facial behavior. In this case ear retraction functions mainly as a visual communicative signal rather than as an acoustic aid. This means that the adaptive functions of the ear musculature have shifted during evolution, for while the ear movements functioned in sound reception in lemurs, they have come to serve visual communicative functions in macaques. The increase in oral mobility is made possible by the loss of the *rhinarium* and *philtrum,* permitting the development of a muscular band (the *orbicularis oris* muscle) all around the mouth (see Figures 17a and b), and the reduction of the *frenulum,* permitting greater freedom of movement of the upper lip. These developments are accompanied by further differentiation and enlargement of the muscles of the mouth and cheeks (compare Figures 16b and 18b). An additional specialization of the facial musculature in the macaques is the development of a cheek pouch. Food is pushed into the cheek pouch from the

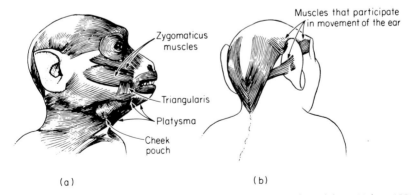

(a) (b)

FIG. 18. Diagrams of the facial musculature of a macaque. (Adapted from Huber, 1931; and Szebenyi, 1969.)
(a) The facial musculature in profile view.
(b) The extrinsic ear musculature.

mouth and temporarily stored there. It is voluntarily returned to the mouth when the animal is ready to eat.

The macaques make approximately a dozen different kinds of facial expressions, with continua of intermediate expressions, or blends, between them (van Hooff, 1967; Chevalier-Skolnikoff, 1971, in press). Table 2 and Figures 19a-k present descriptions and illustrations of a number of these expressions.

A comparison of the facial expressions of lemurs and macaques (see Tables 1 and 2) reveals strong similarities between the corresponding emotional expressions for "confident threat," "subordinate threat," "fear," and "affection." The comparison also suggests that there is considerably more muscular activity about the mouth in macaque expressions than in lemur expressions. The tables also suggest that macaques make more expressions. While these last two impressions are probably correct, one must keep in mind that the descriptions reflect the work of different investigators, whose methods may not yield equally detailed descriptions.

A comparison of the facial musculature of the great apes, viz., the chimpanzee and gorilla, with that of the macaques reveals a further reduction of the ear, scalp, and forehead muscles, and fuller differentiation of the muscles of the midfacial region, particularly around the mouth. The ear muscles in the apes have become smaller, originating closer to the ear and inserting, or attaching, at the root of the ear rather than extending well onto the ear. Consequently there is little leverage, and little ear movement is possible (compare Figures 18b and 20b). Similarly, the extent and consequent potential for movement of the anterior and posterior scalp muscles have been reduced (Huber, 1931).

A number of developments have resulted in increased mobility about the mouth. The *platysma,* as seen in the macaque, is a sheet of muscle that extends from the shoulder anteriorly up the neck, criss-crossing over

---

FIG. 19. Some facial expressions of macaques.
(a) "Stare"; anger, type 1.
(b) "Round-mouthed stare"; anger, type 2.
(c) "Open-mouthed stare"; anger, type 3.
(d) "Bared-teeth stare"; fear-anger.
(e) "Grimace"; fear.
(f) "Teeth chatter" (teeth together); ambivalent affection-fear.
(g) "Teeth chatter" (teeth parted); ambivalent affection-fear.
(h) "Lip smack" (teeth parted); affection, type 1.
(i) "Puckered lips"; affection, type 2.
(j) "Square mouth"; excitement-affection (as displayed by an infant).
(k) "Open mouth eyelids down"; playfulness.
Note–These drawings are presented for illustrative purposes only. They are diagrammatic and do not claim to precisely depict actual expressions of emotion. They are drawn from photographs of Macaca arctoides printed from Super 8-mm motion picture film. All drawings were made from the same angle in order to facilitate comparisons.

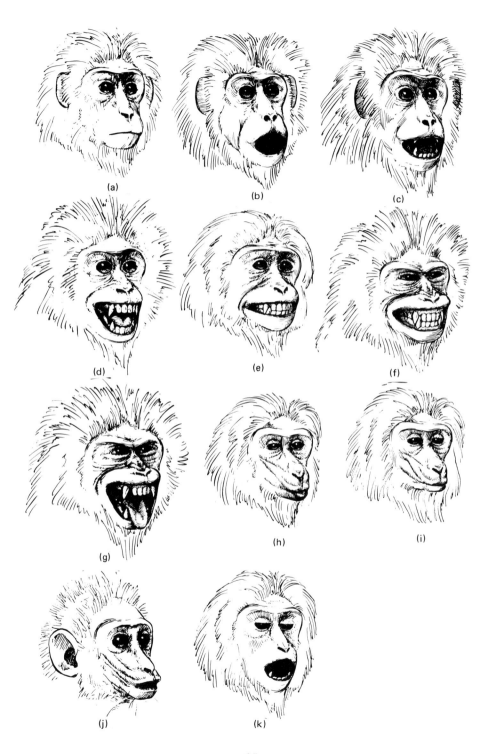

(a)

(b)

(c)

(d)

(e)

(f)

(g)

(h)

(i)

(j)

(k)

65

TABLE 2

Some Facial Expressions of Macaques[a]

Context and emotion	Name of expression	Eyes	Forehead and brow	Ears	Mouth	Vocalization
Confident, dominant threat (anger), type 1.	"Stare" (Chevalier-Skolnikoff, 1971); "tense-mouth" (Van Hooff, 1967).	Wide open; direct gaze, frequently with eye-to-eye contact.	Brow often raised and lowered.	Ears forward.	Jaws closed; lips tightly closed.	
Confident threat (anger), type 2.	"Round-mouthed stare" (Chevalier-Skolnikoff, 1971); "staring open-mouth" (Van Hooff, 1967).	Wide open; direct gaze, frequently with eye-to-eye contact.	Brow raised.	Ears forward.	Jaws open; lips contracted vertically and horizontally, covering the teeth and forming an "o" mouth opening.	Often accompanied by "roar."
Moderately confident threat (anger), type 3.	"Open-mouthed stare" (Chevalier-Skolnikoff, 1971); "staring open-mouth" (Van Hooff, 1967).	Wide open; direct gaze, frequently with eye-to-eye contact.	Brow raised and then lowered.	Ears forward.	Jaws slightly to moderately open; lips moderately contracted vertically, covering the upper teeth, but often not the lower teeth.	Often accompanied by "hoarse roar."
Subordinate threat (fear-anger).	"Bared-teeth stare" (Chevalier-Skolnikoff, 1971); "staring bared-teeth scream" (Van Hooff, 1967).	Wide open; alternation of direct gaze, often with eye-to-eye contact, and gaze avoidance.	Brow lowered; forehead retracted.	Ears back.	Jaws and teeth repeatedly opened and closed; lips retracted vertically and horizontally, displaying the teeth.	Often accompanied by "high-pitched scream."
Extreme submission (fear).	"Grimace" (Chevalier-Skolnikoff, 1971); "silent bared-teeth" (Van Hooff, 1967).	Gaze avoidance most common, but brief direct looks with eye-to-eye contact sometimes.	Brow raised.	Ears back.	Jaws closed or slightly open; lips widely retracted horizontally and slightly to extremely retracted vertically, thereby displaying the teeth in a "grin."	Accompanied only under the most intense circumstances by "high-pitched scream."
As equals, approach and embrace after a fight (ambivalent affection-fear).	"Teeth chatter" (Chevalier-Skolnikoff, 1971, and Van Hooff, 1967).	Eyelids slightly lowered; eye-to-eye contact sometimes (but only at a distance).	Brow lowered extremely.	Ears back.	Jaws opening and closing; tongue alternately protruded and retracted as the jaws open and close; lips widely retracted vertically and horizontally, displaying the teeth and gums.	Usually accompanied by "squeaks."

Non-hostile approach, greeting, grooming (affection), type 1.	"Lip-smack" (Chevalier-Skolnikoff, 1971, and Van Hooff, 1967).	Eyelids slightly lowered.	Brow slightly lowered.	Ears back.	Jaws opening and closing; tongue alternately protruded and retracted as the jaws open and close; as the jaws close, the lips contract horizontally and extend, forming a "pucker."	Accompanied by an unvoiced smacking sound as the tongue breaks contact with the roof of the mouth and is protruded.
Non-hostile approach, greeting, grooming (affection), type 2.	"Puckered lips" (Chevalier-Skolnikoff, 1971); "pout" (Van Hooff, 1967).	Eyelids slightly lowered.	Brow slightly lowered.	Ears back.	Jaws and lips closed; lips contracted horizontally and extended, forming a "pucker."	
Infantile expression (fear-frustration?).	"Bared-teeth gecker" (Van Hooff, 1967).	Eyelids lowered.	Brow sometimes lifted.	Ears back.	Jaws varying from closed to opened; lips vertically and horizontally retracted.	Accompanied by a "gecker."
Excited approach (excitement-affection).	"Square-mouth" (Chevalier-Skolnikoff, 1971); "protruded-lips" (Van Hooff, 1967).	Eyelids slightly lowered.	Brow slightly lowered.	Ears back.	Jaws opened slightly; lips contracted vertically and horizontally and greatly extended, forming a rectangular lip opening ($\square$) in _Macaca arctoides_ and an "o" opening in most other macaque species.	Occasionally accompanied by "faint squeaks and grunts."
Play (playfulness).	"Open-mouth eyelids-down" (Chevalier-Skolnikoff, 1971); "relaxed open-mouth" (Van Hooff, 1967).	Eyelids slightly to extremely lowered; avoidance of direct gaze and eye-to-eye contact.	Brow raised, forehead retracted.	Ears back.	Jaws opened wide; lips slightly contracted vertically, covering the upper teeth but often not the lower teeth.	

[a]The table presents only partial descriptions of the expressions, to convey a general impression of their appearance and permit comparisons between species. The descriptions are abstracted from Chevalier-Skolnikoff's (1971) descriptions of expressions in _Macaca arctoides_ and Van Hooff's (1967) general descriptions of expressions in Old World monkeys and apes.

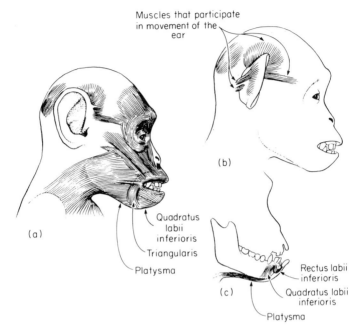

Muscles that participate
in movement of the
ear

(b)

(a)

Quadratus
labii
inferioris

Triangularis

Platysma

(c)

Rectus labii
inferioris

Quadratus labii
inferioris

Platysma

FIG. 20. Diagrams of the facial musculature of a chimpanzee. (Adapted from Huber, 1931.)
(a) The facial musculature in profile view.
(b) The extrinsic ear musculature.
(c) Musculature of the lower jaw and lip derived from the *platysma*.

the midline under the lower jaw and running forward over the lower jaw
(see Figure 18a). In the chimpanzee and gorilla, the *platysma* has become
partly attached to the lower jaw, thereby forming a new muscle, the *quadratus
labii inferioris*, which runs from the jaw anteriorly. In addition, a part of
the new quadratus *labii inferioris, the rectus labii inferioris*, has split away
from the main body of the muscle and participates in the formation of
the lower lip (see Figure 20c). Similar developments have occurred in the
evolution of the upper lip. The *zygomaticus* muscle mass of the macaque
appears as several distinct muscle groups in the chimpanzee and gorilla.
These insert into the upper lip from various angles, thereby providing several
functional muscle bundles capable of moving the lips in different ways.
This group of muscles has been named the *quadratus labii superioris*. A
rectus labii superioris has split off from the *superior quadratus labii* muscles
in the same manner as it developed inferiorly (Huber, 1931). Accompanying
this muscular differentiation is a tremendous increase in the relative size
of the lips.

Behaviorally, the reduction of ear, scalp, and forehead musculature is

TABLE 3

Some Facial Expressions of Chimpanzees[a, b]

Context and emotion	Name of expression	Eyes	Mouth	Vocalization
Confident, dominant threat (anger), type 1.	"Glare" (Van Lawick-Goodall, 1968a); "bulging lips" (Van Hooff, 1971).	Direct gaze.	Jaws closed; lips closed.	
Confident, dominant threat (anger), type 2.	"Waa bark" (Van Lawick-Goodall, 1968a); "woaow-bark" (Van Hooff, 1971).	Direct gaze.	Jaws half open; lips slightly extended and contracted, covering the teeth.	Accompanied by a "bark."
Subordinate threat (fear-anger).	"Scream calls" (Van Lawick-Goodall, 1968a); "staring bared-teeth scream face" (Van Hooff, 1967).		Jaws half or wide open; lips retracted vertically and horizontally, displaying the teeth.	Often accompanied by "screams."
Submission (fear).	"Grinning" (Van Lawick-Goodall, 1968a); "bared-teeth yelp" (Van Hooff, 1971).		Jaws closed to slightly open; lips retracted vertically and horizontally, displaying the teeth and gums.	Accompanied by "squeaks."
Submission, re-assurance, affection, type 1, submission (fear).	"Silent bared-teeth"; "type 1, horizontal bared-teeth" (Van Hooff, 1971); "silent grin" (Van Lawick-Goodall, 1968a).		Jaws closed to slightly open; lips retracted vertically and horizontally, displaying the teeth and gums.	

TABLE 3—(*Continued*)

Context and emotion	Name of expression	Eyes	Mouth	Vocalization
Submission, re-assurance, affection, type 2, appeasement (fear-affection?).	"Silent bared-teeth"; "type 2, vertical bared-teeth" (Van Hooff, 1971); "silent grin" (Van Lawick-Goodall, 1968a).		Jaws closed to slightly open; lips retracted vertically and slightly extended, partially displaying the teeth.	
Submission, re-assurance, affection, type 3 (affection).	"Silent bared-teeth"; "type 3, open-mouth bared-teeth" (Van Hooff, 1971); "silent grin" (Van Lawick-Goodall, 1968a).		Jaws wide open; lips vertically and horizontally retracted, exposing the teeth and gums.	
Submission, re-assurance, affection, type 4 (affection).	"Lip-smacking" (Van Hooff, 1971).		Jaws opening and closing rhythmically.	Teeth often clicking together audibly.
When infants are trying to reach their mothers; when adults are begging (desiring-frustration?).	"Pout face" (Van Lawick-Goodall, 1968a); "pout-moan" and "silent pout" (Van Hooff, 1971).	Eyes open and staring at animal from whom desired goal is sought.	Jaws probably closed or slightly open; lips contracted vertically and extended horizontally and extended at the corners and parted in the middle, forming a pursed appearance with an "o" opening.	In some cases accompanied by "ho" call.

When juveniles are lost or frustrated (frustration-sadness?), type 1.	"Whimper face" (Van Lawick-Goodall, 1968a); "stretched-pout whimper" (Van Hooff, 1971).	Jaws closed or nearly closed; lips slightly retracted horizontally; lips curled outward and protruding with lower lip drawn down.	Accompanied by a "cry."
(Frustration-sadness), type 2.	"Cry face" (Van Lawick-Goodall, 1968a).	Jaws open wide; lips retracted horizontally; lower lip drawn down.	
Excited approach (excitement-affection?).	"Hoot face" (Van Lawick-Goodall, 1968a); "rising hoot" (Van Hooff, 1971).	Jaws slightly to moderately open; lips greatly extended into a "trumpet"; lips sometimes slightly retracted vertically.	Accompanied by a "hoot."
Play (playfulness).	"Play face" (Van Lawick-Goodall, 1968a); "relaxed open-mouth" (Van Hooff, 1971).	Jaws moderately to widely open; lips either retracted horizontally, but remaining relaxed so that the upper teeth are covered while the lower teeth are exposed, or retracted vertically, displaying all the teeth.	Often accompanied by "laughter."

[a] The table presents only partial descriptions of the expressions to convey a general impression of their appearance and permit comparisons between species. The descriptions are abstracted from Van Lawick, Marler and Van Lawick-Goodall (film), Van Lawick-Goodall (1968a), and Van Hooff (1971).

[b] No data were available for the forehead and brow.

correlated with reduction of the mobility of these structures (note that in Table 3 on facial expression in chimpanzees, no ear movements have been described). The behavioral consequence of the proliferation and relative enlargement of midfacial musculature is, however, less clear. While many primatologists have the *impression* that the midfacial region, and particularly the lips, of these great apes is far more mobile and capable of producing a greater variety of expressions than is that of the macaques, the available catalogues of facial expressions list and describe approximately the same number of expressions for both (Reynolds & Reynolds, 1965; Schaller, 1963; van Lawick-Goodall, 1968a; van Hooff, 1971). Comparison of contextually equivalent expressions (Tables 2 and 3) shows them to be also very similar, and an experienced observer of macaque facial expressions could recognize and identify many of the ape expressions. However, detailed examination reveals certain differences in the form of the expressions, and it is the proliferation of the midfacial musculature, particularly around the lips, which makes these differences possible. For example, the chimpanzees' *desiring-frustration* expression ("pout face," van Lawick-Goodall, 1968a), though probably equivalent to the macaque *affection type 2* expressions ("pucker lips"), is characterized by far greater outward extension of the lips. The same is the case with the apes' *excited approach* expression ("hoot face," van Lawick-Goodall, 1968a), probably equivalent to the macaques' *excited approach* expression ("square mouth"), in which the lips are protruded forward "into a trumpet." Similarly, in the chimpanzees' *frustration-sadness* expression ("whimper face," van Lawick-Goodall, 1968a), the lower lip is extended and pulled downward in a manner that is probably impossible for a macaque (see Figures 19 and 21).

FIG. 21. Some facial expressions of chimpanzees.
(a) "Glare"; anger, type 1.
(b) "Waa bark"; anger, type 2.
(c) "Scream calls"; fear-anger.
(d) "Silent bared-teeth"; " type 1, horizontal bared-teeth"; submission.
(e) "Silent bared-teeth"; " type 2, vertical bared-teeth"; fear–affection (?).
(f) "Silent bared-teeth"; " type 3, open-mouth bared-teeth"; affection.
(g) "Pout face"; desiring-frustration (?).
(h) "Whimper face"; frustration-sadness (?), type 1, or type 1-2 transition (infant).
(i) "Cry face"; frustration–sadness, type 2 (infant).
(j) "Hoot face"; excitement–affection (?).
(k) "Play face"; playfulness.
   Note–These drawings are presented for illustrative purposes only. They are diagrammatic and do not claim to precisely depict actual expressions of emotion. They are drawn after photographs and descriptions from van Hooff, 1971; and van Lawick-Goodall, 1968a, b. All expressions were drawn from the same angle in order to facilitate comparisons.

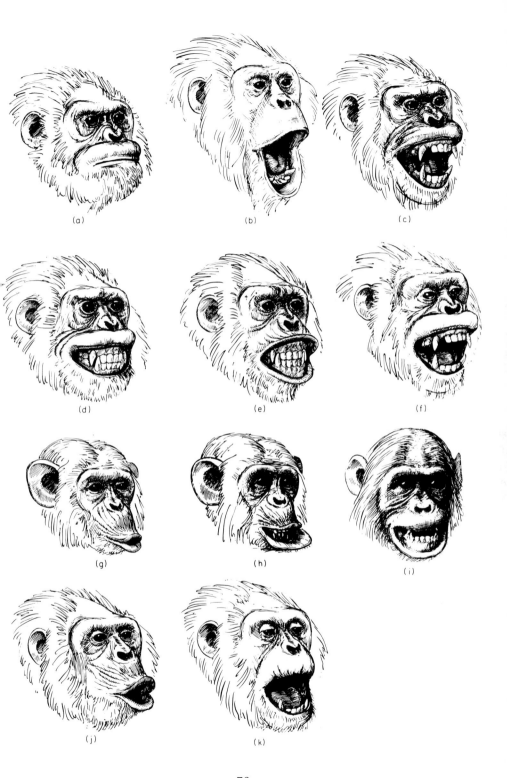

(a)   (b)   (c)

(d)   (e)   (f)

(g)   (h)   (i)

(j)   (k)

While the differences between many of the macaque and chimpanzee facial expressions can be understood in terms of the differentiation of the midfacial musculature, examination of the behavioral evidence does not clarify what the adaptive advantages might have been for further differentiation of these muscles, since the data obtained so far do not show any increase in the number or significant shifts in the kinds of expressions made. It is possible that this muscle differentiation about the lips is an adaptation for feeding; for, despite the ape's relatively skillful use of its hands, the lips are of considerable importance in feeding. For example, van Lawick-Goodall (1968b) reports:

> Some foods are normally prepared before the chimpanzees swallow them, and this is accomplished by a skillful combination of the use of hands, teeth, lips and tongue. The apes use their hands and teeth to tear open large pods and pick out the seeds with their teeth and lips. They pick small pods (some were less than half an inch in length) by mouth and then extract the seeds with their lips, teeth and tongue. They use their teeth and lips to extract pith from a stem which they have picked by hand. They use their canine teeth, and hands, to tear apart large fruits with rough rinds such as those of *Conopharyngia* spp., and scrape out the flesh with their teeth and lips or by hooking movements of one index finger. . .
>
> When a chimpanzee is satiated he may sit or recline, sucking at a wad of skin, seeds or stones in his lower lip. Every few minutes the lip is protruded and the chimpanzee peers down over his nose at the wad [pp. 185-186].

An examination of the facial musculature in man (see Figure 22) shows a continuation of the trends seen in the macaques and the great apes. There is a further reduction in the relative size and extent of the ear and scalp musculature. Concomitantly, there is further muscle differentiation over the anterior part of the cranium into frontal and temporal muscle complexes (a trend already seen in the apes, though less strikingly). The trend in reduction of ear musculature results in nearly total absence of ear mobility (few people can move their ears). The "new" anterior ear muscle, *auricularis anterior,* is actually just a thin fragment that has split off from the muscle, *auricularis superior,* adjacent to it. As is the case with the rest of the ear musculature, it inserts at the perimeter of the ear, and is not capable of making any significant contribution to ear movement. It represents a deterioration rather than an elaboration of the ear musculature. Similarly, the muscular differentiation over the anterior cranial vault does not result in any increase in facial mobility. Rather, it is probably the result of the enlargement of the cranium which is in turn due to the enlargement of the brain. The functional result of this muscular differentiation is a further *reduction* in the mobility of the ears and scalp (Huber, 1931).

In addition to the regression of scalp and ear musculature, there is continued differentiation of the midfacial musculature. The *zygomaticus* muscles

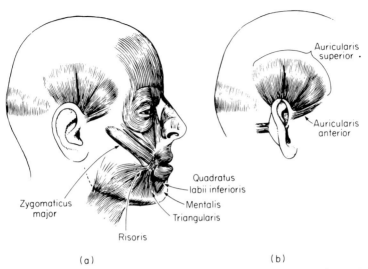

Auricularis
superior •

Auricularis
anterior

Quadratus
labii inferioris

Mentalis

Triangularis

Zygomaticus
major

Risoris

(a)   (b)

FIG. 22. Diagrams of the facial musculature of man. (After Gray, 1930; Huber, 1931; and Sobotta, 1953.)
(a) The facial musculature in profile view.
(b) The extrinsic ear musculature.

become more distinct (Huber, 1931), and provide the potential for even greater diversity of movement of the lips and cheeks (compare Figures 20a and 22a). *Zygomaticus major* becomes capable of drawing the mouth corners backward and upward, as in the human smile (Gray, 1930). Muscular development around the mouth in man also includes more extensive anchorage of the *quadratus labii inferioris* to the lower jaw and further development of *rectus labii inferioris* and *superioris*. In addition, there is considerable architectural change about the corners of the mouth. The base of the *triangularis* muscle becomes fixed to the lower jaw, thereby enhancing its potential for pulling the mouth corners down (Gray, 1930), as in the human "cry face." From the *triangularis,* two new muscles have developed, *risoris* and *mentalis*. *Risoris* pulls the mouth corners laterally, and *mentalis* pushes the lower lip out; consequently, these new muscles provide the potential for new movements. Furthermore, there is a more complex interlacing of the various muscle groups at the mouth corners in man than exists in the apes (Huber, 1931). As was the case with the apes, some of the muscular changes found in man are reflected in his characteristic facial expressions. For example, the down-turning of the mouth corners in the human "sad-face" and "cry-face" is probably a reflection of the evolutionary changes that have occurred in the muscle *triangularis* (see Figure 23d, e, and f).

(a)

(b)

(c)

(d)

(e)

(f)

(g)

(h)

As has already been mentioned, the continued differentiation of the mid-facial musculature in man is, unlike that of the apes, accompanied by a reduction in the size of lip and muzzle musculature and a corresponding reduction in the size of both the underlying bony structure of the mouth region and tooth size. The reduction in the size of the muzzle musculature, jaw bones, and teeth is probably related to the cultural development of tool use, for, with the evolution of man, tools came to be used for most of the functions of food getting and preparation previously met by the teeth and lips (Washburn, 1960). Thus man no longer requires the strength of jaws, teeth, and lips that is still necessary for apes. In addition, there may have been, as Huber (1931) suggested, increased pressure for fine muscular control of the lips in conjunction with the development of human speech.

Whether any of these morphological changes might actually have been an adaptation for facial expression is not exactly clear. Though the human face is capable of producing a vast number of different expressions, human facial expressions have so far been found to be associated with only a small number of emotional states—six to nine states, which is no greater than the number of states that have been described for macaques and apes (Ekman, 1972; Ekman & Friesen, 1971; Ekman, Sorenson, & Friesen, 1969; Izard, 1968; Tomkins & McCarter, 1964). However, in man there is evidently much more variability in the forms of the expressions that signify particular emotional states (Ekman, personal communication). Thus there are a large number of different expressions that all signify anger, and not any other pure emotional state. However, some of them may possibly signify emotional blends (e.g., fear–anger) or other subtle emotional differences. On the other hand, these different expressions may be learned idiosyncracies or learned, culturally prescribed behaviors. Research on human facial expression has not yet clarified the significance of multiple expressions for what appear to be single affect states. Should it be found that these different expressions

---

FIG. 23. Some facial expressions of man.
(a) "Angry face"; anger, type 1.
(b) "Angry face"; anger, type 2.
(c) "Smiling face"; happiness, type 1.
(d) "Sad face"; sadness, type 1 (adult).
(e) "Sad-cry face"; transitional between sadness, types 1 and 2 (adult).
(f) "Cry face"; transitional between sadness, types 1 and 2 (child).
(g) "Crying face"; sadness, type 2 (child).
(h) "Laughing face"; happiness, type 2.
   See Chapter 4, Figures 1, 4, and 5 for illustrations of surprised faces, Figures 4, 5, and 6 for fear faces, and Figures 5, 7, and 8 for disgust faces.
   Note—These drawings are presented for illustrative purposes only. They are diagrammatic and do not precisely depict actual expressions of emotion. They are drawn after photographs. All expressions were drawn from the same angle in order to facilitate comparisons.

TABLE 4

Some Facial Expressions in Man[a]

Context and emotion	Name of expression	Eyes	Forehead and brows	Mouth	Vocalization
Anger, type 1.	Angry face.	Direct gaze; frequently with eye-to-eye contact; no sclera (white part of eye) showing above or below iris (colored part of eye); upper lids appearing lowered; upper lids sometimes tense and squared; lower lids raised and tensed, often producing a squint.	Brows lowered and pulled together.	Jaws clenched; lips contracted vertically and tightly pressed together.	
Anger, type 2.	Angry face.	Direct gaze; frequently with eye-to-eye contact; no sclera showing; upper lids appearing lowered; upper lids sometimes tense and squared; lower lids raised and tensed, often producing a squint.	Brows lowered and pulled together.	Jaws moderately open; lips moderately contracted vertically and horizontally and extended, forming a rectangular opening with teeth showing.	
Fear.	Fearful face.	Eyes open; lower lids tense; sclerae sometimes showing above but not below iris.	Brows raised and drawn together.	Jaws open or closed; lips slightly retracted horizontally.	
Happiness, type 1, positive	Smiling face.	Lower lids often pushed up by lower face, causing wrinkling of skin at		Jaws closed to moderately open; lips retracted horizontally and often vertically as well, ex-	

78

Emotion	Face	Eyes	Brows	Mouth and jaws	
Happiness, type 2, playfulness.	Laughing face.	Lower lids often pushed up by lower face, causing wrinkling of skin at lateral corners of eyes.		Jaws moderately to widely open; lip corners raised; lips perhaps a little retracted, covering the teeth (chiefly in children; silent); or lips moderately to widely retracted vertically and horizontally, exposing the teeth.	Often accompanied by laughter.
Sadness, type 1.	Sad face.	Eyes often directed downward; eyes often showing tears; upper lids often drooping, or tense and pulled up at inner corner.	Brows drawn together with inner corners raised and outer corners often lowered, *or* brows drawn down in middle and raised at inner corners.	Jaws closed or slightly open; if jaws opened slightly retracted horizontally, and lower lip drawn down and trembling; if jaws closed, lip corners pulled slightly down.	
Sadness, type 2.	Crying face (child).	Eyelids closed or nearly closed; eyes often showing tears.	Brows lowered and drawn together.	Jaws closed to widely open; lips retracted horizontally; lower lip drawn down; mouth corners drawn down.	Often accompanied by a cry.
Surprise.	Surprised face.	Eyes wide open; sclera showing above and often below iris.	Brows raised and curved.	Jaws moderately to widely open and lower jaw appearing "dropped"; lips parted.	
Disgust.	Disgusted face.	Lower eyelids raised.	Brows drawn down but not together.	Jaws closed or open; if jaws opened, upper lip raised and lower lip extended; if jaws closed, lower lip pushed up, thereby pushing upper lip up too; tongue sometimes visible.	

[a]The table presents only partial descriptions of the expressions to convey a general impression of their appearance and permit comparisons between species. The descriptions are abstracted from Ekman (1972), Van Hooff (1971), and personal observations.

have subtle functional differences, this would suggest that the continued muscle differentiation about the mouth in man might possibly have been selected for emotional expression as well as for speech.

Six of the emotional states that have been described for man are presented, with nine of their characteristic expressions, in Table 4, and some of these are illustrated in Figure 23. A comparison of the appearance of the face in human and ape expressions shows similarities between six expressions: human anger, type 1, and ape anger, type 1; human anger, type 2, and ape fear–anger; the human "smile" and ape fear–affection, "silent bared-teeth," types 2 and 3; the human child's "cry face" and "crying face" and the ape's frustration–sadness, "whimper face" and "cry face"; and the human "laugh" and the ape "play" expression.

Human anger, type 1, and ape anger, type 1, are both characterized by a direct gaze and clenched jaws with lips compressed. In the apes this expression probably signifies a mild dominant threat, or mild confident anger. In man it also signifies anger, although it is not known whether it relates to any particular kind of anger. Human anger, type 2, and ape fear–anger are likewise similar to each other in appearance, both being characterized by a direct gaze and partly open mouth with lips retracted vertically so that the teeth often show. The ape fear–anger expression is evidently a fear–anger blend, and is often used as a subordinate threat. In man, no functional differences have been distinguished between the two anger expressions. The general formal and functional similarities between the two pairs of anger expressions described above suggest that they are homologous and phylogenetically related (see Figure 10).

van Hooff (1971, 1972) has discussed at length the similarities between the human "smile" and the ape "silent bared-teeth." In both cases the jaws vary from closed to open and the lips are retracted both vertically and horizontally. van Hooff has found that the ape expression has three forms (see Table 3 and Figure 21), and each form functions in a different capacity: The first functions in submission, the second in appeasement, and the third in affection. The human form, like the third ape form, is associated with a general affective attitude. van Hooff has proposed that these two expressions are homologous, and that they represent two levels of phylogenetic development. He speculates that the primate prototype of the human smile is the prosimian and monkey "grin," which functioned as a fear expression, and that with the evolution of the apes the expression came to have three forms, two of which had appeasement and affective functions, and that in man the original fear function has been lost and the grin or smile has assumed its exclusively affective function.

The similarities between the human and ape sadness and cry expressions have not been described before, and must be studied in further detail. Darwin speculated that the grief or sadness expression (which can be distinguished from crying) was unique to man, since

> Our early progenitors, when suffering from grief or anxiety, would not have made their eyebrows oblique or have drawn down the corners of their mouth, until they had acquired the habit of endeavouring to restrain their screams [p.361].

The reason for this, Darwin theorized, was that the brows were lowered and contracted during screaming, in order to protect the eyes, but that if screams were repressed, antagonistic muscles would simultaneously raise the brow, thereby giving the eyebrows an oblique appearance. A preliminary examination of human and ape sad faces suggests to me that the particular muscular contractions which result in obliquity of the eyebrows in man, if present in apes, result in a different appearance of the brows in the very differently shaped head of the ape (apes have little forehead). Nevertheless, the appearance of the ape's face, when sad, shows some suggestion that similar muscular contractions may be occurring, for the eyebrows are elevated, and horizontal wrinkles sometimes appear over the forehead (Figures 21h; 23d and e). In addition, both the human transitional sadness faces, types 1 and 2, and the ape "whimper face" are characterized by an outward extension and drawing down of the lip (Figures 21h; 23e and f). Furthermore, there is a suggestion in the ape as well as in the human cry and transitional sad–cry expressions, of drooping eyelids and wrinkling of the skin near the outer corners and beneath the eyes (Figures 21h and i; 23e, f, and g). The ape and human cry expressions are both characterized by an open mouth, raised upper lip, and depression of the lower lip, which is particularly prominent at the mouth corners in man (Figures 21i and 23g). Thus the human and ape sad and cry faces do show some formal similarities. These ape and human expressions are also functionally similar, for the contexts in which they occur are also similar, and all evidently reflect sadness (see Figures 21 and 23 and Tables 3 and 4). In addition, both the ape sadness, type 2, "cry face," and human sadness, type 2, child's "crying face" are accompanied by similar "cry" vocalizations. Both in the ape and in man, type 1 expressions often intergrade with type 2 expressions, the type 1 expressions being less intense manifestations of sadness than the type 2 expressions. The combination of formal and functional similarities in these two pairs of expressions again suggests that they are homologous and phylogenetically related.

The human "laughing face" and the ape "play face" are also formal equivalents. In both, the jaws are moderately to widely opened, the lips are retracted vertically and horizontally, and vocalizations, in both cases called "laughter" by observers, are often uttered simultaneously. In man the smile–laughter continuum has one general function—to express positive intentions, while the ape formal equivalents, the "grin" and the "play face," have two very distinct functions—to express positive intentions and to signal play. However, Van Hooff has found, chiefly by means of questionnaires, that the expression of positive intentions is primarily associated with the human smile, while both the human smile and human laughter evoke the association of playfulness. This finding suggests that the laugh and the play face are also homologous expressions. It therefore appears that the ape grin and play face have converged in man and have become so highly associated with each other that they essentially form a single facial display. Thus, while in man smiling and laughter form a continuum with essentially a single function, their formal equivalents in the ape are two very distinct expressions, the grin and the play face, which have two very different expressive functions.

Darwin's speculations on the evolution of particular human facial expressions from primate expressions are supported in part by present-day evidence. Laughter was practiced by our nonhuman progenitors—but by our apelike ancestors as they played, and not by the monkeys as they grinned in fear. Darwin would probably be surprised to discover that we now consider the human smile to have derived from what was originally a primate fear expression, which the "grin" certainly is in lemurs and monkeys. Contrary to Darwin's implications, no clear counterpart to the human fear expression has been found among the primate expressions. Today, we agree with Darwin that apes do not weep with tears, but we disagree with Darwin's report that monkeys weep as man does in sadness. Ape whimpering and crying—as distinguished from weeping—and human sadness and crying expressions have contextual similarities, and the cries do have similar vocal aspects as well. But whether these are homologous expressions is still an essentially unexplored area. We agree with Darwin that rage was probably expressed in a similar way by our early progenitors, but it is unlikely that teeth-exposure was a component of pure anger, as Darwin speculated. We also agree with Darwin that monkeys do not open their mouths in astonishment as man does, and in fact no descriptions of surprise expressions in monkeys appear in the recent literature. However, if one observes monkeys as they investigate novel objects, or in a situation that could represent surprise, one may note that the eyes are opened wide and the eyebrows raised, as Darwin also predicted. Contrary to Darwin's expectations, no counterpart to human disgust has yet been distinguished in monkeys. While turning away the eyes is a prominent behavior among the monkeys and apes, it is directed by an animal of low status to another animal of high status and certainly does not signify disgust.

Though our knowledge of the anatomical structure of the face has increased since Darwin's time and a number of investigators have made further speculations on its functional adaptations during evolution, there has not been any great theoretical advance in this area of study. The intimate interrelationships between form and function, which he discussed both in terms of the evolution and production of facial expressions, are still the most significant contribution to the investigation of the anatomical determinants of facial displays.

CONCLUSIONS

After reviewing 100 years of literature on facial expression in nonhuman primates, we must conclude that Darwin's work of 1872 is still the most encompassing work on the subject. In addition, its freshness and high literary quality serve as an inspiration for students of animal behavior today.

Darwin's central hypothesis—that the facial expressions of nonhuman primates and man are similar—has been strikingly confirmed, strongly supporting his theory that human facial expressions have evolved from those of man's nonhuman primate ancestors. This chapter describes many elaborations of Darwin's original hypothesis. The major changes in his theory of emotion have occurred since the striking developments in neurophysiology and genetics. One wonders whether, if these new disciplines had been available to him, there would have been any significant advances since Darwin.

ACKNOWLEDGMENTS

I wish to extend thanks to Paul Ekman, Jack de Groot, Barbara de Pedraza, Karl Pribram, Anna Shannon, and Sherwood L. Washburn, who read and made helpful comments on various versions of this paper. I thank Patricia Garlan for her editorial assistance, Janice Andersen for typing the manuscript, and Eric Stoelting for drawing the illustrations of the facial musculature and facial expressions. The preparation of this chapter was partially supported by the Interdisciplinary Training Program, Langley Porter Neuropsychiatric Institute, University of California, San Francisco; by United States Public Health Services Training Grant #5-T1-MH-7082 from the National Institute of Public Health; and by the Communication Through Nonverbal Behavior Grant #MH-11976 from the National Institute of Mental Health.

REFERENCES

Altmann, S. A. A field study of the sociobiology of rhesus monkeys, *Macaca mulatta. Annals of the New York Academy of Sciences,* 1962, **102**(2): 338–435.

Altmann, S. A. Sociobiology of rhesus monkeys II: Stochastics of social communication. *Journal of Theoretical Biology,* 1965, **8**, 490–522.

Altmann, S. A. The structure of primate social communication. In S. A. Altmann (Ed.), *Social communication among primates.* Chicago: Univ. of Chicago Press, 1967.

Altmann, S. A. Primates. In T. A. Sebeok (Ed.), *Animal communication: Techniques of study and results of research.* Bloomington: Indiana Univ. Press, 1968.

Andrew, R. J. The situations that evoke vocalizations in primates. *Annals of the New York Academy of Sciences,* 1962, **102**(2): 296–315.

Andrew, R. J. Evolution of facial expressions. *Science,* 1963, **142**, 1034–1041. (a)

Andrew, R. J. Trends apparent in the evolution of vocalization in the Old World monkeys and apes. *Symposium of the Zoological Society of London,* 1963, **10**, 89–101. (b)

Andrew, R. J. The origin and evolution of the calls and facial expressions of the primates. *Behaviour,* 1963, **20**(1–2): 1–109. (c)

Andrew, R. J. The displays of the primates. In J. Buettner-Janusch (Ed.), *Evolutionary and genetic biology of primates.* Vol. II. New York: Academic Press, 1964.

Andrew, R. J. The origins of facial expressions. *Scientific American,* 1965, **213**(4): 88–94.

Aronson, L. Functional evolution of the forebrain in lower vertebrates. In L. R. Aronson, E. Tobach, D. S. Lehrman, & J. S. Rosenblatt (Eds.), *Development and evolution of behavior.* San Francisco: Freeman, 1970.

Bard, P. The central representation of the sympathetic nervous system as indicated by certain physiologic observations. *Archives of neurology and psychiatry,* 1929, **22**, 230–246.

Bastian, J. R. Primate signaling systems and human languages. In I. DeVore (Ed.), *Primate behavior: Field studies of monkeys and apes.* New York: Holt, 1965.

Beach, F. A. Evolutionary changes in the physiological control of mating behavior in mammals. *The Psychological Review,* 1947, **54**, 297–315.

Beach, F. A. The descent of instinct. *The Psychological Review,* 1955, **62**, 401–410.

Beach, F. A. Neural and chemical regulation of behavior. In H. F. Harlow & C. N. Woolsey (Eds.), *Biological and biochemical bases of behavior.* Madison: Univ. of Wisconsin Press, 1958.

Bertrand, M. The behavioral repertoire of the stumptail macaque: A descriptive and comparative study. *Bibliotheca Primatologica,* No. 11. Basel: Karger, 1969.

Buettner-Janusch, J. *Origins of man.* New York: Wiley, 1966.

Burrell, H. *The platypus.* Sydney, Australia: Angus & Robertson, 1927.

Busnel, R. G. (Ed.) *Acoustic behaviour of animals.* New York: Elsevier, 1963.

Carpenter, C. R. A field study of the behavior and social relations of the howling monkeys *(Alouatta palliata). Comparative Psychology Monographs,* 1934, **10**(2): 1–168.

Chevalier-Skolnikoff, S. *The ontogeny of communication in Macaca speciosa.* Unpublished doctoral dissertation, Univ. of California, Berkeley, 1971.

Chevalier-Skolnikoff, S. *The ontogeny of communication in the stumptail macaque, Macaca arctoides. Contributions to Primatology,* Basel: Karger, in press, 1973.

Clark, W. E. LeGros. *The antecedents of man.* New York: Harper & Row, 1959.

Collias, N. E. An ecological and functional classification of animal sounds. In W. E. Lanyon & W. N. Tavolga (Eds.), *Animal sounds and communication.* Washington, D. C.: Publication No. 7, American Institute of Biological Sciences, 1960.

Conaway, C. H. & Sade, D. S. The seasonal spermatogenic cycle in free-ranging rhesus monkeys. *Folia Primatologia,* 1965, **3**, 1–12.

Darling, F. F. *A herd of red deer.* London: Oxford Univ. Press, 1937.

Darwin, C. *On the origin of species by means of natural selection; or the preservation of favored races in the struggle for life.* London: John Murray, 1859.

Darwin, C. *The expression of the emotions in man and animals.* London: John Murray, 1872.

Delgado, J. M. R. Effect of brain stimulation on task-free situations. In R. N. Peon (Ed.), *The physiological basis of mental activity,* 1963.

Delgado, J. M. R. Aggression and defense under cerebral radio control. In C. D. Clemente & D. B. Lindsey (Eds.), *Aggression and defense, neural mechanisms and social patterns. Brain Functions,* 1967, **5**, 171–193.

Delgado, J. M. R. Offensive-defensive behaviour in free monkeys and chimpanzees induced by radio stimulation of the brain. In S. Garattini & E. B. Sigg (Eds.), *Aggressive behavior.* New York: Wiley, 1969.

Dethier, V. G., & Stellar, E. *Animal behavior: Its evolutionary and neurological basis.* Englewood Cliffs, New Jersey: Prentice-Hall, 1964.

DeVore, I. *The social behavior and organization of baboon troops.* Unpublished doctoral dissertation, Univ. of Chicago, 1962.

Ekman, P. Universals and cultural differences in facial expressions of emotion. *Nebraska Symposium on Motivation, 1971.* Univ. of Nebraska Press, 1972.

Ekman, P., & Friesen, W. V. A repertoire of nonverbal behavior: Categories, origins, usage and coding. *Semiotica,* 1969, **1**(1): 49–98.

Ekman, P., & Friesen, W. V. Constants across cultures in the face and emotion. *Journal of Personality and Social Psychology,* 1971, **17**(2): 124–129.

Ekman, P., Sorenson, E. R., & Friesen, W. V. Pan-cultural elements in facial displays of emotions. *Science,* 1969, **164**(3875): 86–88.

Gardner, B. T. & Gardner, R. A. Two-way communication with an infant chimpanzee. In A. Schrier & F. Stollnitz (Eds.), *Behavior of nonhuman primates, IV.* New York: Academic Press, 1971.

Gardner, R. A. & Gardner, B. T. Teaching sign language to a chimpanzee. *Science,* 1969, **165**, 664–672.

Gartlan, J. S., & Brain, C. K. Ecology and social variability in *Cercopithecus aethiops* and *C. mitis.* In P. C. Jay (Ed.), *Primates: Studies in adaptation and variability.* New York: Holt, 1968.

Ghiselin, M. T. *The triumph of the Darwinian method.* Berkeley, Univ. of California Press, 1969.

Goy, R. W., & Eisele, S. G. Retention of copulatory ability after ovariectomy in a rhesus monkey. *Anatomical Record, 1964,* **148**, 373.

Gray, H. *Anatomy of the human body.* Philadelphia: Lea & Febiger, 1930.

Gregory, W. K. *Our face from fish to man.* New York: Putnam, 1929.

Hall, K. R. L. Numerical data, maintenance activities and locomotion of the wild chacma baboon, *Papio ursinus. Proceedings of the Zoological Society of London,* 1962, **139**(II): 181–220. (a)

Hall, K. R. L. The sexual, agonistic and derived social behaviour patterns of the wild chacma baboon, *Papio ursinus. Proceedings of the Zoological Society of London,* 1962, **139**(II): 283–327. (b)

Hall, K. R. L. Behaviour and ecology of the wild patas monkey, *Erythrocebus patas,* in Uganda. In P. C. Jay (Ed.), *Primates: Studies in adaptation and variability.* New York: Holt, 1968. (a)

Hall, K. R. L. Aggression in monkey and ape societies. In P. C. Jay (Ed.), *Primates: Studies in adaptation and variability.* New York: Holt, 1968. (b)

Hall, K. R. L., & DeVore, I. Baboon social behavior. In I. DeVore (Ed.), *Primate behavior: Field studies of monkeys and apes.* New York: Holt, 1965.

Harlow, H. F. The development of affectional patterns in infant monkeys. In B. M. Foss (Ed.), *Determinants of infant behaviour I.* New York: Wiley, 1961.

Harlow, H. F. The maternal affectional system. In B. M. Foss (Ed.), *Determinants of infant behaviour II.* New York: Wiley, 1963.

Harlow, H. F., Dodsworth, R. O., & Harlow, M. K. Total isolation in monkeys. *Proceedings of the National Academy of Sciences, 1965,* **54**(1): 90–97.

Harlow, H. F. & Harlow, M. K. Social deprivation in monkeys. *Scientific American,* 1962, **207**(5): 136–146.

Harlow, H. F. & Harlow, M. K. Effects of various mother-infant relationships on rhesus monkey behaviors. In B. M. Foss (Ed.), *Determinants of infant behavior IV*. New York: Wiley, 1969.

Harlow, H. F., Harlow, M. K., & Hansen, E. W. The maternal affectional system of rhesus monkeys. In H. L. Rheingold (Ed.), *Maternal behavior in mammals*. New York: Wiley, 1963.

Harlow, H. F. & Zimmerman, R. R. Affectional responses in the infant monkey. *Science*, 1959, **130**, 421–432.

Hill, W. C. O. *Primates: Comparative anatomy and taxonomy*. Vol. 1. Strepsirhini, Edinburgh: The Edinburgh Univ. Press, 1953.

Hinde, R. A. Ritualization and social communication in rhesus monkeys. *Philosophical Transactions of the Royal Society of London*, 1966, **251**, 285–294.

Hinde, R. A. & Rowell, T. E. Communication by postures and facial expressions in the rhesus monkey *(Macaca mulatta)*. *Proceedings of the Zoological Society of London*, 1962, **138**, 1–21.

Huber, E. Evolution of facial musculature and cutaneous field of trigeminus. *Quarterly Review of Biology*, 1930, **5**(2): 133–389.

Huber, E. *Evolution of facial musculature and facial expression*. Baltimore: Johns Hopkins Univ. Press, 1931.

Huber, E. The facial musculature and its innervation. In C. G. Hartman & W. L. Straus, Jr. (Eds.), *The anatomy of the rhesus monkey*. New York: Hafner, 1933.

Imanishi, K. Identification: A process of socialization in the subhuman society of *Macaca fuscata*. *Primates*, 1957, **1**(1): 1–29. Translated In S. A. Altmann (Ed.), *Japanese monkeys*. Edmonton: The Editor, 1965.

Izard, C. E. The emotions and emotion constructs in personality and culture research. In R. B. Cattell (Ed.), *Handbook of modern personality theory*. Chicago: Aldine, 1968.

Izard, C. E. *The face of emotion*. New York: Appleton, 1971.

Jay, P. C. The common langur of North India. In I. DeVore (Ed.), *Primate behavior: Field studies of monkeys and apes*. New York: Holt, 1965.

Kaufman, I. C. & Rosenblum, L. A. A behavioral taxonomy for *Macaca nemestrina* and *Macaca radiata;* based on longitudinal observations of family groups in the laboratory. *Primates*, 1966, **7**(2): 205–258.

Kaufman, I. C. & Rosenblum, L. A. The reaction to separation in infant monkeys: Anaclitic depression and conservation-withdrawal. *Psychosomatic medicine*, 1967, **29**(6): 648–675.

Kaufman, I. C. & Rosenblum, L. A. The waning of the mother-infant bond in two species of macaque. In B. M. Foss (Ed.), *Determinants of infant behaviour IV*. New York: Wiley, 1969.

Kawai, M. On the system of social ranks in a natural troop of Japanese monkeys: I basic rank and dependent rank. *Primates*, 1958, **1**(2): 111–130. Translated In S. A. Altmann (Ed.), *Japanese monkeys*. Edmonton: The Editor, 1965.

Kawamura, S. The process of subculture propagation among Japanese macaques. In C. H. Southwick (Ed.), *Primate social behavior*. Princeton, New Jersey: Van Nostrand, 1963.

Kawamura, S. Matriarchal social ranks in the Minoo-B troop: A study of the rank system of Japanese monkeys. *Primates*, 1958, **1**(2): 149–156. Translated In S. A. Altmann (Ed.), *Japanese monkeys*. Edmonton: The Editor, 1965.

Kohts, N. Infant ape and human child. *Moscow. Gosudarstvennyi Darvinskii Muzei. Trudy* (English Title: *Scientific Memoirs. Museum Darwinianum Moscow)*, 1935, **3**, 1–596.

Lancaster, J. B. Primate communication systems and the emergence of human language. In P. C. Jay (Ed.), *Primates: Studies in adaptation and variability*. New York: Holt, 1968.

Lehrman, D. S. A critique of Konrad Lorenz's theory of instinctive behavior. *The Quarterly Review of Biology*, 1953, **28**(4): 337–363.

Lehrman, D. S. Hormonal regulation of parental behavior in birds and infrahuman mammals. In W. C. Young (Ed.), *Sex and internal secretions, II*. Baltimore: Williams & Wilkins, 1961.

Leyhousen, P. Das Verhalten der Katzen. *Handbuch der Zoologie*, Berlin, 1956, Bd. VIII, **10**(21): 1–34.

MacLean, P. D. New findings relevant to the evolution of psychosexual functions of the brain. *Journal of Nervous Mental Disease*, 1962, **135**(4): 289–301.

MacLean, P. D., & Delgado, J. M. R. Electrical and chemical stimulation of the frontotemporal portion of limbic system in the waking animal. *Electroencephalography and Clinical Neurophysiology*, 1953, **5**, 91–100.

Marler, P. The logical analysis of animal communication. *Journal of Theoretical Biology*, 1961, **1**, 295–317.

Marler, P. Communication in monkeys and apes. In I. DeVore (Ed.), *Primate behavior: Field studies of monkeys and apes*. New York: Holt, 1965.

Marler, P., & Hamilton III, W. J. *Mechanisms of animal behavior*. New York: Wiley, 1968.

Mason, W. A. The effects of social restriction on the behavior of rhesus monkeys: I. Free social behavior. *Journal of Comparative and Physiological Psychology*, 1960, **53**, 582–589.

Mason, W. A. The effects of social restriction on the behavior of rhesus monkeys: II. Tests of gregariousness. *Journal of Comparative and Physiological Psychology*, 1961, **54**, 287–290.

Mason, W. A. Social development of rhesus monkeys with restricted social experience. *Perceptual and Motor Skills*, 1963, **16**, 263–270.

Mason, W. A. The social development of monkeys and apes. In I. DeVore (Ed.), *Primate behavior: Field studies of monkeys and apes*. New York: Holt, 1965.

Mendel, G. J. *Experiments in plant hybridization*. Edinburgh: Oliver and Boyd, 1965. Translated from the original Versuche uber Pflanzen-Hybriden *Verhandlungen des Naturforschenden Vereins in Brunn*. **4**. 1865.

Michael, R. P., & Herbert, J. Menstrual cycle influences grooming behavior and sexual activity in the rhesus monkey. *Science*, 1963, **140**, 500–501.

Miller, G. A., Galanter, E., & Pribram, K. H. *Plans and the structure of behavior*. New York: Holt, 1960.

Miller, R. E. Experimental studies of communication in the monkey. In L. A. Rosenblum (Ed.), *Primate behavior: Developments in field and laboratory research*, II. New York: Academic Press, 1971.

Miller, R. E., Caul, W. F., & Mirsky, I. A. The communication of affects between feral and socially-isolated monkeys. *Journal of Personality and Social Psychology*, 1967, **7**, 231–239.

Miller, R. E., Murphy, J. V., & Mirsky, I. A. The modification of social dominance in a group of monkeys by interanimal conditioning. *Journal of Comparative and Physiological Psychology*, 1955, **48**, 392–396.

Moynihan, M. Some behavior patterns of platyrrhine monkeys I. The night monkey *(Aotus trivirgatus)*. *Smithsonian Miscellaneous Collection*, 1964, **146**(5): 1–84.

Moynihan, M. Comparative aspects of communication in New World primates. In D. Morris (Ed.), *Primate ethology*. Chicago: Aldine, 1967.

Napier, J. R., & Napier, P. H. *A handbook of living primates*. New York: Academic Press, 1967.

Netter, F. H. *Nervous system*. I. New Jersey: CIBA, 1962.

Nissen, H. W. Axes of behavior comparison. In A. Roe & G. G. Simpson (Eds.), *Behavior and evolution*. New Haven: Yale Univ. Press, 1958.

Noback, C. R., & Moskowitz, N. Structural and functional correlates of "encephalization" in the primate brain. *Annals of the New York Academy of Sciences*, 1962, **102**(2): 210–218.

Papez, J. W. A proposed mechanism of emotion. *Archives of Neurology and Psychiatry*, 1937, **38**, 725–743.

Premack, D. A functional analysis of language. *Journal of the Experimental Analysis of Behavior*, 1970, **14**, 107–125. (a)

Premack, D. The education of Sarah: A chimp learns the language. *Psychology Today,* 1970, **4**(4): 54–58. (b)

Pribram, K. H. Emotion: Steps toward a neuropsychological theory. In D. C. Glass (Ed.), *Neurophysiology and emotion.* New York: The Rockefeller Univ. Press & Russell Sage Foundation, 1967.

Reynolds, V., & Reynolds, F. Chimpanzees of the Budongo Forest. In I. DeVore (Ed.), *Primate behavior: Field studies of monkeys and apes.* New York: Holt, 1965.

Robinson, B. W. Vocalization evoked from forebrain in Macaca mulatta. *Physiology and behavior,* 1967, **2**, 345–354.

Romer, A. S. *The vertebrate body.* Philadelphia Saunders, 1970.

Rose, J. E., & Woolsey, C. N. Organization of the mammalian thalamus and its relationships to the cerebral cortex. *Electroencephalography and Clinical Neurophysiology, 1949,* **1**, 391–404.

Rose, R. M., Holaday, J. W., & Bernstein, I. S. Plasma testosterone, dominance rank and aggressive behavior in male rhesus monkeys. *Nature,* 1971, **231**, (5302): 366–368.

Rosenblum, L. A. *The development of social behavior in the rhesus monkey.* Unpublished doctoral dissertation, Univ. of Wisconsin, 1961.

Rosvold, H. E., Mirsky, A. F., & Pribram, K. H. Influence of amygdalectomy on social behavior in monkeys. *Journal of Comparative and Physiological Psychology,* 1954, **47**, 173–178.

Rowell, T. E. Forest-living baboons in Uganda. *Journal of Zoology (London),* 1966, **149**,

Rowell, T. E., & Hinde, R. A. Vocal communication by the rhesus monkey *(Macaca mulatta).* Proceedings of the Zoological Society of London, 1962, **138**(2): 279–294.

Sackett, G. P. Response of rhesus monkeys to social stimulation presented by means of colored slides. *Perceptual and Motor Skills,* 1965, **20**, 1027–1028.

Sackett, G. P. Monkeys reared in isolation with pictures as visual input: Evidence for an innate releasing mechanism. *Science,* 1966, **154**, 1468–1473.

Sade, D. S. Seasonal cycle in size of testes of free-ranging Macaca mulatta. *Folia Primatologia,* 1964, **2**, 171–180.

Sade, D. S. Some aspects of parent-offspring and sibling relations in a group of rhesus monkeys, with a discussion of grooming. *American Journal of Physical Anthropology,* 1965, **23**(1): 1–18.

Sade, D. S. *Ontogeny of social relations in a free-ranging group of rhesus monkeys.* Unpublished doctoral dissertation, Univ. of California, Berkeley, 1966.

Sade, D. S. Determinants of dominance in a group of free-ranging rhesus monkeys. In S. A. Altmann (Ed.), *Social communication among primates.* Chicago: Univ. of Chicago Press, 1967.

Schaller, G. B. *The mountain gorilla: Ecology and behavior.* Chicago: Univ. of Chicago Press, 1963.

Schnierla, T. C. The relationship between observation and experimentation in the field study of behavior. *Annals of the New York Academy of Sciences,* 1950, **51**, 1022–1044.

Shirek-Ellefson, J. *Visual communication in* Macaca irus. Unpublished doctoral dissertation, Univ. of California, Berkeley, 1967

Simonds, P. *Ecology of macaques.* Unpublished doctoral dissertation, Univ. of California, Berkeley, 1963.

Sobotta, J. *Atlas der deskriptiven anatomie des Menschen. 1. Teil: Regiones corporis, Systema skeleti, Systema musculorum.* Munchen-Berlin: Urban & Schwarzenberg, 1953.

Storer, T. I., & Usinger, R. L. *General zoology.* New York: McGraw-Hill, 1957.

Struhsaker, T. T. Auditory communication among vervet monkeys *(Cercopithecus aethiops).* In S. A. Altmann (Ed.), *Social communication among primates.* Chicago: Univ. of Chicago Press, 1967.

Szebenyi, E. S. *Atlas of* Macaca mulatta. Rutherford: Fairleigh Dickinson Univ. Press, 1969.

Tinbergen, N. 'Derived' activities; their causation, biological significance, origin and emancipation during evolution. *Quarterly Review of Biology,* 1952, **27**, 1–32.

Tinbergen, N. Comparative studies of the behaviour of gulls *(Laridae):* A progress report. *Behaviour,* 1959, **15**(1–2): 1–70.

Tomkins, S. S., & McCarter, R. What and where are the primary affects: Some evidence for a theory. *Perceptual and Motor Skills,* 1964, **18**, 119–158.

Vandenbergh, J. G. Hormonal basis of sex skin of male rhesus monkeys. *General and Comparative Endocrinology,* 1965, **5**(1): 31–34.

van Hooff, J. A. R. A. M. Facial expressions in higher primates. *Symposium of the Zoological Society of London,* 1962, **8**, 97–125.

van Hooff, J. A. R. A. M. The facial displays of the catarrhine monkeys and apes. In D. Morris (Ed.), *Primate ethology.* Chicago: Aldine, 1967.

van Hooff, J. A. R. A. M. *Aspects of the social behaviour and communication in human and higher non-human primates.* Rotterdam: Author, 1971.

van Hooff, J. A. R. A. M. A comparative approach to the phylogeny of laughter and smiling. In R. A. Hinde (Ed.), *Nonverbal communication.* Cambridge: Cambridge Univ. Press, 1972.

van Lawick, H., Marler, P., & Van Lawick-Goodall, J. Vocalization of wild chimpanzees (16-mm film). New York: Rockefeller Univ. Film Service.

van Lawick-Goodall, J. A preliminary report on expressive movements and communication in the Gombe Stream chimpanzees. In P. C. Jay (Ed.), *Primates: Studies in adaptation and variability.* New York: Holt, 1968. (a)

van Lawick-Goodall, J. The behavior of free-living chimpanzees in the Gombe Stream Reserve. *Animal Behaviour Monographs,* 1968, **1**(3): 161–311. (b)

Wallace Laboratories, *The Limbic System: Anatomic Substrate of Emotion.* 1965.

Washburn, S. L. Tools and human evolution. *Scientific American,* 1960, **203**(3): 3–15.

Washburn, S. L., & DeVore, I. The social life of baboons. *Scientific American,* 1961, **204**(6): 62–71.

Washburn, S. L., & Hamburg, D. A. Aggressive behavior in Old World monkeys and apes. In P. C. Jay (Ed.), *Primates: Studies in adaptation and variability.* New York: Holt, 1968.

Wilson, A. P. *Social behavior of free-ranging rhesus monkeys with an emphasis on aggression.* Unpublished doctoral dissertation, Univ. of California, Berkeley, 1968.

Winter, P., Ploog, D., & Latta, J. Vocal repertoire of the squirrel monkey *(Saimiri sciureus),* its analysis and significance. *Experimental Brain Research,* 1966, **1**, 359–384.

Woolsey, C. N. Organization of somatic sensory and motor areas of the cerebral cortex. In H. F. Harlow & C. N. Woolsey (Eds.), *Biological and biochemical bases of behavior.* Madison: Univ. of Wisconsin Press, 1965.

Young, W. C., Goy, R. W., & Phoenix, C. H. Hormones and sexual behavior. *Science,* 1964, **143**(3603): 212–218.

Zuckerman, S. *The social life of monkeys and apes.* London: Routledge & Kegan Paul, 1932.

3

Facial Expressions of Infants
and Children

William R. Charlesworth
Mary Anne Kreutzer
University of Minnesota

INTRODUCTION

This chapter deals with facial expressions of infants and children as they
were observed by Darwin and the researchers who followed him. It is heavily
empirical in the sense that speculations and theoretical interpretations of
the origins and development of such expressions have been given relatively
minor emphasis. The reason behind this is that we feel the best way to
commemorate Darwin's work is to continue the spirit of his approach—a
close and critical documentary look at the phenomenon under study, with
a minimum of theorizing until all the relevant facts are in. Today, 100
years after Darwin, many facts have been collected—some of them relevant
and others irrelevant to his theory. However, a substantial amount of work
has yet to be done in order to test adequately the many ideas he had
concerning the nature and evolution of human expression. The science
of human expression, as he envisaged it, still requires a more solid empirical
basis before it will be possible to make any valid generalizations comparable
in power to his theory of evolution of the physical characters of animals.

Darwin's era began at roughly the same time as that of child psychology.
When he began his studies in the 1830s, the biological and what later
became officially the psychological sciences shared a common tradition
of scientific methodology. Darwin himself experienced no difficulty as a
naturalist collecting data on plants and animals as well as on human beings.
For Darwin and many of his scientific contemporaries, man's behavior was
as much a part of the natural world as that of any object that could be

FORSYTH LIBRARY
FORT HAYS STATE UNIVERSITY

observed. Early infant biographies that formed the starting nucleus of child psychology serve as ample evidence of this.

By the time Darwin's career was well under way, however, psychology more or less officially established itself as an independent scientific discipline, which meant for the most part a separation from philosophy. In doing so, however, psychology became identified as a *Geisteswissenschaft*—a term given to that group of sciences which dealt primarily with matters of mind. In contrast, biology and the other physical sciences were referred to as *Naturwissenschaften* because they dealt primarily with material entities, whether organic or inorganic. Thus the latent gap between psychology and biology, attributable to a long tradition of the mind–body problem that plagued many sciences, grew rapidly almost overnight. This became especially true when psychology began asserting itself as a laboratory discipline. The relevance of Darwin's efforts for the science of human behavior consequently had a very weak start.

The gap between biology and psychology at the turn of the century continued to grow, despite the attempts by such eminent psychologists as Wm. McDougall, James Mark Baldwin, and G. Stanley Hall to emphasize the role of biological factors in human behavior. The idea that much human behavior has an instinctual basis and that such a basis evolved as a result of natural selection had little effect on laboratory psychologists deeply engaged in problems of perception and learning. By the time the twentieth century got under way, Darwin's impact upon the behavioral sciences was further blunted by the rapid ascendancy of behaviorism. Instinct theories, or ideas concerning innate factors, could hardly hold their own against the rigorous experimental research programs inspired by Watson, Pavlov, and others. In child psychology itself, interestingly enough, many researchers were engaged in naturalistic observations of children's behaviors—a research strategy that Darwin approved of and heavily relied upon. However, few of these researchers guided their observations with ideas from evolutionary theory (by searching for high-frequency behaviors and trying to determine their adaptive value, for example) or with data from comparative research with lower animals (see Hilgard, 1960). Neglect of Darwin was perhaps most apparent in the area of emotional and expressive behavior. Of all the studies we reviewed for this chapter, less than a third indicate any direct or indirect influence of Darwin's ideas, even though his book on expressions was available during this period.

Today, however, the scene has changed considerably. As a result of the work of ethologists and geneticists, psychologists are becoming aware of the implications of Darwin's contributions for the study of human behavior. In addition, the renewed interest in nonverbal communication is beginning to direct attention to Darwin's observations of animals in which symbolic, verbal communication is totally lacking.

Important for the present chapter, of course, is the recognition that Darwin shares with child psychologists the insight that a satisfactory understanding of adult behavior requires a solid knowledge of the ontogenesis of the behavior in the infant and child.[1] The one major difference between Darwin and the many child psychologists who eschew the nature–nurture issue is that Darwin saw in the young human infant an excellent opportunity to test his hypothesis about the innateness of behavior. To see in the human infant the "pure" and uninhibited expression of an innate behavior was, for Darwin, one of the most prized moments of research. That the behavior was innate could be demonstrated, he felt, by pointing to its early appearance and to analogous behaviors shared by many animals. Understanding the phylogenesis of behavior through comparative studies of animals was, in his eyes, equally important as understanding its ontogenesis. In this sense, all animal behavior including that of human beings, could be viewed in the same light. Darwin's studies of the expressions of the insane who "were liable to the strongest passions, and give uncontrolled vent to them," and of peoples from over the world completed this perspective. In short, Darwin's approach was broad and unlimited. He considered both ontogenesis and phylogenesis, as well as the deviant and the culturally different. This catholicity, coupled with his insistence on a solid empirical basis for the phenomenon under study, has made his treatise a classic for those interested in facial expressions.

DARWIN'S CONTRIBUTIONS TO OUR UNDERSTANDING OF INFANT AND CHILDREN EXPRESSIONS

Darwin's contribution to the study of expression in human beings had its beginning in two sources: his highly variegated experiences on his voyage on the Beagle, and, to a much greater extent, the diary of observations he made of his own children. As he pointed out in a segment of his diary, which appeared in *Mind* in 1877, he started keeping the diary in 1840—32 years before he completed *The Expression of the Emotions in Man and Animals*. In his usual style he did not rush into publication.

The diary he kept was similar in method and style to other well-known infant diaries kept before and after his time (see, for example, Preyer, 1892, and Shinn, 1900). The diary keeper, usually the parent, faithfully observed and recorded the infant's reactions to his environment; when little happened, attempts were made to elicit new behaviors by improvising changes in stimulation—ringing bells or playing simple games, for example. Interesting

---

[1]Ontogenesis refers to the development of a single individual over his lifetime. Phylogenesis refers to the evolution or development of a species (or other taxonomic unit of plant or animal life) over geological time.

as well as common, everyday reactions were generally noted in great detail. Such an approach to the study of behavior has obvious strengths and weaknesses. A day-by-day, longitudinal account of the infant's development is an irreplaceable record that can be continually referred to for new impressions and hypotheses. However, because of the very nature of this approach, it is impossible to ensure that the parent's observations are reliable. In addition, the changes in stimulation introduced by the observer are a long way from planned experiments aimed at identifying and controlling the many factors that influence behavior; without such experiments no observer can be totally certain of his interpretations.

Such weaknesses are as apparent in Darwin's observations as they are in anyone else's. But Darwin also had another methodological weakness, a habit of recording in his diary things that easily disturb the methodological purist. He could not inhibit himself from making highly speculative and humorous comments about his child's behavior if the situation warranted it. For example, in recording an instance of anger in his 11-month-old son, he noted that his son beat an unwanted object forced upon him (1877). Capitalizing on his knowledge of animal behavior, Darwin added that "the beating was an instinctive sign of anger, like the snapping of the jaws by a young crocodile just out of the egg." Such instances of unscientific color are, happily for the reader, found throughout his observations without abatement. However, they do not damage the scientific value of what he had observed. The rigorous detail characterizing his observations, the careful description of the stimulus conditions under which the behavior took place, the recording of the infant's mood at the time and the infant's age all ensure the reader that a careful scientist was trying his best with a very difficult subject matter.

Today diary keeping does not play a key role in the activity of most students of infant behavior. The rigorous training in scientific methodology now required of most child psychologists has cultivated a healthy, but at the same time limiting, skepticism for one man's observations of his own child. Darwin's observations, like those of all infant biographers, are consequently considered more illustrative and stimulating than conclusive. However, for someone like Darwin, who had reason to trust his own observations, there was a conclusiveness about carefully recorded natural behavior. In his mind, the finished product of all the determinants of behavior one could think of appeared full force in everyday natural situations. It was in these situations that the "pure and simple source" of expressive behavior, which for Darwin lay in the infant's phylogenetic past, could find its release.[2]

---

[2]After his first child was born in 1839, Darwin noted in his autobiographical sketch "I at once commenced to make notes on the first dawn of the various expressions which he exhibited, for I felt convinced, even at this early period, that the most complex and fine shades of expression must have had a gradual and natural origin."

If there were any behavioral universals (that is, phylogenetically determined behaviors shared by different men and to some extent by animals) they would be expressed, he believed, with "extraordinary force" in the infant as he engaged in day-to-day adaptations with his environment. Darwin was convinced that it was in natural situations, free from intrusive experimental equipment and procedure, that the impact of evolutionary determinants could be most readily observed. In this sense, his observations of what went on, if done carefully, were terminal. No new methodology need be, or could be, applied to them to test their validity.

If one joins him in taking this position, what remains is the problem of whether such observations can in any way be replicated. For it is only in replication that science finds the grounds for its claims to generality. The whole of literature on expressive behavior can be viewed in these terms—to what extent are his observations repeated in the work of those who concentrated on the same problem? This chapter has been written with this question in mind. Darwin's observations and those of subsequent researchers will be discussed not only to assess the reliability of Darwin's observations, but also to determine the extent to which subsequent studies have added new information to the corpus of findings that Darwin produced.

One other point should be made before introducing Darwin's findings. The observations of infants and children will be discussed in separate sections of this paper. Although this approach does not provide continuity in the discussion of individual emotions, the infant–child distinction is traditionally made in the field of child psychology. For the most part, this convention is based on the fact that the infant's lack of language and symbolic activity and his relative helplessness makes him quite a different object of study than the highly mobile, verbal, thinking child. This distinction, as will be seen later, has decisive practical implications for the manner in which research is carried out with children. That Darwin himself was influenced by this distinction is evidenced by the fact that he carried out the vast majority of his observations of facial expressions with infants. Older children were only sparsely represented.

DARWIN'S OBSERVATIONS OF INFANTS

It is not possible or appropriate to present an exhaustive catalogue of each of Darwin's infant observations as they appeared in the *Mind* paper, or of those reported in *The Expression of the Emotions*. Instead a number of important and familiar emotions and their expressions in infants and children as described by Darwin will be presented briefly. Hopefully this will serve to set the basis for similar studies of these expressions that were conducted after Darwin's time and that will be reported later in this chapter, as well as illustrate the major problems that arise when attempting to understand the processes and factors involved in judging emotions from expressive behavior.

Darwin (1877) described at least seven common emotional states which are accompanied by distinctive facial expressions. He first noted what he thought was _anger_ in his infant son when he was nearly 4 months old; he also noticed it 3 months later. In both instances, blood gushed into the infant's "whole face and scalp" and the reddening of the face was accompanied by a scream of rage and frustration. At 11 months, the boy began beating things whenever he was angered. Before he was 2 years of age, he also became adept at throwing things at anyone who offended him. Darwin noticed that the same throwing behavior occurred in his other sons, but never in his daughter—an observation, parenthetically, that led him to conclude that throwing objects may be a tendency inherited only by boys. Frowning, lip protrusion, and changes in respiration also accompanied such fits of anger, although the exact age of their occurrence was not recorded.

It should be noted that Darwin did not describe a facial expression that he designated as particularly characteristic of anger. He inferred anger from a number of different expressions as well as from the nature of the particular situation which elicited them. Making such inferences raises interesting questions of a general nature pertaining to the identification of emotional states at different age levels on the basis of different behaviors. Blatant tantrum behavior can easily lead to the inference of anger. However, when such behaviors are absent—as in the infant who does not have the ability to roll on the ground, scratch, and bite—inferring anger is a different matter. Darwin was well aware of this. He observed, for example, that on the eighth day of life, his son "frowned and wrinkled the skin around his eyes before a crying fit." Darwin found it difficult, though, to decide which emotion was behind it; it could have been pain or distress instead of anger. About 9 weeks later the boy frowned slightly while drinking cold milk "so that he looked like a grown-up person made cross from being compelled to do something which he did not like." At both ages the infant frowned, but for Darwin there was no compelling reason to evoke the same emotion.

Despite his penchant for humor and speculation, Darwin wisely avoided committing himself to uncertain inferences. This was clearly a plus for him—the error of evoking the same emotion because the same expression or situation is involved is not easy to avoid, especially if only one pronounced expressive behavior is involved. If more expressive behaviors occur, the probability, obviously, of such errors occurring decreases. An infant's flushed face could suggest many different emotions; but a flushed face accompanied by bright eyes, firmly compressed mouth, and clenched fists restricts the inferences to anger or rage.

The age level of the individual is also an important factor in the process of inferring an emotion. Age level is correlated not only with the maturational status of the individual but also with experiences that have an influence on personality as well as cognitive characteristics. A newborn, for example, may display facial expressions identical to those displayed by a wise and perspicacious adult (see Herzka, 1965, for a wide variety of expressions in the newborn). But the impulse to judge him wise or thoughtful is quickly checked by common sense—an infant obviously could not have the prerequisite knowledge to be wise. Likewise, an adult may act childlike by displaying the appropriate facial expressions, but we would not be inclined to infer that he was experiencing true childlike emotions. In both instances inferences about underlying emotional states are conditioned by knowledge of properties of the individual other than his facial expressions. Darwin did not discuss these problems in any detail, but his observations attest to his awareness of them and the care he took when making his observations.

When studying infants and children, there is the added problem having to do with developmental changes in expressions. Darwin came across this problem in his observations of *fear* and *affection* in his son. The "feeling" of fear, Darwin noted, was probably one of the earliest feelings experienced by infants "as shown by their startling at any sudden sound when only a few weeks old, followed by crying." As he saw it, a startle response followed by crying constituted grounds for inferring fear at this age. When his son was about 2½ months old, Darwin walked backwards toward him and then stood motionless. The infant "looked very grave and much surprised and would soon have cried, had I not turned around; then his face instantly relaxed into a smile." In this instance the behavioral evidence for inferring fear was a grave expression preceding, mixing with, or following surprise, plus tension that was dispelled and followed by a smile. Later, when the child was 2¼ years old, Darwin took him to the zoo and noted that he "was much alarmed at the various larger animals in cages." Afterwards the child said he wished to go again to the zoo, but "not to see 'beasts in houses' and we could in no manner account for his fear." At each of the three age or developmental levels, the behavioral indices of fear were clearly different. It is conceivable that there were other indices which were common across all three levels and Darwin failed either to be conscious of them or to report them. What makes the problem of accounting for the child's behavior, as well as Darwin's evaluations of it, even more complicated is the fact that the stimulus conditions in all three situations were quite different.

Another complex situation which illustrates Darwin's awareness of the problems inherent in judging emotions in infants is exemplified by his observations of *affection*. "This [emotion] probably arose very early in life, if we may judge by his smiling at those who had charge of him when under two months old; though I had no distinct evidence of his distinguishing and recognizing anyone until he was nearly four months old." At nearly 5 months, the same infant showed his wish to go to his nurse, but it was not until he was slightly over a year that he exhibited affection by kissing her several times after she had been absent for a short time. Here we find two different expressive behaviors (smiling and kissing), both giving the impression that they were accompanied by the same emotion.

Apart from anger, fear, and affection, Darwin identified other emotions in the infant which are worth noting because of the early age at which they occurred. What Darwin calls the emotion of *"pleasurable sensations"* was first observed very early (he states no age) during nursing when the infant's eyes were "swimming." Smiles occurred at 45 and 46 days in the same situation, accompanied by transverse nose wrinkles, and bright eyes peeking through closed eyelids. Smiles tended to occur when gazing at the mother, but also occurred afterward when "nothing was happening which could have in any way excited or amused him" and consequently was thought to be the result of some "inward pleasurable feeling."

Amusement as a pleasurable sensation occurred at about 3½ months as a result of a peek-a-boo-like game; smiling was elicited and the infant uttered a little noise which was interpreted as an "incipient laugh." Darwin was surprised at humor being appreciated at such a young age, and could not resist evoking his knowledge of animals to point out that "we should remember how very early puppies and kittens begin to play."

Discomfort or unpleasurable sensations caused by pain or hunger are also obviously observable at birth. Darwin observed crying or screaming and spasmodic breathing in infants' expressions of hunger and pain; these behaviors were accompanied by firmly closed eyes, a frown on the forehead, raised flesh on the upper cheek, and retracted lips. Such detailed observations attest not only to Darwin's observational powers but also to the early fullness and complexity of expressive behavior in the human infant.

When crying in response to stress or discomfort does not immediately occur, the mouth still seems to be the most salient area of the face. Darwin (1872) noted that in the first 2 and 3 months, when the infant is struggling against a crying fit, "the mouth is curved in so exaggerated a manner as to be like a horseshoe; and the expression of misery then becomes a ludicrous caricature." At 1½ years the results of teasing were effective enough to produce oblique eyebrows with "the inner ends of the eyebrows plainly puckered." The corners of the mouth were also drawn as a result of such stress. In his discussion of crying, Darwin noted the possibility that the infant's cries, while at first "instinctive" (like smiling), may become employed as means of communicating his needs to others. This is one of the few instances in which he recognized that expressions could be used intentionally to communicate with others.

Observations of higher, more complex emotions were also made by Darwin. *Jealousy* was "plainly exhibited" by his child when Darwin fondled a large doll as well as when he weighed his younger daughter in front of his son. At this time the boy was 15½ months old. Darwin did not specify what it was about the boy's demeanor that led him to infer jealousy. However, he did make another of his interesting comparisons with animals. "Seeing how strong a feeling jealousy is in dogs, it would probably be exhibited by infants at an earlier age than just specified, if they were tried in a fitting manner." Such a remark is interesting for two reasons: First, it may have been influenced by Haeckel's then popular notion of ontogeny recapitulating phylogeny (if a dog is capable of a certain behavior, then the young human is also probably capable). Second, such a remark actually anticipates psychology's current recognition of the distinction between competence and performance. A person can possess an ability (a competence) to do something, but whether he does it at all during his life depends upon many performance factors that serve as necessary conditions for the ability to be made manifest. Such factors include attentional skills, persistence, memory, the right audience, and motivation. In testing for abilities, a good diagnostician will do his best to optimize testing conditions in order to insure that the negative aspects of these factors do not work to obscure the individual's abilities. In other words, what Darwin meant by his remark was that given enough patience and knowledge of what the infant could perceive as personally threatening in one way or another, it would be possible to elicit jealousy at a very early age.

Darwin saw the first symptoms of *shyness* in his son when the child was 2 years and 3 months old. After being absent from him for 10 days, Darwin returned home; the boy hesitated to approach him and then averted his gaze. A similar but more complicated social emotion was observed even earlier at about 13 months under the rubric of "moral sense." Darwin chided his son for not giving him a kiss, and walked away. This, according to Darwin, "made him feel slightly uncomfortable." Shortly thereafter the boy "protruded his lips as a sign that he was ready to kiss me; and then shook his hand in an angry manner until I came and received his kiss."

Darwin's observations of infant behavior also include notes on the infant's ability to recognize emotional expressions. In the concluding paragraph of his paper in *Mind*, Darwin alludes to what he considered an emotion of the infant that is closely related to his cognitive status—namely, his empathic ability to understand the behaviors of others either as expressions of their emotions or as social signals. He states, "An infant understands to a certain extent, and as I believe at a very early period, the meaning or feelings of those who tend him, by the expression of their features." As an example, he points out that his son at 5 months of age "understood a compassionate expression." When his nurse pretended to cry, the infant responded by assuming a melancholy visage with the corners of his mouth well depressed. Apparently the boy not only had the ability to recognize the plight of the nurse, which today would be viewed as a cognitive skill, but also responded in an appropriate way. Later at almost a year of age he was observed to study the faces of those around him after he just completed performing some new accomplishment.

In current ethological thinking, the ability to recognize and respond appropriately to the expressive behavior of others is viewed as a very important skill. This is especially true in higher animals in which well-regulated social behavior, essential for survival, depends upon the proper sending and receiving of social cues (see Eibl-Eibesfeldt, 1970). It is still very much debatable how early such abilities appear in human beings. More rigorous studies have to be done, since the bulk of what we know about the infant's ability to discriminate and react to facial or postural expressions is still based on anecdote and naturalistic observations similar to Darwin's. Furthermore, whether these abilities are a product of maturation, as appears to be the case in lower animals, or whether they are primarily a product of learning remains to be seen.

In their totality, Darwin's observations touch on most of the major problems dealing with expressive behavior in the infant. What is interesting to note is that many of these same problems were encountered and identified by subsequent researchers who, according to their bibliographies, were not aware of Darwin or significantly influenced by him. A better test for the validity of his method and insights cannot easily be found.

DARWIN'S OBSERVATIONS OF CHILDREN

Darwin's observations of older children were reported mainly in *The Expression* and are less frequent and less systematically obtained than those of infants. Actually, a good portion of the observations were derived from reports made by travelers, doctors, and missionaries who came into contact with children during their various activities. Darwin himself had relatively little new to add to what he had already gathered in infants. This raises the interesting question of whether this was due simply to the nature of the sample of subjects and situations he observed or to the fact that most expressions were already present in the infant. Darwin was inclined to believe the latter; however, not completely. He did note instances of expressive behavior in children which were not observed in infants. These can be dealt with here briefly.

Darwin accepted blushing as an indicator of _shame_, however, evoking it as such an indicator depended upon other factors. In the infant, for example, reddening of the face occurred only in a fit of passion, as evidenced by anger. For blushing to occur as a response to embarrassment, however, the child had to be older. His first observation of it was in two girls between 2 and 3 years (he also stressed that blushing occurred more frequently in females than in males). Unfortunately, in both instances he did not describe the stimulus situation which occasioned the blushing. In a later instance, a 4-year-old girl was observed to blush as a result of being reproved for a fault. It is reasonable to argue that in order for this to occur the girl had to be aware that she fell short of a standard and that this weakness on her part was now exposed to others. This awareness requires a certain level of cognitive development, a level which is certainly not within the capacity of the young infant. Darwin was well aware of this. Probably the closest the infant could get to such an emotion was observed by Darwin (see above, under shyness) when his son at 13 months gave signs of being "uncomfortable" when his father pointed out to him that he did not give him a kiss. Blushing did not occur then, however.

Another emotional expression which is visible after infancy is the reaction subsumed under grief. The facial expressions accompanying grief are quite distinctive—the corners of the mouth are drawn down and the eyebrows are oblique; that is, the inner ends of the brows are plainly puckered, thus drawing them up higher than the outer ends as well as producing rectangular furrows. Darwin pointed out that although this expression occurs relatively infrequently, it can be observed in children who appear to be fighting back tears or overcoming an immediately preceding traumatic experience. He hypothesized that such an expression aided in preventing crying. If he is correct, then the child would have to be old enough to inhibit crying. The age at which this ability first appears is not certain; however, we know it is not present in young infants.

Shrugging the shoulders as a sign of impotence or resignation in children was also reported by Darwin. He noted, though, that it occurred much less frequently in children than it did in adults. Other expressive behaviors observed in young children included jumping up and down, clapping the hands and laughing loudly—all commonplace signs of joy or anticipation. Such patterns of responses obviously could not occur in young infants because of the lack of cognitive skills necessary for recognizing the futility of a situation, or because of physical limitations, e.g., not being able to jump up and down.

DARWIN'S CONCLUSIONS

From his observations of infants and children (as well as observations of adults, the insane, of animals, and of peoples from different cultures), Darwin concluded that human expressive behavior was for the most part innate in the sense that it evolved from more primitive forms. For him the fact that the majority of complex facial expressions observed in adults are already present in the infant or young child suggested strongly that their acquisition was less dependent upon learning than it was on the actualization of innate tendencies. This, he felt, was especially true for the expression of the basic emotions such as pleasure, displeasure, anger, joy, sorrow, and disgust. The expression of more elaborate emotions, he was willing to concede, was subject to social and cultural variations brought about by conscious or unconscious imitation and reward.

Today there is more reluctance to come to such a conclusion. Why this is so can best be answered by sociologists of science. The environmentalistic point of view (man learns most of his important behaviors; the innate plays a very minor role) dominates most of western psychology at present, although there are recent signs indicating that the pendulum is beginning to swing in the other direction.

Whichever viewpoint one adopts, one thing appears certain. As man's knowledge of behavior increases, so does his concern for methodological and conceptual clarity. Since Darwin's time, much progress has been made in establishing such clarity. The question it raises is whether Darwin's relatively simple, subjective observational approach will be seen as having added substantially to our ultimate fund of reliable knowledge about facial expression, or whether what he reported was basically biased by the artifacts of his method, which in turn led him to the wrong conclusions about the innateness of behavior. For the most part, his results have the full backing of common sense observation and intuition. However, common sense is not the ultimate test of a science, as modern physics has clearly demonstrated. The soundness of scientific findings is commensurate with the logical and technical soundness of the methodologies used to produce such findings. Since 1872, the methodologies in the behavioral sciences have become increasingly sophisticated and rigorous in the sense that they are vigorously geared to eliminate or reduce error. The question we attempt to answer in the following pages is whether the improvement in methodology since Darwin's time has led to studies that invalidate his findings in any significant way. Furthermore, we would like to know whether such studies have added novel information to the corpus of knowledge of children's expressions that he has left us.

POST-DARWINIAN STUDIES OF
INFANTS' FACIAL EXPRESSIONS

The literature on emotional expressions of infants consists of a great abundance of observations recorded in baby biographies (in ways very similar to Darwin's) as well as observations made in more controlled and standardized situations. Dennis (1936) compiled a list of 64 such biographies written between 1787 and 1934. It is interesting to note that 61 of these were written after Darwin's. Considering the enthusiasm of parents and the large number of easily observable behaviors that the infant engages in during the first 2 years of life, it is certain that the total number of such biographies today is considerably larger.

The availability of the infant and the easily observable behaviors it engages in makes it an ideal subject to study, but the sheer number of its behaviors—expressive or otherwise—is often not appreciated. Blatz and Millichamp (1935) sampled the behavior of five infants for 3 full consecutive days per month over a period of 2 years; they found that each infant alone was responsible for 3000 to 5000 more-or-less-negative emotional episodes (crying, making a fuss, etc.). It is not certain how many positive episodes occurred, or how many observed episodes did not fit either category. A conservative estimate of the total episode output of an infant during the first 2 years of life would run between 10,000 or 15,000. The interested observer will have no dearth of material if he works with infants.

However, despite the wealth of material infants provide, the task of understanding it is far from easy. Blatz and Millichamp discovered that the episodes themselves were not consistently traceable to known stimuli, nor were they well-defined across ages. The specific form of the emotional behavior changed with age, becoming more complex and varied as well as more appropriately adapted to specific situations. In short, what they discovered was that infant emotional behavior was superabundant, complex, and bore complicated relations to its environment—all properties of behavior that make the job of the researcher very difficult.

To make the matter of understanding such behavior even more complicated, the literature in the field of infant expressions is an amorphous mass of good and bad studies, as well as studies which are impossible to evaluate methodologically. To add to this, many studies are replete with interpretations and generalizations, most of which, in our estimation, are too premature or overdrawn for the amount of reliable data on hand.

In short, a satisfying critical review of the post-Darwinian literature is very hard to come by. Our intent was to present most of the major studies dealing with expression in infants and children, and to cite briefly some of the minor studies and literature reviews which the reader could follow up if he desired. As noted in the introduction, our main goal was to present more facts rather than speculations or theory, hoping that the reader would find post-Darwinian facts about expression in infants and children a more valid comment on Darwin's own data and insights than the untested ideas currently available. The nagging problem though, with such an approach was to know whether or not one was actually dealing with facts. A good portion of the information we have on expression in children comes from studies in which the methodology was not well-described or appeared questionable for one reason or other. This was true, we found, despite the general increase in methodological sophistication that occurred since Darwin's time. However, we felt we could reach confidence if a number of different studies, varying in methodological rigor, still produced common findings. To achieve this, we made a deliberate attempt to search the literature for studies from a wide variety of sources—from the intuitive observations of diary-writing parents to the insights of pediatricians and to conclusions from well-controlled experiments.

The plan for covering the material consists of dividing studies into those which deal primarily with a single expressive behavior such as crying or smiling and those which deal with more global expressions of emotions such as anger, delight, jealousy, and surprise. In contrast to observations of a single expressive behavior, global expressions usually consist of an amalgam of a number of distinct behaviors, and involve more inferences about internal emotional and cognitive states. Although this distinction between a single expressive behavior and a global emotion is often blurred in the studies, it helps somewhat in putting order into an otherwise unwieldy mass of material.

Another distinction made in this chapter is the division between the expression of emotions on one hand and the recognition of expressions on the other. The former refers to the expressive behaviors themselves, whereas the latter refers to an individual's sensitivity to the expressive behavior of others. To illustrate, the infant may smile at his mother as an expression of delight in her presence. Later he may smile only when she smiles, but not respond at all when she frowns or has a neutral expression, thus revealing that he recognizes the difference between her smile and her other facial expressions.

According to our literature search as well as personal observations, there are at least three relatively distinct expressive behaviors that occur very early in the human being and are present until death. They are crying, smiling, and laughing. All three occur with relatively high frequency. They are elicited by a wide variety of stimulus conditions; they constitute parts of many diverse, more global emotional expressions; and they have a wide variety of effects on persons in the immediate environment. To these three behaviors we could logically add a fourth—incipient crying, that is, the crying grimace without the vocal accompaniment; however, this does not seem feasible because of the almost total absence of information on it.

Crying

Crying has the honor of usually being the first distinctive expressive behavior to appear in the human. It generally appears a few seconds or minutes after birth, and is probably considered at this instant as a good sign for the first and last time in the person's life. While the facial expressions and sounds accompanying crying are variable, they are clearly distinguishable from most other expressions the neonate makes. The vocalizations themselves are quite distinctive; the eyes may be tightly closed or slightly open, and the mouth region can assume various shapes—lips pulled back, partly open or protruding slightly (Darwin, 1872; Peiper, 1963). No tears tend to accompany crying until some weeks later. Dennis and Dennis (1937), in their compendium of data from 40 infant diaries, reported that 12 infant biographers noted spontaneous tears for the first time between 2 weeks and 19 weeks (median age of 5 weeks). However, Wolff (1966) claims to have observed them as early as the first day. According to Darwin (1872), tears can be elicited at birth if the eyes are tactually stimulated.

As every parent knows, the frequency of crying in infancy is very high and usually much higher than desired. An infant in the Blatz and Millichamp (1935) study engaged in emotional episodes involving crying at least 4000 times during the first 2 years of life. There are undoubtedly great individual differences in frequencies of crying, but even if an infant cried only half as much, the frequency is sufficiently high to warrant attempts to account for its functional value. In other words, what conceivable purpose does it serve?

The most popular explanation of the function of crying is that it signals a state of discomfort which could be detrimental to the infant's well-being if the condition responsible for it were not removed (see Peiper, 1963). As Wolff (1969) pointed out in his paper on the natural history of crying, the range of causal conditions sufficient to provoke crying in the young infant is very great. Physical pain (caused by puncturing the heel for blood), visceral pain (due to colic), general discomfort, interruption of feeding, and even having a toy or adult removed from sight are all capable of producing crying. In short, crying is a multidetermined response that signals distress and rarely goes unheeded by solicitous parents. In this sense, crying is very adaptive.

It is difficult to determine the time at which crying becomes an instrumental response—that is, the time at which the infant learns to cry to attract attention. Wolff (1969) reported that mothers of 3-week-old infants were convinced that their children were not beyond faking cries to get their attention. In such instances, additional information is of course necessary to validate such claims. Wolff presents at least "circumstantial evidence" from spectrographic analyses indicating morphological differences in crying patterns—patterns which could be used to distinguish instrumental crying from "simple" expressive crying. Work by Lind, Vuorenkoski, Rosberg, Partanan, and Wasz-Hockert (1970), and Wasz-Hockert, Lind, Vuorenkoski, Partanan, and Vallane (1968) tend to support Wolff's finding.

After infancy, crying seems to retain most of its distinctive morphological characteristics (Darwin, 1872). There is some evidence, however, that it begins to lose its high frequency of occurrence as early as the fourth month, and takes on more complicated functions (see Blatz & Millichamp, 1935). No one to our knowledge has made any morphological distinctions between screaming, crying, weeping, and incipient crying, although common sense suggests that screaming can be differentiated by its greater intensity and more extreme use of the facial muscles, and that weeping appears later developmentally than screaming.

In general, the studies on crying tend to support Darwin's observations and in this sense add relatively little that is essentially new.

Smiling

Of all the facial expressions of infants, smiling has been studied most (see Washburn,1929; Spitz & Wolf, 1946, Ambrose, 1961; Wolff, 1963), and also appears to be one of the most complicated expressions in terms of the conditions that precipitate it, the functions it serves, and the developmental vicissitudes it undergoes.

We know of no frequency data on the occurrence of smiling in the naturalistic life situation of the infant comparable to that obtained on crying by Blatz and Millichamp (1935). Guesses could range from no change at all in the total smiling output from infancy to adulthood, to an increase in output followed by a gradual decrease until death. The best guess is that individual differences and life situations vary so greatly that no generalization about trends can be made.

During the first week or two of life, smiling seems to be closely related to internal events occurring mostly during irregular sleep or drowsiness, and seldom or never occurring during regular sleep or when the infant is alert and attentive (Herzka, 1965; Wolff, 1966). At this time smiling appears more reflexive and void of any accompanying emotional state. Spoilsports are wont to point out to pleased parents that early smiles occur merely as reactions to gastrointestinal disturbances; however, there is no evidence to substantiate this.

While the significance of the first smile may be great for the parents, the smile for the infant does not seem to be social until sometime during the second to fourth month (Jones, 1926; Bühler & Hetzer, 1928; Spitz & Wolf, 1946). In most studies the requirements for a social smile, as distinctive from a nonsocial one, are not always spelled out. Whatever the case, the transition from nonsocial to social smiles is less marked by morphological changes than by changes in behaviors that accompany the smile. Gaze fixation on a person's face during smiling seems to be the most important criteria of a "social" smile, (see Rheingold, 1966, 1969), Dennis and Dennis (1937) reported that 20 (out of 40) diaries note that smiling at a person occurred some time between 1 and 10 weeks (median age of 6 weeks). It is important to note, though, that at the same time the social smile becomes convincingly social, the 1-month-old infant may respond with a smile to a simple pattern of dots or angles (see Ahrens, 1954) or to an inanimate object suddenly moving into the visual field (see Wolff, 1966). Since the human face has dot- and angle-like features and moves into the infant's visual field in most experiments, it is possible that the elicited reaction is determined more by nonsocial factors including novelty, surprise, or simply stimulus change. This topic will be touched on later.

The list of stimulus conditions that elicit smiling is very long and could conceivably get longer as experimenters and desperate parents increase their ingenuity. Watson (1925a) seems to be the only one to claim that smiling can be elicited immediately after birth by tickling, shaking, and patting. Gesell (1929) successfully elicited smiling by using squeaking sounds during the sixth week; and Spitz and Wolf (1946) between 2 and 6 months by using a human face or Halloween mask viewed only from the front (a profile face was ineffective). Wolff (1963) discovered that the earliest and most reliable elicitor of smiling was a high-pitched human voice. In an ambitious short-term longitudinal study, Washburn (1929) presented 15 infants with 11 different games over a year's period to elicit smiling. Smiling and clucking on the part of the experimenter, as well as the game of peek-a-boo elicited smiling at 8 weeks; a tinker toy and the experimenter reappearing from behind a cupboard door had a similar effect at 20 to 24 weeks. Washburn also noted that smiling underwent significant qualitative changes between 12 and 20 weeks, although this point was not elaborated. The possibility is raised that social stimulation in addition to physical maturation may have had important influences on shaping the morphology of the response.

Whether there is a true age change in the susceptibility of smiling to inanimate, as differentiated from animate objects, has, in our estimation, not been demonstrated. Rheingold (1966) in an analysis of some of Piaget's (1952) protocols noted that the smiling response tended to be directed more frequently to inanimate objects during the first 4 months, and then began to shift toward the animate. If true, such a change may be due to many different factors. Human faces, voices, and eyes are generally more complex in their stimulus properties than most other objects in the infant's environment and are frequently accompanied by tactile stimulation and feeding. As it now stands, the distinction between social and nonsocial is much too diffuse to provide a reliable means of categorizing stimuli that elicit smiling.

Taken in their entirety, the bulk of studies on smiling makes clear that there is no one-to-one relation between a specific class of external stimuli and smiling. Auditory, tactual, visual, and proprioceptive-kinesthetic stimuli such as helping the infant play pat-a-cake (Wolff, 1963) can produce smiling.

Interestingly enough, Darwin discussed smiling much less than crying or laughter, tending to mention it more or less casually, under such emotions as joy, high spirits, love, and tender feelings. While he acknowledged the possible signal or communicative value of smiling, he did not elaborate upon it. As he viewed it, smiling was primarily an expressive response closely related to laughter, thus having an emotional rather than communicative character. Today the emphasis has been considerably reversed. Psychologists such as Bowlby (1958) and Ambrose (1961), for example, view the smile as an important communication mechanism for controlling parent–infant behavior, a view which is currently shared by those interested in applying ethology to human behavior (see Eibl-Eibesfeldt, 1970).

Laughing

The second best thing that happens to *Homo sapiens* after he starts smiling is that he begins to laugh. Along with the easily recognizable vocal component produced by changes in air intake and expulsion, the features usually constituting laughter include (1) corners of the mouth pulled back and upwards, teeth showing and upper lip tense; (2) raised cheeks pushing up against lower eyelids; (3) partially closed eyes that are often seen as "brilliant," and (4) relatively smooth eyebrows.

It is still not certain when exactly laughing appears for the first time. Darwin (1872) noted "incipient" laughter between 3 and 4 months when his son made little noises during expiration and smiled broadly. Preyer (1892) claims his child laughed already at 23 days of age. Dennis and Dennis (1937) reported on 24 infant diaries, noting that laughing was first observed to occur at the first month or two (between 3 and 22 weeks, with a median age of 9 weeks).

Like smiling, there do not seem to be any solid developmental data on the frequency of laughing in everyday situations. To our knowledge, no studies have been carried out on the factors that reinforce laughing and thereby possibly influence its frequency at different ages. This deficit in the literature may be due simply to the fact that laughing is generally considered as an expression of emotion rather than an instrumental response aimed at achieving a goal. Whereas smiling and crying to some extent have similar expressive qualities, they can be viewed as instrumental ways of controlling the environment.

Most of the research concerning infants' laughing has been focused on different ways of eliciting it. The stimuli eliciting laughter are quite varied, but perhaps to a lesser degree than those eliciting smiling. It appears that the earliest effective stimulus is tickling. Wolff (1969) elicited chuckling and laughing fairly consistently in infants towards the end of the first month by tickling the armpits, groin, or abdomen. Not all infants laughed, however; some showed a negative reaction and some no reaction at all. Tiedemann (1927) obtained laughing during the eight week by tickling the belly; Leuba (1941) obtained the same effect with the same means between 6 and 7 months.

Laughing in response to tickling seems to be contingent upon who does the tickling. Darwin (1872) described a young child who screamed with fear if tickled by a strange man. Washburn (1929), in her intensive study of smiling and laughing, was not successful in eliciting laughter in 6-month-old infants by tickling, although the subjects' mothers had no trouble.

In a pilot study of close to 100 infants, Sroufe (1971) and his collaborators had mothers employ numerous auditory, tactile, social, and visual stimuli to produce laughter. There were very few unambiguous instances of laughter in infants under 4 months. Clear instances of laughter appeared after 4 months and were clearly apparent in most infants by 8 months. This is considerably later than the median onset of 9 weeks reported in baby biographies (Dennis & Dennis, 1937). It is difficult to account for this difference without knowing exactly what criteria for laughing were employed in the baby biographies. Sroufe found that 4 to 6-month-old infants responded with laughter mainly to tickling (tactile–social stimulation). This finding corroborates most of the early studies. In contrast, 7 to 9-month-old infants were most responsive to auditory and tactile stimulation, whereas the oldest infants, those between 10 and 12 months, responded predominantly to nontactile–social and visual stimulation.

The relatively delayed effectiveness of nontactile–social stimuli in eliciting laughter has also been observed by others (see Preyer, 1892; Fenton, 1925). However, Bühler (1931) reported that social smiling (not laughing) begins between 1 and 2 months, and "bodily stimulation" (presumably tickling) becomes effective at about 6 months—the exact reverse of most other studies. While it can be argued that laughing was not mentioned by Bühler in this context, it is difficult to imagine the relative ineffectiveness of tickling to elicit any positive response (smiling or laughing) during the first 6 months of life.

In general, most studies support the observation that laughing appears developmentally later than smiling, and when all stimulus conditions are considered, laughing in young infants occurs more frequently to tactile social stimulation than to most forms of nontactile–social stimulation (a person smiling, for example). With time, however, social stimulation becomes more effective.

There are some hypotheses about the relatively late appearance of laughing as compared with smiling. Darwin (1872) speculated that laughing most probably had to be acquired gradually over time to allow for the articulation of sounds and mouth movements. He also felt that both maturational and experiential factors were involved in the acquisition of laughing. This is an interesting notion in light of the fact that many writers view laughing as a more primitive, expressive response than smiling because once acquired, laughing is less subject to voluntary control and to modification through learning (see Washburn, 1929).

Expressions of Emotions in Infants

What follows is a brief discussion of the most commonly observed emotions in infants. Interestingly enough, nearly all of them were observed by Darwin, even though Darwin's list was intentionally ignored as a guide to our literature search in order that we would have a more objective means of cross-validating his observations. Such a discussion, because of its brevity and arbitrariness, can serve only two functions very modestly: (1) to give some substantive demonstration to the extent to which recent research coincides or fails to coincide with Darwin's findings, and (2) to present an empirical basis for the contention that complex facial expressions and their attending emotional states appear very early in human development.

Before going into the discussion, three rather long prefatory notes are necessary. First, any observer of infant behavior cannot help be aware of the variety of facial expressions that characterize the infant's relatively limited repertoire of total behavior. Some of these expressions can be viewed as grimaces that are neither traceable to any known emotional or cognitive state nor attributable to any external stimulus; others appear as actual expressions of emotions (such as fear or delight) that may be inferred from known stimulus conditions. In either case, such expressions may occur as early as the first few hours of life in full term as well as in premature babies. To our knowledge, there has been only one relatively systematic attempt to document such expressions in the newborn (Herzka, 1965). There are, of course, numerous studies that contain photographs of newborn faces, but they tend to be limited in number or mainly employed for purposes other than documentation. Herzka's effort consisted of observations (made in hospital maternity wards) which were documented by photographic shots of the facial expressions of 38 infants ranging from 1 hour to 29 weeks of age, the result being a compendium of 100 clear photographs. Accompanying each photograph are comments on the expression itself, brief statements about the stimulus conditions thought to have elicited the expression, and inferences about the underlying emotional state, if any. One of Herzka's main purposes was to document facial expressions as early as possible in the hopes of providing a firmer basis upon which to diagnose possible congenital defects or deficiencies that would affect the infant's later development and adaptation. While the actual diagnostic value of the photographic records was not demonstrated at the time his book was published, the value of the photographic records for demonstrating the very early appearance of a wide array of facial expressions was clearly established. The range of variation in facial expressions from the "angelic smile," to the contortions of yawning, the facial expressions accompanying intense visual attention, complicated expressions of disgust and rejection, and to very adult-like appearances of cunning or wisdom powerfully attest to the high degree of facial mobility and neuromuscular organization present already at birth in the human infant. Such evidence suggests strongly that the morphology of many major facial expressions is controlled to a great extent by innate or unlearned factors, a finding that would have greatly pleased Darwin. Herzka's efforts, however, did not deal with the problem of describing the expressions in such a way that precise, objective measurements of them could be made. This brings us to our second point.

   The lack of a systematic and standardized way of describing and measuring facial expressions in the research done until quite recently has made it virtually impossible to generalize across studies and come to any certain conclusions about what is going on in the development of expressions with age. In addition to this lack, there is also the absence of any systematic attempt to establish uniform rules of inference which would link expressions to emotional or cognitive states. Herzka's inferences, for example, about the possible underlying states of certain facial expressions could be subject to other interpretations by observers working within different conceptual frameworks. In general the research literature reveals that the most frequent strategy employed by observers who report their work in the literature is one that relies upon common sense. What is judged, for example, as fear behavior by a majority of trained observers is taken as an overt indicator of the emotion of fear, unless there are good reasons to believe otherwise (for example, that the subject was acting). In light of this lack of organization and standardization in the field, there is little else that can be done at present but to deal with many different studies focusing on purportedly the same emotion and observe the extent to which their findings reinforce or contradict one another. It should be emphasized, however, that this has been the case for past literature. Future literature will most probably be quite different because of the recent efforts of Ekman (as described elsewhere in this book), who has completed a standardized method of describing and measuring facial expressions that would apply to most, if not all, instances of documented facial expression in any human being regardless of age. Also Blurton-Jones (1971) has made a recent attempt to develop criteria for describing facial expressions of children. Working with 500 photos of almost 50 different children ranging from 2 to 5 years,

Blurton-Jones arrived at "52 components of facial expressions" that make a good start towards the complete descriptions of the morphology of expressions, something the field needs before serious work on the causes and effects of facial expressions in childhood can begin.

The third, and final, prefatory note is that there are a number of existing theoretical schemes accounting for emotional expression and development during infancy. Bridges' (1930, 1932) scheme is particularly popular with many textbook writers in child psychology because it depicts emotional development as a gradual evolution and differentiation of behavior over time. According to the scheme, the infant at birth is capable of only general excitement, the behavior for which is so diffuse it is impossible to ascribe any positive or negative hedonic quality to it. Within a short period of time, however, the diffuse behavior indicative of excitement differentiates into clearer signs of distress or delight. Distress becomes apparent first (the infant becomes petulant before feeding, but shows no signs of delight while being fed); and delight emerges some time later (the infant begins to show signs of joy at the sight of the breast or bottle). After some months, fear, disgust, and anger develop out of distress; and elation and affection out of delight. From these proliferate other more complex emotions.

While such a scheme makes much intuitive sense, our feeling is that in reality things are not quite that simple and orderly. The expressive behavior of an infant is so rich and variegated and often highly dependent upon stimulus and subject conditions that it virtually defies any straightforward classification or interpretation that would allow for any easy schematizing of its development. A simple example of what is meant here can be found in discussions of the emotion of disgust. Bridges observed what she called disgust as late as the fifth or sixth month. She considered this expression a developmentally advanced form of behavior that could not appear until other emotions had already developed. In sharp contrast, Stirnimann (1940) and Peiper (1963) noted instances of disgust as early as the first day of life. They accepted pronounced grimaces in reaction to the introduction of certain unpleasant substances in the newborn's mouth as good evidence for it. Bridges, who did not perform this test, arrived at a very different conclusion. We presume that in both instances, disgust was largely inferred from particular mouth movements (see Darwin, 1872) which were to some extent observed by all authors.

Another example of the difficulty of schematizing early infant expressive behavior is evidenced in the controversy generated by Watson's (1919) claim that the infant possesses three clearly recognizable "primary" patterns of emotion at birth. Sherman (1927a, 1927b, 1928) argued that such a claim was clearly unwarranted. Infant emotional behavior, especially in very young infants, claimed Sherman, was ambiguous in its emotional significance. Using four stimulus situations (restraining the head and face, suddenly dropping the infant, pricking with a needle, and hunger) aimed at eliciting four different emotions (anger, fear, physical pain, and hunger pain), Sherman discovered that raters found it impossible to distinguish the different emotions in 8-day-old infants without knowing the stimulus situation. Sherman's conclusion that infant emotional behavior may be very undifferentiated and hence lead to ambiguous judgments, however, hardly seems warranted. As Honkavaara (1961) has pointed out, it would be as equally difficult to judge adult reactions to the same four stimulus situations, all of which are negative in character. Whether Watson or Sherman is correct about infants has still to be determined. Our experience (see below) with infants indicates that judging their emotions without knowledge of the stimulus situation is frequently a difficult task, but it can be done with varying degrees of success.

These, then, are some of the problems that have to be kept in mind when dealing with global emotional expressions of infants. There is no satisfying taxonomy of such expressions and no standard procedure for specifying the stimulus and subject conditions under which they are observed and elicited. Hence, it is almost impossible to make highly general statements about when particular emotions appear during the course of infant development.

Distress and Delight

Distress and delight refer to a multiplicity of behaviors, but each is characterized by certain salient behaviors that distinguish one from the other—distress by crying and grimacing; and delight by smiling, kicking the legs, and flailing the arms. The latter two responses could characterize distress as well, but are not necessarily components of distress. Bridges' notion (1932) that excitement appears before disgust and delight seems arbitrary in light of the fact that crying appears at birth and is used as the first signal of distress. Delight, though, does fit Bridges' scheme by coming later than either general excitement or crying.

Other studies, though, complicate the picture. As noted above, Watson (1919) obtained data for what he claimed were three innate emotions present at birth—love, anger, and fear. Love can be included here as an instance of delight since, as Watson viewed it, it consisted of smiling, gurgling, and cooing responses to gentle tactile stimulation of some erogenous zone. Watson's insistence that love behavior could be found very early challenges Bridges' argument that it first had to be preceded by excitement and developed only gradually over a number of months.

Conceivably future research will resolve the discrepancies between Bridges' and Watson's formulations. It appears to us that reliable judgments of delight and distress will lead us to conclude that both emotional states are well developed at about 2 months, somewhat later than Watson observed (he seems to have read more into a small sample of behavior than was warranted) and somewhat earlier than the time Bridges claims they emerge (she seems to attribute too little differentiation to early behavior).

Anger

Anger was considered by Watson (1919) as one of the triumvirate of emotions appearing at birth as a relatively sterotyped reaction to a specific class of eliciting stimuli. His description of anger involves a stiffening of the body, striking or slashing movements of hands and arms, holding the breath, a flushed face (presumably as a result of checked breathing) and crying, which gradually escalates into screaming. The eliciting stimulus for such a reaction was a restriction of the infant's movements (Watson presumably held the infant's head or limbs quite tightly).

Stirnimann (1940), following Watson's work, pressed the arms of 100 newborns to their sides (not all at once, however) and elicited a range of reactions, some of which were similar to those observed by Watson. Twelve infants cried immediately, two made a pronounced grimace, but most gave a great variety of different reactions. Holding the arms above the infant's head produced a more vigorous reaction: 61 of the 100 infants cried immediately in anger (Wutschreien), 10 cried later, one only whimpered; 12 infants only showed their rage in their faces and 14 did not react (the numbers do not add up to 100). Stirnimann speculated that pain was not necessarily the best explanation for the crying, since this treatment did not waken a sleeping infant of the same age. Stirnimann apparently assumed that any painful stimuli would be of sufficient intensity to waken a sleeping infant. Restraining the arms in an uncomfortable position elicited psychological discomfort which led to anger rather than pain; to experience such discomfort, the subject had to be awake.

Bridges (1932), in contrast, claimed that anger evolved out of distress at about 3 months. As anger became more differentiated, it was characterized less by tearful crying or screaming and more by protest shouts, pushing, and kicking. Anger was also accompanied by flushing of the face—a finding similar to Darwin's observations that his son's face and head reddened with rage at 4 and 7 months.

Despite the variance of the above findings, it is safe to conclude that anger, as inferred from gross behaviors as well as from crying and screaming, is well–developed in infants under 6 months of age. Temper tantrums (which usually involve kicking, scratching, and rolling on the floor) are usually not evident until the beginning of the second year (see Bridges, 1932).

The particular facial expressions involved in anger, apart from those involved in crying, have not been discussed by the above writers. Darwin's (1872) description, based on facial expressions of adults, remains the most detailed. As noted earlier, the fact that Darwin did not describe in detail the facial expression of anger in infants (and no one else seems to have either) suggests that the facial movements in anger may not develop unitl some time in early childhood.

Affection

The earliest apparent sign of affection appears at around 4 months, according to Banham (1950), who made incidental observations of over 900 infants during psychological examinations. The infants generally fixed their gaze on the observer's face, kicked their feet, waved their arms, tried to raise their bodies, and smiled. It could be argued that such behavior is simply delight or joy and that to qualify as affection, active approach behaviors must also be included.

An interesting general question is raised by Banham's observations: What reason, if any, is there for arguing that an early behavior pattern be viewed as a progenitor of a developmentally later and more complete pattern? Most people would confidently judge an infant as affectionate if he reached out and patted or caressed someone and at the same time smiled. At 4 months, though, reaching and touching behavior is a poorly organized, sporadic, hit-and-miss affair. At 6 months, though, reaching and touching improve considerably, and it was at this time that Banham noted her infants periodically trying to pat the other person at the same time that they were engaging in the other so-called affectionate behaviors. The question is whether the 4-month behaviors should be designated as indications of the same emotion as the more complicated 6-month behaviors.

Bridges (1932) supported Banham's findings by observing that affection originated along with delight sometime before 8 months as a response to fondling. After 8 months, affection made a transition from a more passive pattern to a more active pattern involving attempts at caressing. Unmistakable caressing attempts towards adults, as well as mirror images, were observed to appear at 11 to 12 months. Other children (and presumably dolls) became targets of affection a little later.

On the basis of both sets of findings it appears safe to say that by the end of the first year of life and definitely during the second year, infants are capable of expressing affection.

Fear

The fear reaction seems quite different from the foregoing emotions, although it is perhaps most similar to distress. In infants its expression usually involves a momentary decrease in ongoing activity presumably due to startle. The body becomes momentarily rigid; the eyes tend to close somewhat; the head may bend awkwardly; the mouth first contorts into a cry and then crying ensues. In his diary, it can be recalled that Darwin noted that the face can also take on a "grave" expression before crying actually begins.

The first occurrence of fear apparently depends upon who observes it with what criteria in mind. Stirnimann (1940) claims that it can actually be seen on the face during birth, when only the head is visible and the infant is being faced with an oxygen shortage. He also claims that it is especially noticeable in instances of birth trauma in which the infant screams in a most pitiful tone and fear is unmistakably written on his face.

Watson (1919) also noted fear very early and found it readily elicitable by sudden loss of support, a push or a shake, or loud sounds. The reaction he described consisted of a sudden catching of the breath, rapid closing of the eyelids, and puckering of the lips followed by crying. Valentine (1930) also obtained fear responses to loud noises and loss of support during the first month.

Although Stirnimann and Watson felt strongly that fear could be observed very early, there were others who felt just as strongly that fear cannot be observed in young infants. Peiper (1963) flatly asserted that "no expressive movement of fear or horror exists during infancy"; however, his statement appears to rely less on empirical data on fear than on his feeling that cerebral development is not sufficient during the first year to allow the infant to be afraid. It appears, then, that the time when fear first occurs in early infancy is highly debatable. That it appears sometime during the first 6 months is fairly certain.

In the older infant, fear has been studied mostly in terms of the stimulus situations eliciting it and less in terms of its morphological properties. In the bulk of the literature, the overt indices of infant fear are limited mostly to crying, a sober look, cessation of smiling and ongoing activities, tensing of muscles, and averting the head from the fear-arousing stimulus (see Bronson, 1968; Scarr & Salapatek, 1970). Little detailed description is made of the disposition of various parts of the facial muscles or body before and during the fear-arousing event.

The stimulus situations eliciting fear have generally involved presenting the infant with a stranger or with a familiar stimulus in an unfamiliar context, such as the infant being faced with his mother wearing a bathing cap (see Wolff, 1969). Masks and sudden noises are also frequently used. Responses to such stimuli generally indicate that fear as a distinct and easily recognizable reaction appears during the middle of the first year—a period when the infant develops attachments to adults and also has an increased capacity to respond to stimuli in terms of his memory of previous encounters with them.

The literature is not clear on whether there could possibly be two forms of fear in infancy—an early, perhaps more primitive form resulting from the sudden onset of intense or aversive stimuli and a more advanced form of fear resulting from an incongruity between the infant's expectations of a stimulus and the properties of the stimulus at the moment (Jones, 1930; Schaffer, 1969). The facial expressions associated with each form could conceivably differ from one another in as yet unknown respects.

Surprise (Startle)

Surprise has been discussed by some writers (see Berlyne, 1960; Charlesworth, 1969) as an epistemic[3] emotion—one involving the relation between an individual's knowlege or expectations about a particular stimulus and what the stimulus actually turns out to be. Surprise reactions themselves could be followed by additional emotions of fear, delight, and anger as well as the instrumental behaviors of curiosity commonly associated with it. Watson (1919) noted that crying frequently followed surprise. However, the situations which he described appeared to elicit startle rather than surprise per se. The distinction between the two is not clear; while surprise may have a startle component, it can be viewed as a relatively slower, less negatively toned response than startle. Surprise can also be viewed as a response to a misexpected event rather than to a sudden, intense, unexpected event as in the case of startle.

In a study aimed at using surprise responses to diagnose the extent to which infants had expectancies concerning the fate of objects that disappeared from view, Charlesworth (1966) discovered that some facial elements of surprise (as described in adults by Darwin, 1872) were obtainable in infants after 7 or 8 months, but tended to be very infrequent. Raising the eyebrows did not occur in 4- to 12-month-old infants in 132 surprise situations. (This may have been due partly to the fact that infant eyebrows are frequently too fair to see.) However, opening the mouth did occur at times. Sudden immobility of face and posture were seen more frequently, along with quizzical looks and the sudden appearance of looks of puzzlement (difficult to describe in any detail) and an increase in attention. In general, though, the classic surprise response (that is, all the elements of it, as described in adults by Darwin) was not found in infants during the first year.

Peiper (1963) also observed that the expression of astonishment was rare in infants, and noted that the reflex-like raising of the eyebrows and wrinkling of the forehead in surprise appeared at best as a slight trace in infancy. Preyer (1892) also reported what he felt was a reflex movement of surprise (more probably startle) on the twenty-fifth day of life, and astonishment

---

[3]Epistemic: a word derived from the Greek pertaining to knowledge or the conditions for acquiring it. Epistemic emotions refer to those emotions such as interest, curiosity, boredom, and surprise, which have to do with what the individual already knows or desires to know.

at the end of the seventh month; no eyebrows were lifted, however, in the latter, but the mouth was opened.

In general, then, facial surprise responses (as distinct from startle) appear to be present in infants only in a relatively weak and attenuated form, and do not seem to appear in any recognizable adult form until the second half of the first year. Even then, they occur infrequently. This may be due to the infant's not being cognitively equipped to form strong expectancies (the violation of which produce surprise) similar to those formed by older children. A much more parsimonious explanation is that normal 4- to 12-month-old infants have smooth faces because of underlying fat tissues, and that subtle movements in facial musculature in response to a surprising event are best seen when the skin is loose enough to wrinkle.

Jealousy

If one were asked to make a facial expression of jealousy, it would be a very difficult task. To infer that someone is jealous requires more than observing changes in the facial musculature; knowing the situation is very important, as well as observing other things the individual does and says. In this sense, jealousy is comparable to such emotions as sympathy and embarrassment, which are not expressed by distinct, predictable behaviors, but which are nevertheless expressed in the face as well as in other behaviors. As Darwin (1872) pointed out, "Painters can hardly portray suspicion, jealousy, envy, etc., except by the aid of accessories which tell the tale ₄ . ." The observer of jealousy in preverbal children must rely on such gross indices as unhappiness, mild distress, and perhaps poorly concealed acts of aggression.

It can be recalled that jealousy was observed by Darwin (1872) when his son was 15½ months. Bridges (1931) noted its occurrence between 15 and 18 months when some of her subjects became deeply distressed as attention was given to other children. Watson (1930) did not note the first sign of jealousy until around 2 years of age, when it occurred in response to the sight of parents embracing; at 2½ years, the child attacked the father on such occasions, and a few months later would ask the father if he were going to the office. None of the writers describe the facial expressions accompanying such behavior.

Other studies of jealousy are scattered throughout the literature. None, to our knowledge, deal with the phenomenon in any depth, nor supplement the observations of Darwin, Watson or Bridges by defining clearly what distinct facial expressions were involved.

Shyness, Coyness, Embarrassment, and Shame

Darwin (1872) described three behaviors characteristic of expressions of shyness: casting down the eyes, blushing, and moving the body in an awkward, nervous fashion. He observed that it is difficult to distinguish shyness from fear in young children because both presumably involve pronounced avoidance responses. His first observation of shyness, as noted earlier, was in his son's behavior at 2 years and 3 months. Moore (1895) noted shyness in a 1½ year old child who hid his head. In general, most studies suggest that it is possible to elicit shyness sometime during late infancy. However, during this period it is difficult to distinguish shyness from coyness, embarrassment, and shame. Coyness has more of a flirtatious social element, whereas shame has more of a cognitive element—the awareness of having transgressed against a rule. Embarrassment, in contrast, seems to involve more awareness of one's own appearance. Furthermore, shame and embarrassment seem to be more situation-dependent, whereas shyness can be viewed more or less as a persistent personality trait. All four could involve the above three behaviors described by Darwin, hence inferences concerning the emotional state of the infant at the time would depend heavily upon the situation as well as the observers' knowledge about the social and cognitive disposition of the infant.

Sympathy

Like jealousy, sympathy is hardly definable in terms of particular expressive behaviors. The nature of the situation and the behavior of the person toward whom sympathy is displayed are important in determining whether a child is showing sympathy of not. If the child merely mimics someone else, one is not certain that sympathy is being felt. More than mimicking is necessary if one wishes to infer sympathy. However, mimicking may be a necessary developmental prerequisite in the sense that the child must first have the capacity to mimic another's emotion before he can sympathize with him.

To our knowledge there have been no studies beyond infant diary observations of sympathy in infants. Sympathy, as defined in terms of a child sensing or understanding the distress of someone else, seems to begin sometime during the first or second year, as Darwin (1877) illustrated in the observation of his son. Other than that, there appear to be no developmental studies of sympathy in infants. Darwin's achievements in this area do not seem to have been superseded.

THE INFANT'S RECOGNITION
OF EXPRESSIONS

As was noted earlier, Darwin made passing but insightful comments on the importance of the human being's ability to recognize the emotional expressions of others. Studying such an ability in a verbal human being, who can both comprehend verbal instructions and use words to indicate perceived differences and similarities in the expressions of others, has been a relatively difficult task that has at least been partially solved. Testing for such abilities in infants, however, is a different story. It is virtually impossible to know for certain what the infant finds attractive in the visual stimuli of faces peering down at him. As Ahrens (1954) has demonstrated, dotlike figures or angles may hold the infant's attention and elicit a smile more effectively than other stimuli. Even objects moving into the visual field may attract his attention and elicit a smile, as already pointed out.

The problem, though, is larger than merely trying to identify those variables which only the infant perceives as interesting. What responses should be depended upon when we give the infant the task of discriminating between two different facial expressions? As a poorly coordinated, nonverbal, sleep-ridden, and passion-torn organism, the young infant offers relatively few behaviors that may aid even the most skilled diagnostician in identifying his emotional and cognitive states. The older infant is only somewhat less difficult. Looking, smiling, shaking the body, kicking, and changes in ongoing responses such as heartrate or sucking behavior are some of the major behaviors infant testers look to for help, but the relation of these behaviors to recognition has not yet been satisfactorily established.

There are also other factors that make research in this area so difficult. As Kessen, Haith, and Salapatek (1970) point out, the bulk of research in infancy to date has dealt primarily with measures of infant behavior. Relatively little has been done to determine the nature of *stimuli* that play a major role in the infant's world. As a result, almost nothing is known about the kinds and ranges of facial expressions to which the infant is sensitive. Before discussing the few studies that have been conducted, it is instructive to keep in mind that facial expressions of others most probably constitute only a small part of the young infant's stimulus world.

At birth and shortly thereafter the human head and body may be detectable as a simple figure-ground Gestalt aided by movement. Sometime thereafter, the face itself becomes a locus of interesting events, again possibly because of movement as well as such interesting features as moving, glistening eyes and the contrast of the lips and teeth. In addition, facial activity is often accompanied by auditory and tactile stimulation as the person talks to and touches the child. At early ages, it is quite conceivable that the infant reacts in an identical manner to radically different facial expressions on the part of an adult or older child. As playful parents can easily testify, scolding a young infant or speaking to him sweetly can both elicit heartwarming smiles in return. Exactly when the infant begins to respond differentially to certain facial expressions in others has not been well documented. Most studies have concentrated on responses to faces versus nonfaces or to familiar versus strange faces. The few existing studies of recognition of facial expressions, although frequently difficult to evaluate in terms of the rigor of their methodology, are still worthy of our attention.

Bühler and Hetzer (1928) appear to have been the first to do a systematic comparison of infants' reactions to a positive (smiling) face and a negative face (an angry face with lips pressed tightly together, the corners of the mouth pulled down, the brow knitted). The infants' responses were classified into two groups: (1) positive, involving a composite of responses including smiling and moving limbs joyfully, and (2) negative, involving a composite of responses including motionless limbs and crying. In addition to presenting the two kinds of faces, the authors observed infants' reactions to positive and negative voices, presented from behind a screen. Threatening and affectionate arm gestures, acted out silently with a neutral face, were also included in their test battery. Each of the six possible stimulus situations was presented for 30 seconds to 90 different infants, 10 at each age level from 3 to 11 months. Results show that no neutral responses occurred to the angry and friendly face from the third to the end of the sixth month. In the third month, 90% of the reactions to the angry face were positive, 10% negative; in the fourth month 50% positive, 50% negative; in the fifth, sixth, and seventh months, 100% of the responses were negative. After that the responses were more or less split between positive and negative with an increase in neutral responses up to 40% of the total reactions observed. Thus there is clear evidence that by at least the fifth to seventh months, the infants were discriminating between the two facial expressions.

The results for the positive versus the negative voices were (with one exception) identical to those of the facial expressions. Discriminating the significance of the threatening versus the affectionate motor gesture appeared later than discriminating the facial expressions and voices. The average infant, according to the authors, not only discriminated the two gestures by the eighth month, but also comprehended their significance.

Later, Spitz and Wolf (1946) concentrated on 145 infants between 2 and 6 months, and discovered in contrast to the Bühler and Hetzer findings that different expressions on the experimenter's face or on a mask were not effective in producing different reactions in the infants. The classic threat expression used to produce terror down through the centuries succeeded only in eliciting smiles in the same manner that the other expressions did.

Ahrens (1954), working with institutionalized children, obtained some data suggesting that infants around 5 months can discriminate between drawings of a person crying, laughing, and with a neutral expression. At 8 months, a frowning face (with the eyebrows wrinkled more or less vertically) produced distress and avoidance behavior. Although it is not easy to interpret Ahrens' methods or findings, it seems fairly certain that by the second half of the first year, the infants in his study were clearly reacting to differences in facial expressions, and not just to movement or some particular aspect of the face (for example, just the presence of two eyes).

In a more controlled study, Wilcox and Clayton (1968) used visual fixations to determine whether 5-month-old infants could discriminate between smiling, frowning, and neutral expressions presented both as moving and nonmoving pictures. Each stimulus was presented for 28 seconds. Apart from one exception, no significant difference was found in average fixation times to the different expressions. Lack of any demonstrable preference, of course, does not necessarily indicate any failure to discriminate; the infant may quite readily detect the difference between two facial expressions without preferring one expression over the other.

In a more recent study Kreutzer and Charlesworth (1973) confronted 40 infants (10 at 4, 6, 8, and 10 months) with an experimenter who acted out angry, happy, sad, and neutral facial expressions, accompanied by appropriate vocalizations. The infants' responses to the experimenter were recorded on video tape and rated for the amount of attention and activity they engaged in as well as for their emotional responses to the experimenter's expressed emotion. The emotional responses were rated in terms of positive responses (smiling, laughing), neutral responses (relaxed, no expression, or usual expression), and negative responses (cries, almost cries, frowns, very serious). Analysis of the results indicated that the 4-month-old infants responded indiscriminately to the various expressions. In contrast, the 6-month-and-older infants discriminated between the various emotions expressed by the experimenter with attentional and negative affect responses. They also responded, in many cases, with the appropriate emotion, i.e., if the experimenter was sad, the infant appeared sad or very serious. The results of this experiment confirms, in part, Darwin's (1877) observations as well as those of Bühler and Hetzer (1928). What it was exactly about the experimenter's expressions (facial expressions themselves, or voice, or posture) that elicited the responses from the infants was not determined.

It is not easy to reach any firm conclusions from the foregoing studies. The most conservative conclusion is that the infant is most probably making discriminations between some aspects of facial expression during the middle of the first year. By the end of the first year he can undoubtedly recognize expressions quite well, as long as they are pronounced and perhaps accompanied by the appropriate vocalizations and gross gestures.

To our knowledge, no studies have been conducted with one- and two-year-old infants to determine the extent to which they recognize various facial expressions. It seems as if researchers may have taken for granted that children at this age have no trouble in recognizing facial expressions and have therefore concluded it was unnecessary to demonstrate it. The recognition abilities of 3-year-olds has been investigated, however, so perhaps methodological considerations alone account for the lack of research with 1- and 2-year olds. Behavioral indices employed with infants are no longer appropriate to assess the ability of this age group to recognize emotions; yet the verbal techniques employed with older children are also clearly inadequate.

Some Methodological Problems

Most of the foregoing observations were made by a single observer working in naturalistic situations in which, for the most part, the behavior under examination occurred spontaneously. The weaknesses of such a method are apparent. It is possible, for example, that knowledge of the context in which the behavior took place weighed much more heavily in judging the emotions than the facial expressions themselves. As noted earlier, the possibility of contextual or situational cues playing an important role in judging emotions was demonstrated (Sherman, 1927a, b). However, there is evidence to show that facial expressions may be accurately interpreted even when situational cues are absent (see Honkavaara, 1961, for a discussion of this). Goodenough (1931b), for example, demonstrated that when given the task of assigning everyday situations to eight photographed expressions of a 10-month-old girl, judges did significantly better than chance. Clearly the discrepancy between Sherman's findings and Goodenough's requires further attention.

The problem of evaluating expressive behavior is more complicated, though, than trying to assess relative contributions of context and facial expression to valid inferences about infants' emotional states. Making judgments on the basis of motion picture films, one would think, would be easier and more reliable than making judgments on the spur of the moment without such records. However, this may not be totally the case. In Charlesworth's (1966) study of surprise, 80 infants between 5 and 19 months were filmed during a surprise situation. Interrater agreements about the facial expression of each infant ranged from 74% to 95% on such expressions as smiling, crying, surprise, startle, puzzlement, and the absence or presence of a change in affect. While the percentages may be high relative to some other studies, that they are not higher is somewhat surprising, since the raters had the opportunity to replay the film as many times as they felt necessary to arrive at a confident judgment. In numerous instances the behavior was so ambiguous it was impossible to rate it with any degree of consistency or certainty—and this was occasionally true for such seemingly simple expressions as smiling and crying as well as for the more global emotions. All of Charlesworth's ratings were made without knowledge of the stimulus situation; if the raters had had such knowledge and also could have heard the infant's vocalizations, the reliabilities conceivably could have been higher.

The point being made here is that repeated observations of the same expression by the same and different observers do not insure that there will be reliable and valid judgments concerning the nature of the infant's facial expressions and the underlying emotions associated with them. It is possible that early in infancy, facial expressions (as well as other behaviors) are so unstable and undifferentiated that, when taken by themselves (as is often the case with films), an unambiguous interpretation of them is impossible. If infant biographers had had more opportunity to observe such expressions on subsequent occasions without the support of all of the original contextual cues, they would have conceivably been less certain of their final judgments.

In any case, permanent records of expressions are superior to on-the-spot judgments, since they open themselves to repeated evaluation and analysis. However, such records can only be of maximum value if they include as much of the contextual cues as possible as well as the many nonfacial responses that accompany the facial expressions. The infant's inability to tell the observer how he feels or even to express himself fully in nonverbal ways, other than by his facial expressions which in themselves are often inadequate indicators of his emotions, makes the task of inferring infant emotion and cognition a very difficult undertaking.

CONCLUDING REMARKS ON
INFANT EXPRESSIONS

A number of points can be made about the foregoing discussion of facial expressions in infants. Surprisingly little of what has been done in the 100 years after Darwin has added anything substantially new to what he observed; those studies that deal with the same phenomena he observed produce similar findings. In other words, similar expressions are observed in infants at roughly the same ages. This reminds us of a similar case involving Jean Piaget—his early observations of sensorimotor behavior based upon a small number of infants remain, after many years, the core of our knowledge of such behavior. Proportionately little new information has been added to this core despite years of research by many people.

The review of the post-Darwinian literature revealed that three major relatively distinct expressive behaviors (crying, smiling, and laughing) appear very early in the infant. The morphology of these behaviors seems to change little, if at all, during infancy. Their frequency, however, appears to be greatly dependent upon the situations that elicit or reinforce them. Evidence for the appearance during the neonatal period of more complex facial expressions, including grimaces as well as what appear to be emotional expressions, strongly support the view that the morphology of facial expressions is determined before any learning, in the conventional sense of the term, can take place. Furthermore, in light of such evidence facial expressions in later years cannot be accounted for totally by cultural factors without first taking cognizance of the early appearance in the newborn of those complex facial expressions that are clearly similar to those of adults.

The literature review also revealed that many global expressions characteristic of adult emotional expressive behavior also appear in the infant before the end of the second year, thus confirming Darwin's observation about their very early origins. The very early occurrence of such behaviors suggest that extensive learning is not necessary for their emergence. Darwin's hypothesis that such expressive behaviors for the most part are innate has been more directly tested in at least one instance by Freedman (1965), who compared the behavior of identical and fraternal twins. The method of twin comparison used by Freedman is a conventional method employed to assess the relative roles that heredity and environment play in influencing behavior. In a well-controlled study of 11 fraternal and 9 identical twin pairs over the first year of life, Freedman found that identical twin pairs showed significantly greater similarity in social smiling, as well as the intensity and timing of fear reactions towards the investigator. In a later section of this chapter other tests of Darwin's hypothesis will be provided by studies of the effects of the absence and presence of opportunity to learn facial expressions.

When infant recognition of facial expressions is considered, the literature review reveals quite a different level of research achievement than it does for infant expressions. The sparse data on infant recognition do not allow for many conclusions. There seems to be no doubt, intuitively, that infants over a year old are sensitive to facial expressions of others. Outside of everyday observations, however, there is little evidence to support this intuition. Infants under 12 months present an even more uncertain picture; it is impossible to say whether such infants are sensitive to facial expressions per se or if they require the total expressive behavior (facial, vocal, verbal and postural) of those around them before they can discriminate such behavior from other behaviors (instrumental behaviors, for example) and recognize their meaning. Everyday observers of infants frequently feel that even as early as the first few months some infants appear to be dimly aware of the difference between smiles and frowns, but such awareness is transient and very difficult to describe. Whether such observations are totally unwarranted because of their methodological inadequacy cannot be determined. Recognition, like other cognitive acts, is difficult to measure in general; for obvious reasons it is even more difficult to measure in infants.

The question of methodology in measuring expressive behavior as well as recognition is a complex one. To date most methodologies have been insufficient in the sense that they have neither involved permanent visual records of the facial expressions (to allow for greater test of observer reliability); nor have they included enough of the stimulus situation or accompanying behaviors to account satisfactorily for the stimulus and behavioral context in which the expressive behavior itself took place. Such shortcomings are understandably unavoidable in most instances (even filmed records leave much of the context unrecorded); however, until they are eliminated, there will be no adequate picture of expressive behavior and its recognition.

To date, the observations of infant biographers (including Darwin) and naturalistic observers, as anecdotal and uncontrolled as they have been, have not yet been superseded by studies employing more sophisticated techniques. For example, the well-controlled recognition study by Wilcox and Clayton (1968) adds little new information to what we already know as a result of many less rigorous studies done earlier. Nevertheless, the "older studies" disagree sufficiently amongst themselves (for example, Watson's findings compared to Bridges') to suggest strongly that their methodology has a limit to its utility and that new approaches have to be developed. What these new approaches will consist of is difficult to predict; tight experimental designs and the latest cinematographic and video techniques will definitely be included. The impressionistic, naturalistic quality of the early observations must also be somehow included to give the study a solid ground in the reality of everyday infant behavior.

POST-DARWINIAN STUDIES OF
CHILDREN'S FACIAL EXPRESSIONS

Ideally, in this section we would like to be able to follow our discussions of expressions of infancy with a discussion of the expressions which appear in a similar form in childhood, and those which appear later for the first time during childhood. The existing empirical data, however, do not permit such a treatment. There has been little concern on the part of psychologists for developmental changes in the morphological properties of expressive behaviors. Most research seems to have preceded on the implicit assumption that, once established in infancy, the form of expressive behaviors changes little over the years. Thus the research emphasis shifts from morphological characteristics of the expressions of infants to other areas of interest in children's expressions. These areas include the various kinds of situations in which expressive behaviors of children occur and the problem of how often they occur. It is not until adulthood that the research focus is directed back to the morphology of expressive behaviors, as evidenced in the work of such people as Birdwhistell (1970) and other kinesiologists studying nonverbal communication. As a consequence of this shifting of focus, the developmental continuity of expressive behavior between infancy and adulthood is broken. This represents a loss of information necessary for full understanding of expressive behavior. As Peiper (1963) and others have argued, adult expressive behaviors cannot be fully understood in the absence of a longitudinal approach beginning with the first years of life.

Despite the lack of systematically collected data, several authors, nevertheless, have given impressionistic accounts of age trends in expressive behavior (Murphy, Murphy, & Newcomb, 1937; Allport, 1961; Peiper, 1963). In general, infants and very young children are believed to be more expressive than older children and adults. It is observed that children's expressions of emotions tend to be more diffuse and much more motoric, in contrast to the differentiated and subtle expressions of more mature individuals. For example, infants or young children may flail their limbs in bursts of crying; similarly during expressions of joy, the entire body of the child is activated. This is usually not the case with older children or adults; their responses are much more subdued.

Several factors bring about these developmental changes. Increased fine muscular control is likely to contribute in part to the relatively more refined and subtle ways in which older children and adults express their emotions. In addition, social pressures are likely involved. For example, males are warned that "big boys" do not cry in our society—they may clench their hands or bite their lips, but may not whine, scream, or show other pronounced signs of pain or sadness. Greater subtlety of expressions with age and their relatively lower frequency are also influenced by the increasing role that cognitive factors play in regulating emotions and their facial displays. Changed cognitive abilities enable the child to respond to a wider range of stimuli; furthermore, the child can respond to past as well as present events. Expressive behaviors no longer bear one-to-one relationships to contemporaneous internal physiological states or environmental events, as appears to be the case in infancy. Emotional outbreaks in older children are frequently inhibited and replaced by cognitive and instrumental acts. A simple instance of this, for example, is the child who refuses to cry when he loses a game, and either rationalizes his failure and does nothing, or admits he did not do well enough and works harder to improve himself. Another trend noticed is that with increasing development, the child no longer exhibits the rapid onset or the sudden shift of emotional expressions characteristic of infancy. Here again social, cognitive, and volitional skills play an important role in creating such a difference. The ability to simulate

emotions also increases with age; the control and mental development necessary for the voluntary expressions of most emotions are clearly beyond
the capabilities of infants. Unfortunately, observations of these trends, as
already noted, have been mainly anecdotal and impressionistic; there are
no solid empirical data to support them. Hence there is no way of knowing
how reliably they portray what really happens during childhood.

To parallel the preceding discussions of expressions in infants, the following treatment of research on expressions of children will deal first with
the studies of a single expressive feature—crying, smiling, or laughter—followed by studies concerning the expressive features of more global emotions.

Crying

Darwin (1872) observed close parallels between crying and laughter,
which have also been observed and corroborated later by Crile (1915) and
Peiper (1963). Tears, characteristic of most instances of crying, are
sometimes associated with laughter; and both crying and laughter have
similar respiratory patterns, although the mouth movements in each
can differ considerably. In children, crying and laughter are readily in-
terchangeable within a very short period of time (seconds in some instances)
and frequently the onset patterns of each are difficult to distinguish from
one another. In cases of grief that involve intense and often prolonged
crying, the forehead assumes a configuration not found in laughter. As Darwin
described it, the forehead develops vertical, central, and transverse furrows
resembling a horseshoe or triangle. This pattern, Darwin noted, was less
marked in children than adults, and he hypothesized that this was due to
greater skin resilience in children and a corresponding decreased tendency
of children's skin to wrinkle.

Since Darwin, research on crying has largely focused on frequency data
and the situations in which crying most frequently appears. Peiper (1963)
has noted that the incidence of crying in adults is relatively small in contrast
to smiling and laughter; whereas observations of infants seem to suggest
that the first few months of life are dominated by expressions of distress.
Brackett (1933) reported that the frequency of crying in nursery school
children decreases with age, and the frequency of laughter increases. According to Bridges (1931), children over 3 years rarely cry more than 4 to 5
times a month in nursery school. Not only does the child become less
distressed by nursery school routines, but he also finds more adaptive means
of dealing with difficult situations.

Blurton Jones' (1967) ethological observations of nursery school children
are unique in their attention to the form of expressive behaviors in addition
to the situations and concomitant behaviors. He reported that crying,
retaliation, or pleas for help occur in response to physical attack by peers,

or threatened loss of property. Prior to and during crying, puckering of the brow and reddening of the face as well as relative immobility were noted; these observations agree with Darwin's (1872).

Bridges (see Murphy et al., 1937) and Watson (1925b) have catalogued the situations in which crying most frequently occurs in young children. The 25 situations delineated by Bridges include contexts from which we would commonly infer fear, pain, sympathy, anger, frustration, distress, displeasure, and anticipated displeasure. These situations, no doubt, change as the child grows older; Brackett (1933), for example, observed that following adjustment to new nursery school routines, children cried most frequently during free play. Brackett's observations also suggest that although crying does not appear to occur frequently in the presence of close friends, crying is essentially a social phenomena. More than 78% of all instances observed occur during social interactions.

The intricacies of children's instrumental control of crying do not seem to have been investigated. The crying of infants has been treated as an expressive response, although, as mentioned earlier, 3-week-old infants may be capable of instrumental crying (Wolff, 1969). Any parent will attest to their preschooler's histrionic abilities and manipulative control of crying; however, these more creative aspects of crying have not received any attention in research.

Smiling and Laughing

Darwin discussed laughter and smiling as expressions of joy and happiness; he also recognized the presence of smiling in tender feelings of love. In contrast, most research with children has tended to treat smiling merely as a milder form of amusement, joy, or happiness. As a result, the many subtle nuances of smiling have tended to be neglected. Variations of smiling have been observed in adults' greeting behaviors, appeasement, and flirting behavior (see Eibl-Eibesfeldt, 1972); smiling can also signal assurance. Yet, with the exception of the observations of Blurton Jones (1967), these various facets of smiling have not been translated into research. Blurton Jones reported two patterns of greeting behaviors when children met their parents at the end of a school day. One pattern was a quick approach to the parent, accompanied by smiling and touching. The other pattern did not involve smiling.

As for laughter, Darwin mentioned the situations in which it tended to occur. He maintained that "it is chiefly the anticipation of a pleasure, and not its actual enjoyment, which leads to purposeless and extravagant movements of the body, and to the utterance of various sounds."

Post-Darwinian research on children's laughter seems to have been dominated by a concern with the context in which smiling is most frequently elicited. This emphasis parallels the attention given to the adequate stimuli that elicit smiling in infancy. In general, however, the research on children's laughter has not completely supported Darwin's claim; the anticipation of an event is *one* situation in which laughter occurs, but numerous other situations also elicit laughter. For a comprehensive account of these situations, the reader is referred to Kenderdine's (1931) study, which summarized laughter-eliciting situations under three general rubrics: motor activity, humorous situations, and situations that the child recognized were unacceptable.

Laughter appears to show some consistency within the child; children who tended to laugh frequently during free play also laughed frequently during routine activities (see Brackett 1933). There is also general agreement that laughter is principally a social response. Of the 223 instances of laughter she observed in the preschool, Kenderdine (1931) reported that only 6.3% occurred when children were alone. The distribution of laughter is usually confined to a few children, however (see Brackett, 1933).

Age trends have been noted in the situations that elicit laughter and the frequency with which laughter occurs. Bridges (1931) reported that 3- and 4-year-olds laugh increasingly at absurdities and incongruities. This trend is probably attributable to cognitive factors undergoing maturational change at the time and the concomitant formation of expectancies. The reported age differences in frequency of laughter are equivocal. Kenderdine (1931) found that 2-year-olds laughed on the average of 14 times within 5 hours of observation. Three- and 4-year-olds laughed fewer than seven times within the same period. Gregg, Miller, and Linton (1929) also reported less laughter in kindergarten and first-grade children in situations in which one child was already laughing. These age differences could be attributable to maturational or situational variables, and therefore are difficult to interpret. Enders (1927) and Ding and Jersild (1932) found a curvilinear relation between age and frequency of laughter. Three-year-olds laughed less frequently than 2-, 4-, and 5-year-olds. Ding and Jersild suggest that situational factors are responsible for these age differences. Three-year-olds are no longer pampered, and are forced into serious interactions with older children as equals.

Attempts to correlate laughing and smiling with intelligence have been equally equivocal. Kenderdine (1931) found that children with IQs over 140 laughed more than twice as frequently as children with IQs between 100 and 130. In contrast, Ding and Jersild (1932) reported a nonsignificant relation between frequency of smiling and laughter and IQ.

Delight

Darwin (1872) recognized laughter as a central component of expressions of delight. In children, he observed that in expressions of joy, laughter usually was accompanied by dancing about, clapping hands, and other motor movements. A 4-year-old described "good spirits" to Darwin as "'laughing, talking, and kissing.'"

Although a plethora of studies, as just noted, deal with children's laughter, little research has been conducted on children's expressions of delight since Darwin. Bridges (1931) reported that in some children, delight and joy are expressed as the child becomes familiar with a situation. Bridges made a fairly complete analysis of facets of expressions of delight and the changes that occur with age. Characteristic behaviors accompanying the expressions of delight include increased motor activity (noted by Darwin), slight flushing of the face, and raised lower eyelids—probably a concomitant of smiling and laughter. According to Bridges, 2- and 3-year-old children manifest delight in smiling, laughing, motor activity, and greeting behaviors. Four-year-olds supplement these behaviors with verbalizations, and motor activity becomes increasingly directed. Diffuse motor responses are increasingly replaced by anticipatory gestures as getting dressed for an outing or fetching books to be read.

Surprise

Darwin's contribution to our understanding of surprise has been theoretical as well as empirical (see Charlesworth, 1969). He saw surprise as playing a significant role in aiding the organism to perceive and react to novel stimuli as quickly and as adaptively as possible (opening the eyes and mouth widely and raising the eyebrows, presumably to enhance perception, and arresting ongoing behavior—freezing—apparently to avoid detection). As noted earlier, such responses appear in infants, but they do not appear frequently and intensely (at least as far as the face is concerned). Most studies of surprise, outside of those with infants, have involved adults (see Desai, 1939); for the most part they verify Darwin's observations and lend considerable credence to his theory.

Work on surprise in children has been relatively sparse until quite recently, when it has been used for diagnostic purposes in the area of cognitive development. Charlesworth (see below) has emphasized the importance of describing the facial response of surprise in children, rather than whether or not surprise merely occurred. Global estimates of whether surprise occurs or not are relatively easy to make (from films or in experimental situations) if the judge knows the stimulus situation and knows exactly when the reaction takes place (see Charlesworth, 1964; Charlesworth & Zahn, 1966). However, when film raters are asked to rate subjects blindly (that is, without knowledge of the stimulus situation), ratings show considerably less agreement (Charlesworth, 1971). Facial expressions of surprise in elementary school children tend to be more distinguishable than those in infants and are very similar to the adult reactions Darwin describes. Charlesworth found that the most sensitive facial area to surprise in the child is the mouth, and of the mouth reactions, the smile is the most frequent. There are relatively few eyebrow and forehead reactions. The incidence of the classic surprise reaction described by Darwin (mouth open, eyes opened wider; raised brows, momentary freezing) interestingly enough did not occur as frequently as expected (no more than 3–7% of the total responses) and did not change much from infancy through the sixth grade. Charlesworth also found that surprise reactions varied greatly in their intensity according to the kind of surprise event and also according to the particular individual.

Anger

Perhaps the most colorful and succintly detailed account of behaviors observed in expressions of anger was advanced by Darwin (1872): "Young children when in a violent rage roll on the ground on their backs or bellies, screaming, kicking, scratching, or biting everything within reach." Darwin observed similar behaviors cross-culturally, as well as in young primates.

Research to date on expressions of anger in children has focused on who expresses anger, what specific behaviors are observed, and how these expressions of anger change with age. McFarland (1938) studied social behavior of sister pairs at home. Half the cases of rivalry noted were material rivalry, and half were social rivalry—with the older sister of the pair responsible for initiating 84% of the total episodes. Several studies have reported a decrease in the frequency of conflicts with age (see Ricketts, 1934; Jersild & Markey, 1935). The latter reported that older nursery school children tended to respond differently than younger children in conflict situations; older children employed more verbalizations and fewer instances of screaming, crying, and calling for help. More striking age differences are reported by Goodenough (1931a) on the basis of parents' records of their children's outbursts of anger. Specific behaviors observed included kicking, stamping, jumping up and down, striking, making the body limp, refusing to move, struggling, and running for help. Facial expressions noted are mentioned briefly. These included: closing the mouth firmly, crying, frowning, making faces, pouting, and sulking. With age, explosive outbursts become less frequent. Children display less purely expressive behavior and manifest increasingly more instrumental control to the point of reacting with symbolic forms of behavior, or laughter "intended to irritate or annoy." Bridges (1931) noted the tendency of more mature nursery school children to settle conflicts by means of compromise instead of angry outbursts.

Another age-related trend in expressions of anger in children is in the precipitator of outbursts of anger. Two- and 4-year-olds most frequently become angry at other children, whereas children between 2½ and 3½ years tend to display more anger towards interference by adults (Bridges, 1931).

The importance of extending observations of children's expressions beyond nursery school settings has been highlighted in a study by Ricketts (1934), which compared expressions of anger in nursery school and home settings. In both situations, angry facial expressions were the most frequent manifestations of anger, followed by crying. Although crying was observed in 69% of angry outbursts occurring in home settings, only 39% of nursery school outbursts involved crying. This difference indicates the pervasive influence of the environment on children's expressions, and emphasizes the dangers of overgeneralizing from studies of children in nursery school settings.

Affection

Darwin mentioned little about expressions of affection specific to children. He considered affection, joy and sympathy as "tender feelings" and emphasized touching as an associated behavior; he mentioned nothing about specific facial expressions.

Research on affection after Darwin has been very limited. Bridges (1931) treated affection as a form of delight children express as they give or receive embraces, thus emphasizing the importance of touching. She also reported that 2-year-old children direct affectionate responses largely towards adults. This could be related to their extensive dependence on adults at this age. In 3- and 4-year-olds, affectionate behavior becomes more peer-directed, frequently in association with a nurturant, maternal attitude displayed toward younger children. McFarland (1938) found that older sisters exhibited almost three times the number of displays of affection shown by younger sisters. With age, dispensing affection appears to become as satisfying as receiving embraces.

A somewhat surprising finding is Berne's (1930) report of a positive relationship between IQ and teacher ratings of *lack* of affection in nursery school children. This could be a reflection of the more intelligent child's greater independence and his greater immersion in activities at preschool, resulting in fewer social contacts.

Fear

Darwin made no specific reference to expressions of fear in children. These behaviors have been described in a fairly detailed account provided by Bridges (1931). She characterized intense expressions of fear by "momentarily checked breathing, tearless screaming, inhibition of movement, opened eyes and often pallor of the face." Milder expressions of fear are described as involving "stiffening of the body, cessation of movement, and opening of the eyes, followed by crying and protesting, exclaiming or calling for help." These behaviors are most frequently observed in children under 3 years. Older children when frightened tend to react with fewer intense emotional behaviors, and make more instrumental responses directed toward avoidance of the situation. To our knowledge, there are no detailed accounts of fear behavior in older children, although several studies of children have made intensive investigations of the situations which arouse fear (see Jersild, Markey, & Jersild, 1933; England, 1946).

Most research on children's fears includes descriptions of frightening objects and events as well as the particular behaviors displayed in expressions of fear. Through records of children's fears kept by parents, teachers, and nurses, and through parent interviews, retrospective statements by adults, statements by children, and experimental observations, Jersild and Holmes (1935) made an exhaustive catalogue of situations eliciting fear and their relative frequencies. For a group of 105 children aged 24 to 71 months, dogs, snakes, and dark rooms proved to be the most frightening experimental manipulations—with fear shown by 50% of the children in response to a large dog, by 44% in response to a snake, and 41% in response to a dark room. Parents' records of these preschoolers indicate an average of approximately one fear every 4½ days, a frequency the authors consider relatively low in contrast to the frequency of expressions of anger in children this age.

There have been early attempts, on the part of behaviorists, to describe how situations come to elicit fear. Watson (1930), in a series of conditioning studies, attempted to demonstrate the pervasive influence of learning on the acquisition of fears. Children, according to Watson, are not "naturally" frightened of snakes and other animals; they learn it through conditioning. Interestingly enough, Watson did not mention whether the expressive reactions to conditioned stimuli were in any way different than the reactions initially elicited by the unconditioned stimuli—loud noise and loss of support. Chances are that Watson's conditioning paradigm is an oversimplification—it is unlikely that the development of fears can be totally traced to pairing neutral stimuli with loud noises and loss of support. In addition, Watson's paradigm cannot totally discount the possible role of maturation in the development of fear, as evidenced by the relatively sudden appearance of fear at certain ages without any prior conditioning with the fear object (see James, 1891; Jones & Jones, 1928; Valentine, 1930).

Jealousy

As noted earlier, Darwin remarked that jealousy has no characteristic expression. Despite statements like "green with envy," Darwin asserted that, if visibly expressed, jealousy takes the form of another emotion—rage. Thus, judgments of these behaviors as indicative of jealousy are dependent on knowledge of the situation or the person. To our knowledge, Darwin did not discuss jealousy in children.

Watson (1925b) recognized the response of jealousy as being very similar or identical to rage—facial discoloration, clenched hands, heavy breathing, and verbal accusations. He felt that the main stimuli eliciting jealousy were the "sight or sound of a loved one being tampered or interfered with." For example, he observed jealousy in children from 2 to 3 years when their parents feigned attack (presumably on each other) or embraced each other. Although these events can be considered adequate for the arousal of expressions of jealousy, it is unlikely that they are necessary. Young children are frequently jealous of a strange child with an interesting new toy, for example. The literature search for studies of the expressions of jealousy in children revealed nothing after Watson's work.

Shyness, Coyness, Embarrassment, and Shame

According to Darwin, blushing is present in expressions of shyness and shame and appears to be a uniquely human activity. It does not occur in other higher primates, nor does it occur in children under 2 to 3 years. Darwin evidently discounted the reddening of passion found in monkeys and infants as true instances of blushing; blushing, he felt, implied self-attention. This means, in the context in which he used the term, that the organism had to be sufficiently developed mentally to realize that he was being observed. According to his observations, very young children or infants demonstrate no self-attention: "It is one of their chief charms that they think nothing about what others think of them. At this early age they will stare at a stranger with a fixed gaze and unblinking eyes, as on an inanimate object ... " Not until 2 to 3 years do young children show the approach-avoidance characteristic of shyness, coyness, and embarrassment. The child wishes to avoid the eyes of the stranger or person causing the embarrassment, yet, at the same time, attempts to look at this person. This, Darwin observed, produces restless eye movements and attempts at concealment. Behaviors accompanying blushing include hiding or lowering the face, and rapid blinking or averting the eyes.

Observations of coy and shy behaviors in young children have been made by Marvin, Farris, and Bates (1971). Like Darwin, these authors also conclude that no approach–avoidance behaviors referred to as "self-attention" appeared in children younger than 2 years. In 3- and 4-year-olds, coy behaviors observed included smiling, lowering and tilting the head submissively, lowering the eyes and peering through the eyelashes, and tongue protrusions (which Darwin considered rudimentary forms of rejection). Additional awkward movements which Darwin claimed were the result of self-attention were observed in the 3-year-olds and particularly in the 4-year-olds. These behaviors included touching the body and hair, squirming, and adjusting clothing. Responsiveness of the 3- and 4-year-olds to a mirror within the experimental situation provided further evidence for increased self-attention in older children.

Sympathy

To our knowledge, Darwin did not discuss sympathy in much detail; when he did, he viewed it as a complex of experiences involving a person's feelings about another's welfare. Among other things, he noted that persons react with sympathy to individuals undergoing great moments of happiness or good fortune as well as suffering. He also pointed out that young children can feel immediate sympathy toward themselves if pitied: "Everyone must have noticed how readily children burst out crying if we pity them for some small hurt."

As far as we could ascertain, no reference was made by Darwin to how developmentally advanced the child would have to be to express sympathy in various situations. It can be recalled that Darwin observed the beginnings of sympathy in his 5-month-old son when his nurse pretended to cry. It is difficult to imagine the child showing similar feelings at the same age, or even 1 or 2 years later, when the nurse experienced great happiness. As noted earlier, the maturational status of children's cognitive skills are clearly linked with their ability to express sympathy.

In his discussion, Darwin made no lengthy description of facial expressions in sympathy other than the fact that tears were involved. This he felt was true for instances in which the person being sympathized with was experiencing great happiness or great misfortune. Presumably a sad face and nurturant behavior are also generally considered as sufficient indicators of sympathy if no tears are shed. However, such behaviors, one would think, would characterize sympathy only with instances of misfortune rather than with instances of good fortune.

The post-Darwinian research literature is not clear about what sympathetic behavior looks like in children or when it first appears. It is general knowledge that playing with dolls is frequently accompanied by signs of affection and sympathy; hence such behavior must certainly appear no later than the second year. Murphy and Murphy (1931) and Murphy et al. (1937) report clear instances of sympathy in nursery school children and high reliabilities (between 94 and 99%) in ratings in free situations. They make no mention, however, of the behavioral and facial details that distinguish sympathy from other emotions. The same is true for most studies dealing with sympathy. Apparently the behavioral criteria for sympathy (sad face, crying, and

nurturant acts) were considered so obvious most researchers felt they were
not worth mentioning.

REMARKS ON METHODOLOGY AND
SUBSTANTIVE GAPS IN STUDYING
CHILDREN'S EXPRESSIONS

As noted in the introductory remarks to this section, there are only a
few parallels between research on the expressions of emotions in infants
and research in children. Not only is there a partial change in emphasis
upon *what* is studied during the two age periods, but also a change in
how facial expressions are studied. There is no doubt that both kinds of
changes reflect changes in the characteristics of the subjects themselves.
As the child becomes more cognitively mature, there is a corresponding
increase in the number of new and different ways one can elicit and assess
his expressive behavior. Such cognitive maturity also poses certain problems
for measurement, however.

One major specific change in the child deserves special attention because
it has a direct methodological influence on many different aspects of research
on facial expressions. This change is the sharp increase in the child's mobility
once he can walk and is given the opportunity to move about in a relatively
wide, unrestricted space. Under such circumstances, it becomes increasingly
difficult for an observer to focus for any length of time on the child's face
in order to obtain reliable measures of its activity. Not only is the distance
between the observer and subject greatly increased when the child begins
to walk, but also there is an increased probability that the child's face
will be obscured from view. Even the most highly trained observer and
photographer cannot avoid frustrations under such circumstances. The infant,
in contrast, presents a much more manageable subject for the observer.
The relatively slow pace of his movements and the more or less two-
dimensional space imposed on him by his supine or sedentary position
make it much easier for an observer to catch the full play of his facial
expressions. It is not surprising, then, that as the child grows more active,
researchers change their tactics. Descriptions of the nuances of expressive
activity characterizing the child's face give way to simple frequency counts
of more grossly described facial expressions such as smiling or crying, and
the various situations in which they occur.

Of course, with age also comes the possibility of increased control over
the child's behavior. Because of his newly acquired language skills, it is
possible to instruct the child to sit or stand in a two-dimensional space,

to perform certain tasks which will increase the probability that a wider variety of facial expressions will occur, and to instruct him to act or imitate the expressions of others. All these possibilities are especially enjoyed by researchers who have experienced the difficulties of working with infants. However, those interested in catching facial expressions at their purest—as Darwin was—like to point out that the older the child, the more sensitive he is to being observed. And with an increase in such sensitivity, he becomes more capable of suppressing or simulating his expressive behavior. In research, as in life, everything has its advantages and disadvantages.

As the studies reported in this section indicate, researchers appear to have done the best they could to meet the particular problems posed by children. However, despite these efforts, the literature still has many substantive gaps. In our estimation, one of the most salient gaps is the developmental one. Nowhere is there any indication of a systematic longitudinal or cross-sectional approach to the problems of the origins and ontogenesis of facial expressions. Unlike students of children's bones and endocrine glands, students of expressive behavior cannot boast of a longitudinal tracing of facial expressions from infancy through childhood to adolescence. The natural history of the smile—perhaps man's most important single facial expression—from birth to adulthood has still to be written. The changes in its personal and social significance as the child makes his way to maturity still elude us. And the same can be said for all the other facial expressions that make the child such an interesting object of study.

Two other gaps in the literature are worth mentioning. One deals with the fact that a great bulk of the subjects studied were nursery school children in a nursery school setting. While such a setting may offer rich opportunities for expressive behavior to occur, they constitute only a small part of the average child's life experiences. To this extent our understanding of the child's full potential for expressive behavior is limited.

The other gap in the literature is less methodological. It reflects a lack of substantive concern for an increase in the functional role expressive behavior assumes after infancy. The guileless infant presents an innocent picture compared to the young child who has learned how to control his facial expressions for his own advantage. The increase with age in the use of the face as a means of communication must certainly bring about changes in facial expressions worth recording. No research to our knowledge has examined what surely must be interesting morphological differences between spontaneous expressions and those the child has just learned to exhibit to disguise his real motives. The intricacies of a child's use of these behaviors has also been neglected.

These, then, are some of the gaps in the literature. In light of them, we are just at the beginning of our understanding of what happens to facial expressions over the course of development.

THE CHILD'S RECOGNITION
OF EXPRESSIONS

The ability of the child to recognize emotions has received more attention in the research literature than the child's expression of emotions. As was noted earlier, the reverse is true for infants. It is difficult to determine why this is so. One possibility is that the shift of research emphasis from expression of emotions in infancy to recognition of emotions during subsequent years actually reflects a true developmental trend rather than some historical trend in research. One could argue, for example, that by 2 years of age, most expressive behaviors have been established in at least rudimentary form; however, the infant's recognition of emotions in others remains very primitive during this period. Many social experiences seem to be necessary before he will develop the ability to recognize and interpret the expressive behavior of others. In addition to these experiences, appropriate cognitive skills are also necessary. According to Piaget, these skills are not acquired rapidly, but develop as a result of an extended period of interaction with the environment.

This argument raises the interesting point, which Darwin himself seriously pondered—the different roles nature and nurture may play in the development of expressive behavior as contrasted with the development of the ability to recognize the expressions of others. As Honkavaara (1961) points out in her summary of this issue, the American view is that recognition "is learned, despite the fact that most expressions as overt manifestations of emotions are generally accepted to be innate reaction patterns." In contrast, the European view is much more nativistic about the recognition of expressions. This view is based primarily on the research concerning infants' recognition of expressions (already discussed). It should be pointed out that the total reliance upon research on early infant recognition to support the European viewpoint could be misleading. The absence of behavioral indices in the first few months does not mean that the infant is incapable of recognizing emotions. He may be able to recognize emotions, but lacks the behaviors which observers accept as evidence of his ability to make these differentiations.

It is equally possible to argue that the development of expression and recognition of emotions is parallel—the observed lag in ability to recognize expression could be merely an artifact of the lack of adequate methodology to measure infant recognition. Observing facial expressions of infants poses fewer problems. The problem of obtaining subjects for experimental investigations of recognition may also play a role in influencing the types of results that have been obtained. It is no coincidence that, with the exception of a few studies, there are no data from American research concerning the ability to recognize emotions until 3 years—the age when many children enter preschool programs and become part of a captive subject pool. Children and infants under 3 years have (historically at least) been much more difficult to obtain. However, even if children under 3 could have been obtained in reasonable numbers, the young child's attention span and limited or nonexistent verbal capacities make it difficult to impose conventional tests of emotion recognition upon him. Not until we can develop appropriate nonverbal techniques (for example, preference measures and response conditioning) will he become a good subject for a recognition study.

Whatever the case may be, it is remarkable that after approximately 50 years of research on older children's recognition of emotion and a recent increase in methods of measuring infant abilities, so few methods appropriate for assessing the sensitivity of younger children to the emotions of others have been developed. It seems particularly ironic that nonverbal methods of judging pictures of facial expressions, such as the sorting technique devised by Hulin and Katz (1935), have been employed almost exclusively with adults. If similar methods were adapted to use with young children and infants, it is possible that we would discover that the development of recognition and expression of emotions is more parallel than is currently believed.

Research that has been conducted on children's recognition of facial expressions can be considered under three general rubrics: developmental studies of judgments of facial expressions and vocal expression, investigations of the correlates of this performance, and studies dealing with the salience of expressive cues for young children.

Darwin (1872) was one of the first to employ photos to assess the ability of adults to recognize facial expressions. Gates (1923) appears to be the first to extend this technique to a developmental study. Gates assessed the ability of 458 children (age 3 to 14 years) and 36 adults to identify the facial expressions displayed on six Ruckmick photographs. For example, the children were asked "What is this person doing?" if further prompting was required, the child was asked to describe what the person was thinking about or how she felt. Although the scoring procedures employed by Gates were fairly liberal, especially for the expressions of laughter and pain, the child was required not only to recognize the expressions, but also to communicate this expression adequately to the experimenter.

Gates' results indicated that adults could recognize the six facial expressions with 84% to 100% accuracy. Results with the children revealed a developmental trend, as expected. Fifty percent or more of the children below 3 years of age could recognize laughter, but not until 5 to 6 years of age were 50% or more of the children able to recognize pain. Using the same criterion, recognizing anger appeared next at 7 years; fear followed at 9 to 10 years, and surprise 1 year later. Recognizing scorn was the most difficult; it could be identified by fewer than 50% of children at 14 years of age. In general, the results show an overall increase with age in the ability to recognize emotions. The strength of these findings, however, is open to question as Jenness (1932) has pointed out; since only one photograph was used for each emotion, it is possible that age changes may be partly due to the quality of the pictures (some may have had sharper, more clear-cut expressions than others). Such a criticism is justified. Intuitively, however, Gates' developmental progression makes sense. Laughter and pain seem easier to recognize than surprise and scorn.

Dashiell (1927) later modified Gates' technique so that performance would not be influenced so pervasively by the child's verbal skills. Dashiell's method required the child to select an appropriate picture for each story presented by the experimenter. Thus, although this method reduced the role of verbal production, the child's performance was dependent on his verbal comprehension, and his ability to translate cues from the stories into facial expressions. Unfortunately the ages of the children included in this study, the story content, the data and other relevant details of this "classic" study are unpublished. In the résumé of a convention presentation, however, Dashiell concluded that with this method, young children demonstrated improved performance in the recognition of subtle emotions.

Using Dashiell's technique, Ekman and Friesen (1971) were able to test the recognition ability of 130 children from an isolated group of peoples (Fore) living in the highlands of New Guinea. Six emotions (happiness, anger, sadness, surprise, fear, and two versions of disgust) were described in stories to each child whose task was to pick one of two photographs of faces—one photo depicted the emotion related to the story and the other photo, unrelated emotion. In all 17 combinations of emotions, the percentages of children picking the correct photograph were significantly above chance (percentages ranged from 76 to 100% with a mean of about 90%). To test for age of developmental differences, Ekman and Friesen compared the performance of 6- to 7-year-olds with that of 14- to 15-year-olds and found no difference. This finding demonstrates the relatively early appearance of the ability to recognize that particular facial behaviors are associated with particular emotions. That the children were also virtually isolated from the outside world, especially from the Caucasian world where the photographs were made, and could still associate facial expressions with emotions strongly supports the view that such an association is universal and may therefore be innate, as Darwin hypothesized. This possibility will be brought up later in this chapter when discussing the absence and presence of opportunity to imitate facial expressions of others.

Honkavaara (1961) conducted a series of studies on the development of the ability to recognize facial expressions. Positing that perception of objects and colors precedes recognition of facial expressions, Honkavaara studied subjects from 5 to 6 years to adulthood cross-sectionally. She discovered that perception of friendly-hostile and happy-miserable was more difficult in general than the perception of colors; with age, this difference decreased, as perception of friendly–hostile became more accurate.

Honkavaara also employed a three-choice discrimination task to assess developmental trends in recognition of expressions. On each of three boxes was a painting of a girl with a happy, sad, or neutral expression. The experimenter stated that candy was placed under the happy or sad face, and the task of the subjects was to retrieve the candy. Performance increased with age, but decreased again in 50- to 80-year-old adults with limited education. Three- and 4-year-olds, and 5- to 6-year-olds performed with approximately 40 and 65% accuracy respectively—somewhat lower than what one would expect from Gates' results, especially since Honkavaara's technique was intended to optimize the relevance of the task for young children. However, the stimuli were schematized in her study, thus making any direct comparisons with Gates' results difficult.

Another study by Honkavaara indicated that children's judgments of facial expressions are easily influenced by external variables like the color of the model's accessories, for example. More than 50% of 3- to 4-year-old children mistakenly identified a sad girl in a red dress as happy. Honkavaara employed data from another study to challenge the assumption that happy expressions are recognized earlier than unhappy expressions. Although her data indicate a definite response bias of young children to give "happy" answers more frequently, a problem with her study could be the nature of the stimuli employed. The two pairs of stimuli illustrated in her monograph depict the moods of infants; and as Darwin (1872), Crile (1915), and Peiper (1963) have noted, it is sometimes very difficult to differentiate the onset patterns of laughter and crying in infants or young children.

A fourth study of Honkavaara's demonstrated that children develop the ability to perceive the action of laughing and crying first, followed by the ability to perceive the expressions of sadness and happiness. Children of 3 to 6 years will state that the person in the picture is laughing; yet when questioned about the person's mood, the child will frequently answer that the same person is miserable. The discrepancy between accuracy of labelling *actions* and *expressions* decreases with age. In general, this tendency to understand actions earlier is consistent with children's early acquisition of verbs and their tendency to define objects in terms of their functions. The thought of the young child appears to be very action-oriented. In the sphere of expressions, he first perceives the action (laughing or crying); not until later does he develop the ability to attach the appropriate interpretation, thus giving emotional significance to these behaviors.

Staffieri and Bassett (1970) compared 10- and 11-year-olds on their ability to recognize facial expressions of adults and children of both sexes. This is a novel study, since the stimuli employed by Gates (1923) were pictures of adults, yet it is sometimes assumed that children are more accurate judges of the expressions of other children. Staffieri and Bassett reported significant age differences in recognition of the expressions of male or female children, but no corresponding age differences in the judgment of expressions of adults. The authors did not present any specific error data, so it is not possible to draw any conclusions regarding the relative identifiability of expressions of adults and children from these age differences. Sex differences were also reported. Children were more accurate judges of the expressions of adults of the *opposite* sex.

In a recent study of recognition of facial expressions, Odom and Lemond (1972) examined the ability of 32 kindergarten and 32 fifth-grade children to recognize eight facial expressions and produce them in a posed setting before a camera. While the older children made more correct recognitions of the 32 standard photographs of human faces (based on Izard, 1971) than the younger children and also tended to produce expressions more correctly, both groups showed a significant lag in their ability to produce expressions correctly as compared to their ability to recognize them.

In other words, both groups did less well at posing expressions than they did at recognizing them. This finding would at first seem to contradict our earlier suggestion that spontaneous expression precedes recognition. Earlier in this chapter, it was pointed out that the infant has a limited ability to recognize the expressions of others, yet at the same time is capable of producing a wide variety of expressions himself. What must be kept in mind, though, in interpreting the gap between recognition and production reported by Odom and Lemond is that their method defined ''adequacy of production'' in terms of adult raters' ability to recognize and evaluate the child's posed expressions. Acquiring such an ability was accomplished by pretraining on Izard's (1971) photographs, a set of idealized facial expressions—i.e., easily distinguishable expressions that most probably do not occur frequently as such in normal life situations. Comparing the children's productions, the majority of which were most probably not as idealized as Izard's, with Izard's less ambiguous photographs not surprisingly would lead raters to judge such productions as not very adequate. While the question of absolute adequacy is, of course, an empirical question, the adequacy of the child's production was relative in the sense that it was compared with the adequacy of his recognition. Since the childrens' recognition of expressions were based on Izard's photographs, it is not surprising that their recognitions were superior to their productions. It is much easier to recognize an ideal form than to produce one. In order to have a fair comparison of recognition and production abilities, it is essential that in a recognition task a more representative set of photographs be used (i.e., not idealized ones). Since the child's productions are less idealized (i.e., more representative of a wide range of variations of an ideal form), they are also more ambiguous and hence will be more frequently misjudged. Hence if a wide range of variations of an emotional expression (i.e., one more representative of the child's productions) was used in the recognition task, it is highly probable that the child's ability to recognize would not be significantly greater than his ability to produce.

In a more recent study of developmental changes in expression recognition (using techniques similar to those of Dashiell), Izard (1971) confirmed early findings indicating that, across the age of 2 to 9 years, older children recognize expressions significantly better than younger children. Studying French and American children, Izard found no significant cultural differences in the developmental trends of the ability to recognize emotions. He did find, though, that French children did better than American children in recognizing contempt and disgust.

Izard also extended his research to developmental changes in the young child's ability to label expressions (using the traditional methods employed in most of the studies already discussed) and found changes between 2 to 5 years of age. He found no significant age changes after 5 years. His overall findings on developmental trends indicate that recognition skills are acquired earlier than labeling abilities, a find which seems plausible because of the greater dependency of labeling upon the mastery of skills involving the production of language, which develop later than recognition. Izard did note that the ability to recognize and label emotions is significantly and positively correlated with intellectual development in middle-class preschool children.

With the exception of the above studies, the mass of observations conducted during the 40 or more years after the pioneering efforts of Gates have not added extensively to Gates' efforts in providing us with knowledge of developmental trends in the recognition of facial expressions.

Darwin considered vocalizations accompanying facial expressions important communicators of affect; yet this facet of the recognition of emotions has received relatively little attention. Gates (1927) compared children's recognition of nine vocal expressions with recognition of corresponding facial expressions. These data are also unpublished; thus a discussion of this research is restricted to the conclusions presented in the abstract of this study. Gates concluded that performance on the recognition of vocal expressions improved with age, and that some vocal expressions were easier to judge than others. These findings parallel previous conclusions on the recognition of facial expressions, mentioned in the foregoing discussion. Another finding was that facial expressions were more readily interpreted than vocal expressions. Similar results have been reported for college students (Dusenbury & Knower, 1939). However, the generality of this superiority of facial expressions has yet to be ascertained. Dusenbury and Knower reported that the extent of the superiority of facial over vocal expressions depended on the particular emotion expressed as well as on the performer.

A limited number of studies have investigated correlates of the child's ability to interpret vocal and facial expressions of emotion. Considerable individual differences in these skills have been observed; yet our knowledge of the characteristics of the sensitive individual is extremely limited. Witkin, Dyk, Fattuson, Goodenough, and Karp (1962) suggest that field-dependent individuals are more socially oriented than field-independent individuals, and, as a result, would possess heightened sensitivity to facial expressions and other clues indicative of moods and attitudes. No related research has been conducted with children; however, Messick and Damarin (1964) found that field dependence was significantly related to college students' memory for faces. Staffieri and Bassett (1970) did not find evidence to support the hypothesis that later-born children would be more accurate judges of facial expression than first-born children because of their greater exposure to peers, whose moods are more labile than those of adults. Gates (1927) briefly stated that the "more intelligent" children in grades 3 to 8 were superior to the "less intelligent" on judgment of vocal and facial expressions; as mentioned previously, no data were cited, however. Gates (1925) also reported that judgment of facial expressions by kindergarten children correlated ".20 with chronological age or mental age and with estimated physical or mental maturity, and about .46 to .60 with estimated social maturity." Further details were not presented. Gates (1923) reported no consistent sex differences, although boys were more accurate judges of fear expressions. Gates (1923) also reported no social class differences in the ability to interpret facial expressions in 3 to 14-year-olds. In a very different experimental task, Kashinsky and Weiner (1969) reported that lower-class children are more sensitive than middle-class children to the tone of voice in which experimental instructions are delivered.

Now that it has been established that children *can* judge emotional expressions, a question that deserves consideration is whether children *do* attend to these nonverbal cues in natural situations. Given an array of stimuli as complex as those that occur in social interaction, will facial expressions and other nonverbal cues be very salient to the young child? To date, this question has been examined infrequently, and then only indirectly, by a variety of tasks fairly remote from real-life interactions.

It appears that with age, there is a general progression from external variables (clothing, accessories, actions) to increased use of cues from facial expression. Children become increasingly attuned to the thoughts and feelings of people in TAT-like cards, and attend less to the objective action and external detail (Amen, 1941; Dymond, Hughes, & Raabe, 1952; Gilbert, 1969). It could be argued that these developmental trends are merely a function of increased ability to express more abstract thoughts; however, studies employing nonverbal sorting tasks have also reported similar age transitions from pairing stimuli on the basis of accessories, sex, and age, to pairing stimuli on the basis of emotional expressions (Levy-Schoen, 1961; Gilbert, 1969; Savitsky & Izard, 1970).

GENERAL REMARKS ON RECOGNITION
OF EXPRESSION

It is interesting that almost 50 years after Gates's (1923) initial study of the recognition of emotions by children, our knowledge in this area has not progressed much further than Gates's statement that with increasing age, children become increasingly skilled at identification of the emotions. There have been a few methodological innovations—tests of vocal expression (Gates, 1927), and comparisons of children's judgments of expressions of adults and children (Staffieri & Bassett, 1970); however, for the most part, this area of investigation tends to lack the richness of methodological variations apparent in parallel studies of recognition of expressions by adults. In studies of adult recognition, the range of stimuli includes moving pictures of emotions (Dusenbury & Knower, 1938), as well as emotions depicted by live actors (Thompson & Meltzer, 1964). There have been attempts to take a less psychometric approach and examine the *types* of errors people make instead of simply calculating percentages of correct responses (Woodworth, 1938); investigators have also questioned subjects to determine the basis of judgments of emotions. Other problems that have been examined in research with adults' recognition of emotion include the relative role of context and facial expression in judgments (Goodenough & Tinker, 1931), and the relative contributions of the eye region and the mouth region (Ruckmick, 1921; Buzby, 1924; Dunlap, 1927; Coleman, 1949).

Perhaps a more glaring flaw than the methodological specificity of this area of research with children is the possible inadequacy or inappropriate use of the methods that have been employed. Hebb (1946); for example, is perhaps the most outspoken critic of our lack or ecological validity in research on recognition of facial expressions: ''The persistent idea that the recognition of emotions can be fully tested by allowing the judge to see the subject's behavior for a moment or so, even by means of a picture showing the subject as he was at a single instant, has dominated every experimental investigation of the problem." Ordinarily when a child assesses an individual's emotions, he has a wealth of cues in addition to a fixed facial expression. He sees the patterning of the facial expression from its onset to its peak with concomitant grosser body movements, and sometimes with verbal statements. These cues are supplemented by his knowledge of the context of the emotional response, and sometimes, by knowledge of the individual's past behavior and general dispositional traits.

Interestingly enough, Darwin has been erroneously held responsible for this methodological cul de sac. Bruner and Taguiri (1954); for example; state: "Historically speaking, we may have been done a disservice by the pioneering efforts of those who, like Darwin, took the human face in a state of arrested animation as an adequate stimulus situation for studying how well we recognize human emotion." It must be emphasized here as a corrective that Darwin himself employed a variety of approaches to the study of expressions; the studies of recognition of photographs were merely one aspect of his research. These findings were supplemented by observations of infants, the insane, people in different cultures, and comparative studies. Numerous investigators after Darwin, however, have overemphasized the importance of this technique by rigidly applying it and then concluding that recognition of facial expressions is not innate because of the low accuracy of judgments and individual differences in performance. For example, the studies of Gates (1923, 1925) and Dashiell (1927) have frequently been cited as evidence that recognition of facial expressions must be learned. In view of the methods they employed and the deficiencies of these methods, such conclusions are hardly warranted. It is corrct to state on the basis of their findings that the data on children's recognition do not permit the conclusion that recognition is innate; but the corollary is also correct—we can not conclude that recognition is *not* innate. One reason we cannot come to such a conclusion is that still photographs may be hardly adequate stimuli for the young child, who has not yet developed the capacity to extract the necessary information out his everyday experiences with faces to make a judgment on that basis. If Gates and Dashiell had used motion pictures of facial expressions in action, they may not have obtained the developmental trends they observed; the younger children may well have been able to recognize all the facial expressions if they saw them in action.

The issue of the validity of using still photographs versus motion pictures is hardly resolved, however. It can be recalled that Ekman and Friesen (1971) used photographs in an effective manner in the sense that the preliterate children they tested did not find the photographs artificial or impoverished. If they had, they could have hardly done as well as they did in matching the photographs to the appropriate emotion-arousing situations. Clearly the young children they tested (the 6- to 7-year-olds) were developmentally mature enough to find the photographs meaningful. Whether 2- to 3-year olds would have done so is another question. That studies have not been made comparing the usefulness of motion picture versus photographic representations of facial expressions in detecting the earliest age at which the young child can recognize different expressions is a curious lacuna in the body of infant research.

ABSENCE AND PRESENCE OF OPPORTUNITIES
TO LEARN FACIAL EXPRESSIONS

The foregoing studies give only circumstantial evidence for the hypothesis that facial expressions—and possibly their recognition—are innate. The earliness with which most of the common, primary expressions appear is good, but not convincing, evidence that the capacity to produce such expressions is not learned. One could always argue that rapid learning takes place, although this argument has its weaknesses as well. As already noted, Darwin was convinced that most, if not all, of the basic expressions were innate, but he also knew that under normal conditions the child has ample opportunity to learn facial expressions from others. Although he probably did not put much weight on the possibility that the latter was true, he still had to make a special effort to obtain information on individuals who had little or no opportunity to learn facial expressions. Only by doing this could he convince those who did not believe as strongly as he did that the innate hypothesis was the correct one. He turned to infants, young children, the blind . . . in short to anyone who may have had no opportunity or limited opportunity to observe facial expressions in others. He also turned to cultures that were sufficiently isolated from one another in the sense that they did not provide each other with opportunities to learn common expressions.

It should be noted here that considering Darwin's convictions, it is not surprising that he did not spend much time examining the possibility that subtle learning processes may be responsible for the appearance of facial expressions in the child. However, a complete analysis of the origins of facial expressions must include the possibility that such processes could be operating. In the two sections that follow we will discuss studies that shed light on both hypotheses—studies that involve both the absence and the presence of opportunities to learn facial expressions.

Absence of Opportunity

Because of obvious ethical considerations, most psychologists are reluctant to create deprivation situations to test the absence-of-opportunity hypothesis. However, such deprivations do exist in conditions outside the laboratory. The environments of feral children, institutionalized children, and congeni-

tally blind children are sufficiently devoid (in varying degrees) of opportunities to learn facial expressions from others; the expressive behavior of
such children therefore afford insight into what may be the necessary factors
in the development of facial expressions.

Feral Children

Reports of feral children are obviously difficult to verify and hence must
be taken as tentative. Usually abandoned by parents during infancy or early
childhood, the feral child reputedly is left to fend for himself with or without
the help of other animals. Thus, any opportunities to learn from human
beings are usually restricted to early infancy. When initially discovered,
the feral child's behavior typically bears little resemblance to the behavior
of a socialized child of the same age, a fact which most probably accounts
for the rigorous training program to which he is usually submitted. Most
of this training focuses on instrumental behaviors—including how to talk,
walk upright, and put on and tie shoes; little or none, interestingly enough,
is focused on expressive behavior.

In a review of the characteristics of 31 feral children observed by different
people as early as 1657, Zingg (1940) concluded that such children do
not initially cry or laugh. Such a finding supports the position that they
do not have to cry or laugh because there is no one to respond to such
behavior (other animals are tuned in to other kinds of signals) hence it
is never rewarded. This finding does not support Darwin's notion that laughing or crying reduces tension (and hence could be conceivably rewarding).
Outbursts of extreme anger and impatience, however, have been observed
in such children, and this finding can be seen as supporting the notion
that such behavior may be maintained because it releases energy stored
up by frustrating circumstances. Singh and Zingg (1945), for example,
reported than an 8-year-old girl, purported to have been raised by wolves
since infancy, was observed to feign death or react with temper tantrums
when frightened. Such behavior could have been adaptive in situations
where she was preyed on by other animals; feigning death may have helped
conceal her from animals, while throwing tantrums could have frightened
animals that detected her. The girl would also extend her tongue and pant
during warm weather or after expenditures of great effort; presumably this
could have been learned from the wolves.

A more reliable case study of a feral child than most (in the sense that
it was systematically documented by a careful observer) has been presented
in the diary of Itard (1932), a French physician. Itard tried to socialize the
Wild Boy of Aveyron, an 11- or 12-year-old feral child discovered in the
late eighteenth century in the forests of southern France. In his chronicle,
Itard reported:

"In short, he [the Wild Boy] was destitute of all means of communication and attached neither expression or intention to his gestures or to the movements of his body. He passed rapidly and without apparent motive from apathetic melancholy to the most immoderate peals of laughter." His lack of communication through expression or gestures suggests, as with the girl noted earlier, that communication was of no value because there was no one with whom to communicate. That he could laugh violently and appear melancholy suggests that such behavior, for him at least, may have served some expressive function. This is in contrast to the conclusions we could draw from Zingg's report.

In light of such findings and others of roughly a similar nature, it appears that feral children do possess at least a limited range of expressive behaviors that are usually interpreted as anger, shyness, joy, depression, and impatience. Whether the range is much broader is not known because of the limited number of situations in which their behaviors were observed and the obvious deficiencies of the records.

Institutionalized Children

Institutionalized children and children reared at home under conditions of isolation provide additional data on the effects of minimal social contact and reward on expressive behaviors. Davis (1940, 1947) discovered an illegitimate child, Anna, whose mother had confined her to a single room with minimum care and social contact for almost the first 6 years of her life. According to Davis (1940), the first time he saw Anna several days after her removal to a county home, she "neither smiled nor cried in our presence . . . she did frown or scowl occasionally in response to no observable stimulus. Otherwise she remained expressionless." A day later, Anna "did not smile except when coaxed and did not cry." Later, she smiled more frequently; and after approximately 6 weeks, she laughed when tickled. From Davis' records, it is not possible to determine whether this occasion marked the first time Anna was tickled, or the first time she laughed when tickled. As with cases of feral children, the possible contributions of extreme isolation and congenital mental defects are difficult to untangle in Davis' study. Because Anna's mother was severely retarded (IQ of 50) and her father possibly syphilitic, Davis admits that congenital deficiency cannot be totally discounted.

A clearer statement on the effects of minimum social contact is provided by Dennis (1938). Beginning at 1 month of age, a pair of identical twins was reared for 7 months with adequate care for their physical needs, but severely restricted social contacts. The infants' caretakers did not smile at the twins, play with them, or talk to them; the twins spent entire days in their individual cribs, separated by an opaque screen. Although one twin experienced intracranial birth injury, Dennis found that, in comparison to data from 40 baby biographies and Shirley's developmental scales, the twins showed no retardation in the development of numerous behaviors including the appearance of tears, smiling at persons, laughing, crying at sounds and strangers, and the cessation of crying upon presentation of music. Thus, it appears from this study at least, that imitation and reward are not essential for the normal development of expressive behaviors in the first 8 months of life.

Questions, however, have been raised concerning the actual degree of social deprivation experienced by the twins in this study. The conditions under which Dennis reared the twins were later relabeled "controlled environmental conditions" by Dennis and Dennis (1951), and "minimum adequate social stimulation" by Stone (1954). However, since the conditions preclude any visual contact with the facial expressions of the caretakers as well as reward for any expressions other than crying (which was responded to neutrally by physical caretaking), these relabelings do not diminish the importance of Dennis' findings for our discussion.

The development of the smile in institutionalized infants has been the focus of relatively numerous investigations. Gewirtz (1965) and Ambrose (1961) have examined the onset and frequency of smiling to an unresponsive human face in institutionalized and noninstitutionalized infants. Gewirtz found that infants raised in a kibbutz began to smile at a human face earlier than institutionalized children, but the frequency of their smiling was somewhat depressed. Gewirtz also noted that institutionalized children smiled less frequently at an unresponsive face, and reached their peak smiling frequency approximately 4 weeks later than children reared in families or in a kibbutz. Ambrose (1961) corroborated Gewirtz's findings by noting the earlier onset and peak frequency of smiling in home-reared infants.

Gewirtz (1965) reported further differences in the development of the smile in institutionalized infants. Once the smiling response reached its peak frequency in institutionalized infants, there was a consistent decline in mean frequency. A similar decline was *not* noted in infants reared at home or in a kibbutz. Gewirtz assumes this decline represented a general decreased responsiveness to caretakers in the institution. In contrast, Ambrose reported similar declines in frequency of smiling following peak levels in *both* home-reared and institutionalized infants. He maintained, however, that this decline was specific to the experimental situation. The infants' nurses and mothers reported that their infants were smiling with equal, if not greater, frequency than in previous weeks.

Thus although there is no clear agreement on the postpeak shapes of the smiling curves, there is evidence that institutionalized infants show later onset and peak frequencies of smiling to an unresponsive human face.

Despite fewer opportunities to observe facial expressions of others, institutionalized infants are still capable of smiling. The observed differences in the rate of the development of smiling in this situation could be a reflection of decreased exposure to expressive faces, a decrease in emotion itself which usually characterizes such children, or decreased probability of a social reward from others. Ambrose's research especially highlights the sensitivity of the smile to social rewards, a finding that converges with Davis' more naturalistic observations.

Blind Children

Congenitally blind children (without form vision) have no visual opportunity to imitate expressive behaviors in others. Thus any strengthening of their expressive behavior is limited to auditory and tactile-kinesthetic channels, a highly ineffective way to learn expressive behaviors compared to visual imitation. For this reason, such children are viewed as good sources of information that may shed light on the extent to which such expressions are innate or acquired through imitation.

Freedman's (1964, 1965) observations of four congenitally blind infants and a review of the literature on the development of the blind led him to conclude that smiling is an innate response. According to Freedman (1965), congenitally blind infants "smile at the usual time, but their early social smiles are fleeting, much like normal eyes-closed smiling in the first month." By 6 months, the fleeting social smiles of blind children are replaced by normal social smiling of a longer duration. An interesting phenomenon Freedman noted in one blind female was the accompaniment of her social smiling by a gaze in the direction of the person interacting with her, thus making her expression especially difficult to distinguish from that of a sighted child.

Thompson (1941) reported more extensively on the development of facial expression in blind children in a study of a heterogeneous group of 26 blind children, ranging in age from 7 weeks to 13 years 6 months. Eleven were congenitally blind; eight were blinded by 6 months; and seven were blinded before 3 years. Four children were deaf and blind. As a group, their intelligence was equally heterogeneous—ranging from the imbecile level to above average. Sighted control subjects were equally as varied. The children were filmed chiefly in their natural activities; a few situations were specifically designed to elicit emotional responses.

The data from this study strengthened Darwin's (1872) hypothesis that crying, smiling, and laughing were innate. Although there were few instances of each expression observed, the amounts of involvement of eighth facial features (e.g., elevation of eyebrows, changes in the nasolabial fold) were remarkably similar for both groups. Thompson's other findings suggest that the range of inherited expressions may be more extensive than those just mentioned. She found that displays of anger, annoyance, and sulkiness in the blind closely resembled those of sighted children and, furthermore, appeared in appropriate situations. However, as noted earlier, evaluating such global responses, may be criticized on the basis of underestimating the role the knowledge of the situation plays in making judgments and overestimating the role of the facial expression themselves.

Thompson (1941) also reported that there were decreases with age in facial activity in smiling and laughter in the congenitally blind. Since a comparable decrease was not observed in sighted children and a less marked decrease was noted in children who once had vision, Thompson, interestingly enough, attributed this change to maturation. In sighted children, these maturational phenomena are purported to be masked by the effects of social mimicry. An equally plausible interpretation, however, is that the decrease in facial activity in the blind relative to the sighted could be attributable to the absence of reinforcement via the facial expressions of others.

In addition to preventing a decline in facial activity with age, Thompson claimed that social mimicry served to stylize facial expressions. Evidence for this claim was the fact that sighted children showed less variability in facial expression than blind children, visual experience presumably having the effect of shaping a person's expressions to conform to more standardized expressions of others.

In view of the comparability of Thompson's sighted and blind groups on total facial activity and the relatively small number of instances of each expression, it is unlikely that the differential age trends in the blind and sighted were as significant as she believed. Also, from the data given, it is difficult to make conclusions concerning the variability of expressions in the blind and sighted that would produce a better picture of the extent to which both groups were really similar across the various ages. Thus, the age data are not easy to interpret confidently. However, Thompson's group data on behavior changes during laughing, smiling, and crying do appear sound and emphasize the close similarities between the blind and sighted, despite the lack of social mimicry in the former.

Thompson's observations of blind children's facial expressions of sadness, anger, and sulkiness were confined to children under 6 years (with the exception of one blind-deaf child). However, Goodenough (1932), Charlesworth (1970), and Eibl-Eibesfeldt (1970) have all noted fairly normal expressive responses in older blind children. Goodenough (1932) reported expressions of laughing, mild and intense resentment, anger, and astonishment in a 10-year-old girl, congenitally blind and deaf. The expressive responses were appropriate to the situation; however, a few expressions were not normal. What appeared to be aberrant expressions of mild resentment were noted—gaze aversion, frowning, or pouting; at other times crouching in a bizarre position with the head resting on the knees, or thrusting a thumb and index finger into the nostrils. In light of all of Goodenough's detailed descriptions, it appears that although there may be some atypical behaviors in emotions of less intensity, most expressions seem to be independent of the opportunity for visual learning.

Experimental research conducted by Charlesworth (1970) provides further support for the parallels in facial expressions of blind and sighted. Surprise responses to two standard task situations involving the confirmation and violation of expectancies (a coin that disappears mysteriously from a box and the unexpected presence of water in a jar from which metal objects were lifted on ten previous trials) and to the presentation of a stimulus designed to elicit startle (a form of Jack-in-the-box) were compared in 11 normal and 14 congenitally blind children, 6 to 14 years of age.

Detailed analyses of filmed responses revealed no significant differences between the two groups in the pattern of behaviors, nor the amount of facial activity observed. The possibility that some of the behaviors (such as smiling) may have been social responses to the experimenter was not overlooked. Smiling may have also been due to the subject finding the violation of expectancies an amusing trick. An unexpected finding was the absence of a stereotyped surprise reaction or startle response. Considerable variability in responses was obtained within each subject (across the three tasks) as well as between subjects, thus suggesting that if such responses are not learned during ontogenesis, they are not necessarily linked to any single set of stimulus conditions, as an innate theory may posit.

The findings of Goodenough (1932) and Charlesworth (1970) are corroborated by Eibl-Eibesfeldt's (1970a) film analysis of two deaf–blind children. He reported that the "motor patterns of laughing corresponded in all details to those of normal children." Other expressive behaviors were also like those of sighted children, although their vocal expressive behaviors were different.

In a clinical study of eight blind infants, Fraiberg (1968) reported that rage or aggressive reactions of the blind infants were different from those of normal sighted infants. Rage reactions, for example, in an 18-month-old boy tended to consist mainly of yelling and were not accompanied by more stereotyped responses as kicking, banging the floor, or facial expressions of rage or anger. One 18-month-old girl expressed her anger at toilet training with primitive tic-like behavior. It is not easy to use these findings to test Darwin's hypothesis that rage reactions for the most part are unlearned. What the children's rage reactions were before 1 year of age were not reported. Hence, it is possible that the blind showed typical rage reactions early, as Darwin would have predicted, and then ceased over time to exhibit them because of the lack of visually mediated reinforcement. Also no detailed descriptions of the facial reactions were given for a basis of comparison with other studies of rage. Taken as a whole, Fraiberg's observations indicate that some of the congenitally blind child's expressive behaviors are either undeveloped or aberrant. This finding is counter to most of the conclusions of the authors mentioned above. Part of this discrepancy may be accounted for by differences in the ages of the subjects in the various studies (Fraiberg's tended to be younger) as well as to the fact that Fraiberg relied heavily upon instrumental expressions of anger (hitting, kicking) rather than on its facial expressive components, which was the main emphasis of the other writers. Also it is not possible to ascertain exactly what kind of situations (and what was the infant's disposition at the time) actually preceded the expressions Fraiberg observed. Since it does not appear that Fraiberg intentionally manipulated the situations, as most of the other researchers did, there is no way of knowing for certain exactly what situations actually elicited the reactions. Such knowledge is obviously important in making inferences about what emotion was elicited.

In general, then, results show that in the majority of instances the blind and sighted do not vary significantly in many of the facial expressions of emotion. However, this is the case when the expressions are spontaneous; when the emotions are voluntary or acted, differences between blind and sighted become apparent.

In the case of the blind, there are a few studies involving acting. Dumas (1932) asked 33 congenitally blind persons, mostly between 12 and 20 years old, to act afraid, sad, angry, and happy (more specific expressive responses such as smiling, crying, and laughing were not included). According to the observations of sighted people living with them, the blind studied by Dumas showed no deficits in normal spontaneous expression of emotions—thus supporting the studies noted above. However, the results of Dumas' acting experiment indicated that the blind were totally unable to act out appropriate emotional expressions. For example, one subject stated that although he knew what the experience fear was, he did not know what a frightened face was like. When asked to describe the expression of happiness, subjects focused exclusively on more global body movements (for example, clapping the hands for happiness), giving no acknowledgement of changes in facial expressions.

This study was partially supported by unreported side observations made in Charlesworth's (1970) study of surprise noted above. After the surprise experiment, the blind and sighted children were asked to act out such expressions as surprise, rage or anger, and sadness. Some blind children could produce recognizable surprise responses; others found this task totally impossible to do, and if they succeeded in producing an expression it was markedly distorted. Similar variability was found in the voluntary expressions of the other emotions. The sighted children did somewhat better than the blind, despite the fact that they appeared to be more inhibited.

Part of the variation in acting ability among the blind children themselves could be accounted for by age factors, although this was not certain. Mistchenka's (1933) study is relevant in this respect. On the basis of a study of 61 blind children ranging in age from 4 to 18 years, Mistchenka contended that the ability to control various facial movements is significantly related to chronological age as well as age at the onset of blindness. No differences were found between the youngest blind child and the youngest sighted child' however, with age, blind children showed increased deficits in motor mimicry. Less deterioration was evident in children who became blind later in life.

Fulcher (1942) conducted an investigation of the voluntary expression of emotions in 118 sighted children, age 4 to 16 years, and 50 blind children (having no more than light perception), age 6 to 21. All children were of normal intelligence. Motion pictures were made as the children portrayed the emotions of happiness, sadness, anger, and fear. The films of posed facial expressions were carefully analyzed; included were measurements of total facial activity, specific muscular involvement, specific movement of facial features (for example, lips round, lips parted), and estimates of the adequacy of the observed facial expressions in comparison to a description of appropriate movements in various facial expressions. On the basis of these data, Fulcher concluded that although blind children exhibit less facial activity than sighted children, blind children are capable of voluntary expressions of emotion. There is a marked similarity in the patterns of expressive behaviors between blind and sighted. Fulcher also reported that facial activity increased with age in sighted children and decreased with age in blind children.

Unfortunately, it is not easy to make firm conclusions about Fulcher's findings. Apart from some methodological weaknesses in his study, his findings have not been submitted to statistical tests. From their appearance in tabular form, the differences in amount of facial activity and age trends noted in the blind and sighted do not seem to be as significant as he believes. Also, there is reason to believe (as Fulcher himself suggests) that the instructions may have elicited more spontaneous than voluntary behaviors in some children. Initially Fulcher used instructions which explicitly differentiated between "looking" and "feeling" happy, sad, angry, and afraid. These instructions had to be discarded because they were too difficult for young children to understand. Instead, the experimenter gave appropriate emotional situations as he instructed the subject to perform. For example, the children were told: "You are afraid when you are nearly hit by a car." Although these instructions made the task comprehensible to the youngest children, the distinction between voluntary and spontaneous expressions may have been blurred if the instructions were sufficient to arouse emotional feelings.

Thus methodological variations may account for the difference between Fulcher's findings and some of those mentioned earlier. In Charlesworth's (1970) study, narratives of the appropriate situations were employed (as in Fulcher's), hence it is likely that the expressions in some of the blind children could have been more spontaneous than voluntary. This may account for some of the similarities between the two studies. Dumas (1932), in contrast, did not employ narration, but instead asked his subjects to display a happy, sad, angry, or frightened face—a task designed to elicit purely voluntary expressions; and his blind subjects were unable to act the appropriate expressions. In all such studies part of the problem in obtaining valid data may be due to the child's inability to comprehend what is required of him. Only better controlled studies with a more precise definition of the various possible factors involved will be able to clarify this problem.

Taken as a totality, the data on the blind are heavily in favor of Darwin's hypothesis that spontaneous expressive behaviors in the blind (and in the sighted, too, for that matter) are not dependent upon visual learning for their appearance and are, therefore, most probably a result of the operations of innate factors. Voluntary expressions of emotions are more difficult to interpret in terms of the various studies because of methodological variations. The fact that there is a difference in the blind child's ability to act out an emotion and his ability to express it spontaneously does not necessarily weaken Darwin's hypothesis. It could be argued that voluntary or acted expression requires being able to reproduce a model of the desired expression. One could acquire such a model by observing other persons over a long period of time, or one could acquire it from himself in the form of the sensations he receives from his face while the facial muscles are activated during an emotion. If good acting depends on having a good model, then the blind child is at a disadvantage since he has only one source of information to construct such a model while the sighted child has two—visual information from others as well as the information from his own face. Individual differences among the blind could exist because of differences in learning ability, but the overall difference between blind and sighted would nevertheless remain. In the studies covered, the sighted never do poorer than the blind; but the reverse is true in some cases. Darwin, it should be emphasized, never discounted the role that learning could play in the formation or shaping of facial expressions. It can be recalled that he considered many expressive behaviors—especially those related to elaborate emotions—subject to cultural conditioning.

Presence of Opportunity

There is no reason to go into a lengthy account of the importance of social imitation in the acquisition of many salient and common human behaviors. The fact that man is the most culturally conditioned of all animals is sufficient proof that his behavior is highly susceptible of being molded by tradition. The research literature is replete with studies demonstrating how this molding takes place during childhood. Interestingly enough, though, the extent to which expressive behaviors are known to be imitated is quite restricted. Only a relatively few studies have been devoted to determining how facial expressions could be acquired during early childhood and when such acquisition actually begins.

There is some evidence that imitation can take place at a very early age. Piaget (1962) noted that imitation of another child's crying could well take place during the first few days of life. However, as Walters and Parke (1965) point out, what appears to be imitative crying may simply be a distress reaction to a loud sound. However, infants less than a month of age have been observed by Zazzo (1957) to engage in imitative tongue protrusions, and Gardner and Gardner (1970) observed what may well have been imitation in an infant as young as 6 weeks of age. In the latter study, four responses, two of which were facial expressions (tongue in/out and mouth open/close), were produced by the parent and followed by similar responses on part of the infant. Although Gardner and Gardner do not attribute such behavior to "direct" imitation, they feel that the child at that age may be capable of partial imitation of may be sensitive to the "modal properties" of the model's behavior.

Guernsey (1928) observed 200 infants from 2 to 21 months old in more than 20 different stimulus situations designed to elicit imitation. According to her, at 2 months the infant engages in reflexlike or passive imitation; at around 4 months, imitation becomes conscious or active; at 8 months, delayed or memory-based imitation begins. Interestingly enough, Guernsey discovered that the best time to study pure imitation was before the eighteenth month; after that she found it very difficult to isolate imitation from the infant's play and social behavior. Piaget (1962) observed similar stages of imitation and also obtained, for example, clear evidence of his daughter imitating his lip movements at 8 months. Bridges (1932) noted that 10-month-old infants mimic other baby's calls and laughter, and also pat, bang, and laugh in imitation of each other. Bühler and Hetzer (1928) reported that during the fifth and sixth months, infants imitated the behavior of the eperimenter when the latter made faces; closing the mouth, protruding the lower lip, furrowing the brows occurred in infants when face to face with the same expression of the experimenter.

In short, there is evidence that by the time the infant is approaching the end of his first year he can effectively imitate the expressions of others.

It can be recalled from the studies on infant recognition that during this time there is also evidence of the infant's ability to discriminate between expressions as well as recognize their significance.

To our knowledge, there are only two major studies involving the development of imitation or mimicking ability in children; one mentioned earlier (Fulcher, 1942) actually involved sighted and blind children voluntarily making facial expressions (the assumption here being that the subject needed some form of internal model—a visual, kinesthetic proprioceptive image—to copy as he performed the task). The other study, by Kwint (1934), was a direct attempt to examine age changes in the ability to mimic facial movements.

Fulcher's (1942) normal sighted subjects (118 of them between 4 and 16 years) showed an increase in total voluntary facial activity with age; the blind subjects (60 between 6 and 21 years) showed a decline with age, although as noted earlier we are not certain of the statistical significance of these data. There was no noticeable change in the form of expressions in both sighted and blind children with age, and large individual differences were also obtained. Such findings suggest that experience may be related to how much facial activity the child displays in such a task. The blind, presumably because of no experience, engages in progressively less facial activity with age as compared to the sighted.

In Kwint's (1934) study of 476 children between 4 and 16 years, each child was asked to perform a particular facial movement (e.g., lift the brows, draw corners of the mouth down and back, etc.). The child was required to watch the experimenter make the facial expression and then perform the same expression while watching himself in the mirror. Kwint found that the ability to mimic increased with age (until puberty, when it showed a slight decrease). Older children could not only mimic more facial movements, but were also capable of mimicking more complicated expressions. Brighter children did better than children of average intelligence at each age level. Kwint felt that maturational processes—physical as well as cognitive—were responsible for the development of the ability to mimic.

Both studies document developmental trends and suggest that these changes are related to experiences that influence both the amount of facial activity the individual produces in a given situation and his ability to mimic a diversity of expressions in someone else.

GENERAL REMARKS ON ABSENCE AND
PRESENCE OF OPPORTUNITY

Studying the absence and presence of opportunity to acquire and use facial expressions, as noted earlier, sheds light on the questions of the origins of such expressions. The dearth of longitudinal studies involving the close observation of expressions over time in the child, however, makes it impossible to infer with any certainty what mechanisms could conceivably be involved. In light of the findings showing age changes in ability to produce facial expressions, it is difficult to rule out either learning or maturation. However, as noted earlier in the discussion of smiling, there is clear evidence that smiling is influenced by variations in the reinforcing properties of the infant's environment. Hence learning most probably plays a significant role. There is no reason why the same thing could not happen with other specific responses as well. On the other hand, the similarities in the kinds of expressive behaviors of both sighted and blind suggest that learning experiences involving visual models are not necessary for their first appearance.

In light of both sets of findings, the most satisfying conclusion (one reached by a number of investigators—e.g., Peiper, 1963) is that both the environment and innate fators have effects on expressive behavior. The environment may influence the time at which a behavior appears (many smiling individuals around a newborn may accelerate the appearance of the first social smile) and may determine how often the behavior occurs once it first appears. The innate factors, on the other hand, seem to be mainly responsible for the morphological characteristics of expressive behaviors (and hence the fact that they occur at all as such) and for the connections such behaviors have to the emotional states associated with them. Such a conclusion simultaneously acknowledges the significance of the data from the absence-of-stimulation studies as well as the relative ease with which many different kinds of environmental stimuli can elicit and strengthen expressive behaviors once they occur.

At present we feel such a conclusion is justified; however, we also feel that the more interesting problem of how the various factors (innate and learned) interact with each other during the ontogenesis of the individual has still to be attacked.

CONCLUSIONS

While writing this chapter we wondered what Darwin, if he were alive today, would have thought as he read it through to its final pages. Would he have been impressed with the strides the behavioral sciences have made in their study of expressive behavior in children, or would he have experienced some mild disappointment? We think his reaction would have initially been one of mild disappointment, accompanied by some feelings of pride in the validity and generality of his own observations. His reaction would have also been accompanied by some feelings of optimism.

If one measures the progress science makes by the extent to which it reveals novel information about the empirical world and consequently restructures our thinking about it, then Darwin's disappointment would have been justified. A century after his book, there is actually little new information on facial expressions in infants and children in the sense that such information would surprise Darwin or any well-trained observer of human behavior. The majority of observations made after Darwin either agree with or expand upon his; few diverge in any significant way. On these grounds Darwin could feel a sense of pride about the contents of his diary and the other observations he made. As for his hypothesis concerning the innateness of many of the primary emotions, we feel it has been challenged and has and has come away very much intact.

Where his disappointment would lie, we feel, would be in the fact that no one as yet has attempted to study the ontogenesis of many important facial expressions—for example, of pity, shyness, embarrassment, cruelty, or threat behavior, or all those subtle expressive behaviors that promote or inhibit aggression, nurturant behavior, or other social behaviors in persons. These behaviors, as Darwin intuited in his writings, have significant adaptive value for the maintenance of a social life necessary for the survival of the human species. It has been only lately that scientists, many of whom have been trained in zoology, have recognized the important signal value such expressions conceivably could have for the regulation of social behavior.

The failure to fulfill and extend Darwin's empirical work cannot be attributed to anything inherent in his basic approach. His belief that expressions were mostly innate cannot be interpreted to mean that there is nothing new to discover about them. As we understand him, Darwin considered his belief a hypothesis that was well tested by the standards of this time, but which was also subject to future examination by the scientific community. He was well aware that his observations of expressions in children were mere sketches of a vast, uncharted area and hardly comparable, in either detail or latitude, to his monumental mapping of the properties of the behavior of lower animals.

It has often been said that in the field of child behavior, no one has yet attempted to build systematically a complete taxonomy of natural behavior and that until this is done the science of the developing child will remain incomplete. While this is a difficult task, it is true that to make progress, any science must have as complete a description of the phenomena under study as possible. Such a description is still lacking in many areas of child development, although here and there a small corpus of information about a particular class of behaviors is gradually being developed (see Hutt & Hutt, 1970). In the area of expressive behaviors of children there is only the beginnings of a dictionary of facial expressions representative of children at different ages. Child psychologists have a long way to go until they can match the botanist or zoologist in this respect.

Despite the relatively limited progress that has been made in the empirical domain of child expression, Darwin, we think, would have been pleased by the conceptual advances in the area of relating adult facial expressions to emotions, and the factors influencing both made by such persons as Tomkins (1962, 1963), Frijda (1968), Izard (1969), and Ekman, Friesen, & Ellsworth (1972). He would have also been pleased to see that cinematographic technology has now made it possible to record as well as to display expressive behaviors in the most rigorous and detailed manner possible. If he acquainted himself further with recent efforts in child psychology, he would also be pleased at the degree of sophistication—theoretical as well as technical and methodological—that characterizes such efforts.

In our estimation, the current state of the behavioral sciences dealing with children and the increasing interest on the part of behavioral scientists in the work of ethologists finally make it possible to realize Darwin's vision of a rigorous approach to studying the development of expressive behavior in man.

ACKNOWLEDGMENTS

Support for writing this chapter was provided the senior author by Research Grant 5PO1 HDO 5027-02 from the National Institute of Child Health and Human Development and by The Human Etiology section of The Max-Planck-Institute for Behavior Physiology, Percha Starnberg, West Germany. The authors wish to extend their gratitude to Dr. Philip Salapatek, Dr. Paul Ekman, Prof. Dr. I. Eibl-Eibesfeldt, to Ms. Ruth Dickie who was so helpful in typing the manuscript, and to Ms. Liz Burkhardt who assisted in innumerable ways.

REFERENCES

Ahrens, R. Beitrag zur Entwicklung des Physiognomie - und Mimikerkennens. *Zeitschrift für experimentelle und angewandte Psychologie,* 1954, **2,** 412–454.

Allport, G. *Pattern and growth in personality.* New York: Holt, 1961.

Ambrose, J. A. The development of the smiling response in early infancy, In B. Foss (Ed.), *Determinants of infant behavior.* London: Methuen, 1961, 179–196.

Amen, E. W. Individual differences in apperceptive reaction: A study of the response of preschool children to pictures. *Genetic Psychology Monographs,* 1941, **23**, 319–385.

Banham, K. M. The development of affectionate behavior in infancy. *Journal of Genetic Psychology,* 1950, **76**, 283–289.

Berlyne, D. E. *Conflict, arousal, and curiosity.* New York: McGraw-Hill, 1960.

Berne, E. V. C. An experimental investigation of social behavior patterns in young children. *University of Iowa Studies in Child Welfare,* 1930, **4**(3), 1–96.

Birdwhistell, R. L. *Kinesics and context.* Philadelphia: Univ. of Pennsylvania Press, 1970.

Blatz, W. E., & Millichamp, D. A. The development of emotion in the infant. *University of Toronto Studies, Child Development Series,* 1935, No. 4.

Blurton Jones, N. G. An ethological study of some aspects of social behavior of children in nursery school. In D. Morris (Ed.), *Primate ethology.* Chicago: Aldine, 1967.

Blurton Jones, N. G. Criteria for use in describing facial expressions of children. *Human Biology,* 1971, 43(3), 365–413.

Bowlby, J. The nature of the child's tie to his mother. *International Journal of Psychoanalysis* 1958, **39**, 350–373.

Brackett, C. W. Laughing and crying of pre-school children. *Journal of Experimental Education,* 1933, **2**, 119–126.

Bridges, K. M. B. A genetic theory of the emotions. *Journal of Genetic Psychology,* 1930, **37**, 514–527.

Bridges, K. M. B. *The social and emotional development of the pre-school child.* (1st ed.) London: Kegan Paul, 1931.

Bridges, K. M. B. Emotional development in early infancy. *Child Development,* 1932, **3**, 324–341.

Bronson, G. W. The development of fear in man and other animals. *Child Development,* 1968, **39**, 409–431.

Bruner, J. S. & Tagiuri, R. The perception of people. In G. Lindzey (Ed.), *Handbook of social psychology.* Vol. 2. Reading, Massachusetts: Addison-Wesley, 1954, 634–654.

Bühler, C. The social behavior of the child. In C. Murchison (Ed.), *A Handbook of child psychology.* (1st ed.) Worcester, Massachusetts: Clark Univ. Press, 1931. Pp.392–431.

Bühler, C. & Hetzer, H. Das erste Verständnis für Ausdruck im ersten Lebensjahr. *Zeitschrift für Psychologie,* 1928, **107**, 50–61.

Buzby, D. Interpretation of facial expressions. *American Journal of Psychology,* 1924, **35**, 602–604.

Charlesworth, W. R. Instigation and maintenance of curiosity behavior as a function of surprise versus novel and familiar stimuli. *Child Development,* 1964, **35**, 1169–1186.

Charlesworth, W. R. Persistence of orienting and attending behavior in infants as a function of stimulus-locus uncertainty. *Child Development,* 1966, **37**, 473–491.

Charlesworth, W. R. The role of surprise in cognitive development. In D. Elkind & J. H. Flavell (Eds.), *Studies in cognitive development.* New York and London: Oxford Univ. Press, 1969, 257–314.

Charlesworth, W. R. Surprise reactions in congenitally blind and sighted children. National Institute of Mental Health Progress Report, 1970.

Charlesworth, W. R. Unpublished research, 1971.

Charlesworth, W. R. & Zahn, C. Reaction time as a measure of comprehension of the effects produced by rotation on objects. *Child Development,* 1966, **37**, 253–268.

Coleman, J. Facial expressions of emotions. *Psychological Monographs,* 1949, **63**, (Whole #296, No. 1).

Crile, G. W. *The origin and nature of the emotions.* Philadelphia: W. B. Saunders, 1915.

Darwin, C. *The expression of the emotions in man and animals.* London: Murray, 1872.

Darwin, C. A biographical sketch of an infant. *Mind,* 1877, **2**, 285–294.

Dashiell, J. F. A new method of measuring reactions for facial expressions of emotions. *Psychological Bulletin,* 1927, **24**, 174–175.

Davis, K. Extreme social isolation of a child. *American Journal of Sociology,* 1940, **45**, 554–565.

Davis, K. Final note on a case of extreme isolation. *American Journal of Sociology,* 1947, **52**, 432–437.

Dennis, W. A bibliography of baby biographies. *Child Development,* 1936, **7**, 71–73.

Dennis, W. Infant development under conditions of restricted practice and of minimum social stimulation: A preliminary report. *Journal of Genetic Psychology,* 1938, **53**, 149–158.

Dennis, W., & Dennis, M. G. Behavioral development in the first year as shown by forty biographies. *Psychological Record,* 1937, **1**, (21), 349–361.

Dennis, W., & Dennis, M. G. Development under controlled environmental conditions. In I. W. Dennis (Ed.), *Readings in child psychology.* Englewood Cliffs, New Jersey: Prentice-Hall, 1951.

Desai, M. H. Surprise: A historical and experimental study. *British Journal of Psychology,* 1939, **22**, 1–124.

Ding, G. & Jersild, A. A study of the laughing and smiling of pre-school children. *Journal of Genetic Psychology,* 1932, **40**, 452–472.

Dumas, G. La mimique des aveugles. *Bulletin de l'Acadé*mie de Médicine, 1932, **107**, 607–610.

Dunlap, K. The role of eye and mouth muscles in the expression of emotions. *Genetic Psychology Monographs,* 1927, **2** (3), 195–233.

Dusenbury, D. & Knower, F. H. Experimental studies of the symbolism of action and voice. I. A study of the specificity of meaning in facial expression. *Quarterly Journal of Speech,* 1938, **24**, 424–435.

Dusenbury, D., & Knower, F. H. Experimental studies of the symbolism of action and voice. II. A study of the specificity of meaning in abstract tonal symbols. *Quarterly Journal of Speech,* 1939, **25**, 67–75.

Dymond, R., Hughes, R. & Raabe, V. Measurable changes in empathy with age. *Journal of Consulting Psychology,* 1952, **16**, 202–206.

Eibl-Eibesfeldt, I. *Ethology: The biology of behavior.* New York: Holt, 1970.

Eibl-Eibesfeldt, I. *Love and hate.* New York: Holt, 1972.

Ekman, P. & Friesen, W. V. Constants across cultures in the face and emotion. *Journal Personality & Social Psychology,* 1971, **17**, 124–129.

Ekman, P., Friesen, W. V., & Ellsworth, P. *Emotion in the human face: Guidelines for research and integration of findings.* New York: Pergamon Press, 1972.

Enders, A. A study of the laughter of the pre-school child in the Merrill-Palmer Nursery School. *Papers of the Michigan Academy of Science, Arts and Letters,* 1927, **8,** 341–356.

England, A. O. Non-structured approach to the study of children's fears. *Journal of Clinical Psychology,* 1946, **2**, 364–368.

Fenton, J. C. *A practical psychology of babyhood.* Boston: Houghton Mifflin, 1925.

Fraiberg, S. Parallel and divergent patterns in blind and sighted infants. *Psychoanalytic Study of the Child,* 1968, **23**, 264–300.

Freedman, D. G. Smiling in blind infants and the issue of innate versus acquired. *Journal of Child Psychology and Psychiatry,* 1964, **5**, 171–184.

Freedman, D. G. Hereditary control of early social behavior. In B. Foss (Ed.), *Determinants of infant behavior.* London: Methuen, 1965, 149–156.

Frijda, N. H. Recognition of emotion. In L. Berkowitz (Ed.), *Advances in experimental social psychology.* New York: Academic Press, 1968.

Fulcher, J. S. "Voluntary" facial expressions in blind and seeing children. *Archives of Psychology,* 1942, **38** (272), 1–49.

Gardner, J., & Gardner, H. A note on selective imitation by a six-week-old infant. *Child Development,* 1970, **41**, 1209–1213.

Gates, G. S. An experimental study of the growth of social perception. *Journal of Educational Psychology,* 1923, **14**, 449–461.

Gates, G. S. A test for ability to interpret facial expression. *Psychological Bulletin,* 1925, **22**, 120.

Gates, G. S. The role of the auditory element in the interpretation of emotion. *Psychological Bulletin,* 1927, **24**, 175.

Gesell, A. Maturation and infant behavior pattern. *Psychological Review,* 1929, **36**, 307–319.

Gewirtz, J. The course of infant smiling in four child-rearing environments in Israel. In B. Foss (Ed.), *Determinants of infant behavior.* London: Methuen, 1965, 205–248.

Gilbert, D. Young child's awareness of affect. *Child Development,* 1969, **40**, 629–640.

Goodenough, F. L. *Anger in young children.* Minneapolis: Univ. of Minnesota Press, 1931a.

Goodenough, F. L. The expressions of emotions in infancy. *Child Development,* 1931b, **2**, 96–101.

Goodenough, F. L. Expression of the emotions in a blind-deaf child. *Journal of Abnormal and Social Psychology,* 1932, **27**, 328–333.

Goodenough, F. L., & Tinker, M. A. The relative potency of facial expression and verbal description of stimulus in the judgment of emotion. *Journal of Comparative Psychology,* 1931, **12**, 365–370.

Gregg, A., Miller, M., & Linton, E. Laughter situations as an indication of social responsiveness in young children. In D. S. Thomas (Ed.), Some new techniques for studying social behavior. *Child Development Monographs,* 1929, **1**, 86–98.

Guernsey, M. Eine genetische Studie über Nachahmung. *Zeitschrift für Psychologie,* 1928, **107**, 105–178.

Hebb, D. O. Emotion in man and animal: An analysis of the intuitive processes of recognition. *Psychological Review,* 1946, **53**, 88–106.

Herzka, H. S. *Das Gesicht des Säuglings: Ausdruck und Reifung.* Basel/Stuttgart: Schwabe, 1965.

Hilgard, E. R. Psychology after Darwin. In Sol Tax (Ed.), *Evolution after Darwin.* Chicago: Univ. of Chicago Press, 1960. Pp.269–287.

Honkavaara, S. The psychology of expression. *British Journal of Psychology Monograph Supplements,* 1961, **32**, 1–96.

Hulin, W., & Katz, D. The Frois-Wittman pictures of facial expression. *Journal of Experimental Psychology,* 1935, **18**, 482–498.

Hutt, S. J. & Hutt, Corinne, *Direct observation and measurement of behavior,* Springfield, Illinois: Thomas, 1970.

Itard, J. *The wild boy of Aveyron.* New York: Appleton, 1932.

Izard, C. E. The emotions and emotion constructs in personality and culture research. In R. B. Cattell (Ed.), *Handbook of modern personality theory.* Chicago: Aldine, 1969.

Izard, C. E. *Face of emotion.* New York: Appleton, 1971.

James, W. *Principles of psychology.* Vol. II. London: Macmillan, 1891.

Jenness, A. Differences in the recognition of facial expression of emotion. *Journal of General Psychology,* 1932, **7**, 192–196.

Jersild, A. T., & Holmes, F. B. Children's fears. *Child Development Monographs,* 1935, **20**, 1–296.

Jersild, A. T., & Markey, F. V. Conflicts between pre-school children. *Child Development Monographs,* 1935, **21**, 1–181.

Jersild, A. T., Markey, F. V., & Jersild, C. L. Children's fears, dreams, wishes, daydreams, likes, dislikes, pleasant and unpleasant memories. *Child Development Monographs,* 1933, **12**, 1–172.

Jones, M. C. The development of early behavior patterns in young children. *Pedagogical Seminary,* 1926, **33**, 537–585.

Jones, M. C. The development of basic emotions. *The child's emotions.* Proceedings of the Midwest Conference on Character Development. Chicago: Univ. of Chicago Press, 1930.

Jones, H. E., & Jones, M. C. A study of fear. *Childhood Education,* 1928, **5** (3), 136–143.

Kashinsky, M., & Weiner, M. Tone in communication and performance of children from two SES groups. *Child Development,* 1969, **40**, 1193–1202.

Kenderdine, M. Laughter in the pre-school child. *Child Development,* 1931, **2**, 228–230.

Kessen, W., Haith, M. M., & Salapatek, P. H. Human infancy: A bibliography and guide. In P. Mussen (Ed.), *Carmichael's Manual of Child Psychology.* (3rd ed.) Vol. 1. New York: Wiley, 1970. Pp.287–445.

Kreutzer, M. A., & Charlesworth, W. R. Infants' reactions to different expressions of emotions. Paper presented at the Society of Research in Child Development, Philadelphia, March 1973.

Kwint, L. Ontogeny of mobility of the face. *Child Development,* 1934, **5**, 1–12.

Leuba, C. Tickling and laughter: Two genetic studies. *Journal of Genetic Psychology, 1941,* **58**, 201–209.

Levy-Schoen, A. Une mimique perçue comme critère de choix: Son émergence dans l'évolution génétique de divers comportements de choix. *Psychologie Française,* 1961, **6**, 32–46.

Lind, J., Vuorenkoski, V., Rosberg, G., Partanan, T. J., Wasz-Hockert, O. Spectographic analysis of vocal response to pain in infants with Down's Syndrome. *Developmental Medicine & Children's Neurology,* 1970, **12**, 478–486.

McFarland, M. Relationships between young sisters as revealed in their overt responses. *Child Development Monographs,* 1938, **23**, 1–230.

Marvin, R., Farris, D., & Bates, E. The development of coyness and greeting behaviors in 2-, 3-, and 4-year-olds. Unpublished research, 1971.

Messick, S., & Damarin, F. Cognitive styles and memory for faces. *Journal of Abnormal and Social Psychology,* 1964, **69**, 313–318.

Mistschenka, M. N. Ueber die mimische Gesichtsmotorik der Blinden. *Folia Neuropathologica Estoniana,* 1933, **13**, 24–43.

Moore, K. C. The mental development of a child. *Psychological Review,* 1895, **1** (Monograph Supplement 3), 37–41.

Murphy, G., & Murphy, L. B. *Experimental social psychology.* New York: Harper, 1931.

Murphy, G., Murphy, L. B., & Newcomb, T. M. *Experimental social psychology.* (Rev. ed.) New York: Harper, 1937.

Odom, R. D., & Lemond, C. M. Developmental differences in the perception and production of facial expressions. *Child Development,* 1972, **43**, 359–369.

Peiper, A. *Cerebral function in infancy and childhood.* New York: Consultants Bureau, 1963.

Piaget, J. *The origins of intelligence in children.* New York: International University Press, 1952.

Piaget, J. *Play, dreams and imitation in childhood.* New York: Norton, 1962.

Preyer, W. *The mind of the child.* New York: D. Appleton & Co., 1892.

Rheingold, H. L. Development of social behavior in the human infant. *Monographs of the Society for Research in Child Development,* 1966, **31** (5, Whole no. 107), 1–17.

Rheingold, H. L. The social and socializing infant. In D. Goslin (Ed.), *Handbook of socialization theory and research.* Chicago: Rand McNally, 1969, 779–790.

Ricketts, A. F. A study of the behavior of young children in anger. In L. Jack *et al.* (Eds.), *University of Iowa Studies: Studies in child welfare,* 1934, **9**(3), 163–171.

Ruckmick, C. A. A preliminary study of the emotions. *Psychological Monographs,* 1921, **30**, 30–35.

Savitsky, J. C., & Izard, C. E. Developmental changes in the use of emotion cues in a concept-formation task. *Developmental Psychology,* 1970, **3**(3), 350–357.

Scarr, S. & Salapatek, P. Patterns of fear development during infancy. *Merrill-Palmer Quarterly,* 1970, **16**(1), 53–90.

Schaffer, H. R. Cognitive structure and early social behaviour. Paper presented at a study group on "The origins of human social relations," London, July 1969.

Sherman, M. The differentiation of emotional responses in infants. I. Judgments of emotional responses from motion picture views and from actual observation. *Journal of Comparative Psychology,* 1927, **7**, 265–284. (a)

Sherman, M. The differentiation of emotional responses in infants. II. The ability of observers to judge the emotional characteristics of the crying of infants, and the voice of an adult. *Journal of Comparative Psychology,* 1927, **7**, 335–351. (b)

Sherman, M. The differentiation of emotional responses in infants. III. A proposed theory of the development of emotional responses in infants. *Journal of Comparative Psychology,* 1928, **8**, 385–394.

Shinn, M. W. *The biography of a baby.* New York: Houghton Mifflin, 1900.

Singh, J. A., & Zingg, R. M. *Wolf children and feral man.* IV. Contribution of the University of Denver. New York and London, 1945.

Spitz, R. A., & Wolf, K. M. The smiling response: A contribution to the ontogenesis of social relations. *Genetic Psychology Monographs,* 1946, **34**, 57–125.

Sroufe, L. A. Research on infants' laughter. Personal communication, 1971.

Staffieri, R., & Bassett, J. Birth order and perception of facial expressions. *Perceptual and Motor Skills,* 1970, **30**, 606.

Stirnimann,-F. *Psychologie des neugeborenen Kindes.* München, Germany: Kindler Verlag, 1940.

Stone, L. J. A critique of studies of infant isolation. *Child Development,* 1954, **25**, 9–20.

Thompson, D., & Meltzer, L. Communication of emotional intent by facial expression. *Journal of Abnormal and Social Psychology,* 1964, **68**, 129–135.

Thompson, J. Development of facial expression in blind and seeing children. *Archives of Psychology,* 1941, No. 264, 1–47.

Tiedemann, O. Beobachtungen über die Entwicklung der Seelenfähigkeiten bei Kindern. Published 1787. (Translated by C. Murchison & S. Langer. *Pedagogical Seminary,* 1927, **34**, 205–230.)

Tomkins, S. S. *Affect, imagery, consciousness. Vol. 1. The positive affects.* New York: Springer, 1962.

Tomkins, S. S. *Affect, imagery, consciousness. Vol. 2. The negative affects.* New York: Springer, 1963.

Valentine, C. W. The innate bases of fear. *Journal of Genetic Psychology,* 1930, **37**, 394–420.

Walters, R. H. & Parke, R. D. The role of the distance receptors in the development of social responsiveness. In L. P. Lipsitt & C. C. Spiker (Eds.), *Advances in child development and behavior,* New York: Academic Press, 1965, **2**, 59–96.

Washburn, R. W. A study of the smiling and laughing of infants in the first year of life. *Genetic Psychology Monographs,* 1929, **6**, 398–537.

Wasz-Hockert, O., Lind, J., Vuorenkoski, V., Partanan, T., & Vallane, E. *The infant cry: A spectographic and auditory analysis.* London: Heinemann, 1968.

Watson, J. B. *Psychology from the standpoint of a behaviorist,* Philadelphia: Lippincott, 1919.

Watson, J. B. Experimental studies on the growth of the emotions. *Pedagogical Seminary,* 1925, **32**, 326–348. (a)

Watson, J. B. Recent experiments in how we love and change our emotional equipment. *Pedagogical Seminary,* 1925, **32**, 349–371. (b)

Watson, J. B. *Behaviorism.* New York: Norton, 1930.

Wilcox, B. & Clayton, F. Infant visual fixation on motion pictures of the human face. *Journal of Experimental Child Psychology,* 1968, **6**(1), 22–32.

Witkin, H. A., Dyk, R. B., Fattuson, H. F., Goodenough, D. R., & Karp, S. A. *Psychological differention: Studies of development.* New York: Wiley, 1962.

Wolff, P. H. Observations on the early development of smiling. In B. M. Foss (Ed.), *Determinants of infant behavior.* II. London: Methuen, 1963, 113–133.

Wolff, P. H. The causes, controls, and organization of behavior in the neonate. Psychological Issues, 1966, 5(1, Whole No. 17), 1–99.

Wolff, P. H. The natural history of crying and other vocalizations in early infancy. In B. M. Foss (Ed.), *Determinants of infant behavior.* IV London: Methuen, 1969. Pp.81–109.

Woodworth, R. S. *Experimental Psychology.* New York: Holt, 1938.

Zazzo, R. Le problème de l'imitation chez le nouveau-né, *Enfance,* 1957, **10**, 135–142.

Zingg, R. M. Feral man and extreme cases of isolation. *American Journal of Psychology,* 1940, **53**, 487–517.

4

Cross-Cultural Studies of Facial Expression[1]

Paul Ekman
University of California, San Francisco

INTRODUCTION

Are facial expressions of emotion the same for all men? When someone is surprised, for example, will we see the same facial appearance no matter what his country, race, or culture? Are facial expressions of emotion unlike verbal behavior, where people in different cultures learn different words for saying the same thing? Is it true that we can understand a foreigner's emotions if we observe his facial expressions, that we need no special facial language school, tutoring us as to what these expressions mean in each culture?

If facial expressions are universal, does that mean they are innately determined? Is learning unimportant in determining facial expressions of emotion? Does man inherit particular facial muscular movements for anger, and surprise, and sadness, etc.? Is it our genes that determine which facial muscles move when we feel one way or another?

And, if facial expressions of emotion are universal and innately determined,

[1]The preparation of this chapter was supported by a Career Scientist Award, 5-KO2-MH06092. My own research, reported within this chapter, was supported by a grant from the Advanced Research Projects Agency, administered by the Air Force Office of Scientific Research, AF-AFOSR-1229-67. I am grateful to Patricia Garlan for her editorial help, and to Karl Heider, Jerry Boucher, and Michael Ghiselin for their comments.

have they evolved with man from his animal progenitors? Are man's facial expressions of emotion similar to those shown by other primates? Do the principles that explain why our lips turn up rather than down when happy also explain the facial muscular movements of the chimpanzee or the wolf? Does man show these facial muscular movements for emotion because he has evolved from other animal species?

Darwin thought the answer to all these questions was yes. Furthermore, he believed that a positive answer to the first set—facial expressions are universal—necessarily led to a positive answer to the second set—that they are innate. And, if universal facial expressions are innate, a positive answer to the third set of questions may be inferred—that they are the product of evolutionary pressures. We shall not be concerned with this last matter, for Chevalier-Skolnikoff has discussed in Chapter 2 the relationship between the facial expressions of man and the other primates. Instead our primary focus shall be on the first set of questions, the possible universality of facial expressions. We shall see that a positive answer to the question of universality does not necessarily require a positive answer to the question of innateness, as Darwin thought it did, although it does increase the probability that genetic factors are important determinants of facial expression. The question of innateness will not be of major concern to us, for reasons to be explained shortly.

In Darwin's time, according to his own report, most people accepted the notion that facial expressions are universal, even though there was scanty evidence for such a claim. Darwin obtained some new evidence to prove the universality of at least some facial expressions,[2] although his methods of study were vulnerable to many sources of error. In the century following Darwin's book on expression, his views came to be largely ignored, and credence was instead given to those who claimed, with evidence as faulty as Darwin's, that facial expressions of emotion are specific to each culture and that there are no universals. The dominant view became "what is shown on the face is written there by culture."[3] Only in the last year or two has sufficient evidence been accumulated to refute that view and to show that Darwin was indeed at least partially correct. Even now, many scientists not familiar with all the new evidence to be described here scoff at the notion that there are universal facial expressions of emotion.

---

[2]Darwin considered only the "chief" facial expressions to be universal, although he often failed to include the qualification, thus giving the false impression that he thought all facial expressions were universal.

[3]This quote has been attributed to Otto Klineberg. Klineberg recently told Izard that he had never made the statement, and my own reading of Klineberg's writings failed to yield anything like such an over-simplification.

DARWIN'S VIEW AND HIS
EVIDENCE ON UNIVERSALITY

In *The Expression of the Emotions in Man and Animals,* Darwin, referring to the general unsubstantiated acceptance of the idea that facial expressions of emotion are universal, stressed the usefulness of cross-cultural studies in determining *which*are universal and, by inference, innate:

> ... It seemed to me highly important to ascertain whether the same expressions and gestures prevail, as has often been asserted without much evidence, with all the races of mankind, especially with those who have associated but little with Europeans. Whenever the same movements of the features or body express the same emotions in several different races of man, we may infer with much probability, that such expressions are true ones—that is, are innate or instinctive. Conventional expressions or gestures, acquired by the individual during life, would probably have differed in the different races, in the same manner as do their languages ... [1965, pp. 14–15].[4]

There were but two choices as Darwin saw it. If facial expressions vary from one culture to another, then they must be learned within each culture and, like language, learned differently. Or, if facial expressions are universal, then they are not like language, where the vocabulary is culture specific, and cannot be acquired in a fashion that would vary with culture. For this reason, Darwin infers, they must be inherited. This last step in Darwin's thinking can be disputed. Universality increases the *likelihood* that inheritance determines the form and appearance of facial expressions, but it does not *prove* an innate[5] basis of facial expression since there are other explanations available. Universality requires only the postulate that whatever source is responsible for the origin of facial expressions, it must be constant, not variable, for mankind. Inheritance is one such source, and a likely one; but other constants that all human beings experience in their interactions with their environment may possibly be the source of universal facial expressions. We (Ekman, 1972) have outlined four alternative explanations that could account for universal facial expressions and for an unvarying association between a particular emotion and a particular facial configuration. One of these explanations emphasizes species-constant learning experiences; the others consider different inherited mechanisms. We believe that some universal facial expressions may be best accounted for by one

---

[4]All of the page references for our quotations from Darwin's *The Expression of the Emotions in Man and Animals* are from the 1965 University of Chicago Press edition.

[5]Argument continues about the usefulness of the terms "innate" and "instinctive." Lehrman (1953) and Beach (1955) provide two strong attacks on such terminology, while Lorenz (1965) provides a strong defense.

explanation, and other facial expressions by the other explanations. We do not believe, however, that there is yet definitive evidence to allow a choice among explanations as to the origin of facial expressions. We need more research on the very early stages of life, to examine not only the smile or fear of stranger response, but the variety of facial expressions that have been studied in the adult. Such research should examine facial expressions in the neonate and infant in more than one culture, and among the blind as well as the sighted. Research on brain stimulation and brain lesions and facial expression would also be relevant to understanding the origin of facial expressions.

Definitive data are now available on the question of universality, and that is the issue and evidence with which we shall be concerned. Let us turn now to examine Darwin's method for studying facial expressions across cultures.

Darwin sent a list of 16 questions about facial expressions to people working in other countries. Here are two of the 16 questions:

> (1) Is astonishment expressed by the eyes and mouth being opened wide, and by the eyebrows being raised? (2) When in low spirits, are the corners of the mouth depressed, and the inner corner of the eyebrows raised by that muscle which the French call the "grief muscle"? The eyebrows in this state become slightly oblique, with a little swelling at the inner end; and the forehead is transversely wrinkled in the middle part, but not across the whole breadth, as when the eyebrows are raised in surprise [1965 p.15].

Darwin received answers from 36 different observers, some of whom, he noted, worked with isolated peoples. Darwin placed more confidence in replies that described both the circumstances in which the expression occurred and the expression itself. Here is an example of one of the better descriptions:

> Mr. J. Scott, of the Botanic Gardens, Calcutta has obligingly sent me a full description . . . He observed during some time, himself unseen, a very young Dhangar woman from Nagpore, the wife of one of the gardeners, nursing her baby who was at the point of death; and he distinctly saw the eyebrows raised at the inner corners, the eyelids drooping, the forehead wrinkled in the middle, the mouth slightly open, with the corners much depressed. He then came from behind a screen of plants and spoke to the poor woman, who started, burst into a bitter flood of tears, and besought him to cure her baby [1965, pp.185–186].

By current scientific standards, and even by those of Darwin's day, even such full descriptions can only be considered suggestive, since they are vulnerable to error in perception and bias in interpretation. Such observations cannot be the only evidence to resolve a controversial question. For those who doubt the universality of facial expression (and they would be many, if not most, behavioral scientists in the past four or five decades), the observations of Mr. Scott of the Botanic Gardens in Caluctta and those of all of Darwin's other sources are open to the charge of bias. All of them knew from the questions he sent them what facial muscular pattern Darwin thought was associated with each emotion. Mr. Scott may have seen the "grief muscle" so clearly in the Dhangar woman because he knew that that was what he might expect to see—what Darwin thought he would see.

Darwin's own descriptions of the difficulties in observing facial expression could be marshalled by those who doubt the universality of facial expression to discount his cross-cultural evidence completely. They could say that the expressions are hard to see: "The study of expression is difficult, owing to the movements being often extremely slight, and of a fleeting nature [Darwin, 1965, p.12]." Or, that the observer's own immediate emotional reaction may obscure his impression: "When we witness any deep emotion, our sympathy is so strongly excited, that close observation is forgotten or rendered almost impossible [Darwin, 1965, p.12]." Finally, the observer must be blind to what the hypothesis is, for if he knew what facial expressions were expected, he might imagine it: "Our imagination is another and still more serious source of error; for if from the nature of the circumstances we expect to see any expression, we readily imagine its presence [Darwin, 1965, pp.12–13]."

The problems raised by Darwin could be partially resolved by having multiple observers who do not know the hypothesis under study. If, for example, more than one observer has witnessed and described in the same terms the reactions of the Dhangar woman from Nagpore, there would be more reason to have confidence that the report was not the product of the emotional reactions or idiosyncrasies of one observer. Having more than one observer does not, however, guard against the other type of error mentioned by Darwin—the observer's imagination. If many observers had witnessed the Dhangar woman, but if, like Mr. J. Scott, all had known Darwin's hypothesis about the facial muscular movements universally associated with grief, we might well suspect all of their reports.

It is difficult for an observer in the situation not to know the hypothesis under study, just as it is difficult to arrange for many observers from one culture to hang around together, scientifically loitering in another culture so that they might jointly witness a facial expression. The use of motion picture film and photographs, a technique unavailable, of course, to Darwin, does help to solve these problems. A single observer can film the event. The filmed facial expression can then be shown to multiple observers without information about what it is supposed to depict, and without information about what transpired immediately before or after the filmed facial expression. The use of film or videotape also allows slow motion and repeated viewing to catch the fleeting expressions mentioned by Darwin.

We shall shortly see that Darwin's current chief antagonists on the issue of universality—Klineberg, LaBarre, and to some extent Birdwhistell—used the same highly suspect, casual methods of obtaining evidence as did Darwin. In fact, until very recently there has been no incontrovertible evidence, free of bias, to settle the question of universality.

It is amazing that Darwin was so uncritical in his acceptance of the rough observations from his sources in different cultures, since he had an alternative method. He himself was the first to apply this method to the study of facial expression, and it was free of many of the charges of bias that could be levelled against his cross-cultural sources. Darwin was the first to conduct what is now called a judgment study of the face, in which observers are shown photographs (or films) of facial expressions, are not told what emotion the investigator thinks the face shows, and are asked to supply their own interpretation. Darwin found that observers in England did agree in their interpretation of the emotion shown in particular facial photographs. He *could* have supplied such photographs to his contacts in other countries, not telling them what emotion he thought was shown in each photograph, but asking them to obtain interpretations of the pictures from natives within their country. If the people from these different countries all interpreted the same facial photographs as showing the same emotion, that would be strong and unbiased evidence of universality. This very method, the judgment study of the face, which Darwin first used in England and could have but did not use cross culturally, is the method employed in all but one of the experiments that have finally settled the issue of universality of facial expression.

THEORISTS OF THE
CULTURE-SPECIFIC VIEW

In the last 30 years, three behavioral scientists—Klineberg, LaBarre, and Birdwhistell—have directly challenged Darwin's view of facial expressions of emotion. They have been extremely influential, asserting that the existence of universal facial expressions is dubious or disproved. The popularity of their view and the ready rejection of Darwin has not been due to their providing irrefutable evidence, for their evidence is tentative at best and subject to the same types of error as was Darwin's. The ready acceptance of their view has more probably been due to its congeniality with other theories in vogue in psychology and anthropology. At a time when much of psychology emphasized learning as the only important influence on man's behavior, behaviorists would have found Darwin's emphasis on innate, unlearned determinants repugnant, and Klineberg's assertion that emotional expressions are also the product of learning more satisfactory. Similarly, LaBarre and Birdwhistell's claims that facial expressions of emotion differ in each culture was harmonious with the emphasis on cultural relativism in anthropology. There might be reason to worry that again the popularity of certain ideas in science has changed our view of Darwin—for now bio-psychology, behavior genetics, and ethology all make universality and innate determinants more respectable in at least some scientific circles—if it were not that now, as we shall see later in this chapter, there is conclusive scientific evidence to resolve the question of universality.

Klineberg and the Issue of Display Rules

Klineberg (1938) examined descriptions of facial expressions of emotion in Chinese literature and found both similarities and differences with Western facial expression. The fear expression, crying, and laughter seemed similar, but some accounts of the facial expressions for anger and surprise seemed quite unrecognizable to the Western eye. In his social psychology textbook (1940), Klineberg gave two types of evidence for his "tentative conclusion that the weight of evidence is . . . in favor . . . of the hypothesis of cultural or social determination of emotional expression [p.180]."[6] The first type of evidence was the report of observers in other cultures. For example, he quoted from a report by Williams (1930) of a festive ceremony among the Melanesian Orokaiva:

> The guests, arriving in their several parties, come riding single file into the village, each party headed by its man of first importance, befeathered club on shoulder. No smile adorns his face, but rather an expression of fierceness, which however unsuited it may seem to the hospitable occasion, is nevertheless Orokaivan good form [Williams, 1930, p.29; Klineberg, 1940, p.194].

Klineberg then comments:

> Not only may joy be expressed without a smile, but in addition the smile may be used in a variety of situations in a manner quite different from what appears to be its original significance. Even in our own society, we know that a smile may mean contempt, incredulity, affection, and serve also as part of a purely social greeting devoid of emotional significance . . . [quoting from Lafcadio Hearn's observations of the Japanese]. "Samurai women were required, like the women of Sparta, to show signs of joy on hearing that their husbands or sons had fallen in battle; to betray any natural feeling under the circumstances was a grave breach of decorum [Hearn, 1904, p.193; Klineberg, 1940, pp.194–195]."

[6]This, and other quotations on the following pages are taken from O. Klineberg. *Social Psychology*. New York: Holt, 1940. Used with permission of the Publisher.

The reliability of these observations, their accuracy, and their generality are all questionable, since Klineberg, like Darwin, accepted the informal report of single observers in the cultures he discusses. But let us suppose that these are accurate descriptions of what typically occurs: Do they refute the notion of universality of facial expressions of emotion? The Orokaiva men with the fierce look on their faces would be damaging evidence if we assume that festive occasions must evoke happiness or joy in every culture. Klineberg himself (1940) noted that "there are obvious differences between communities as to the situations which give rise to the various emotions [p.168]." More recently, our "neurocultural theory" of facial expression (Ekman, 1972) has sought to reconcile the views of Klineberg, LaBarre, and Birdwhistell with those of Darwin by acknowledging that the events which elicit an emotion will usually vary from culture to culture. Even though what calls forth a given emotion may differ across cultures, the facial expression for the emotion will be the same, with one further proviso.

Display Rules

Cultures can also differ in what we (1967, 1969b) have called *display rules,* norms regarding the expected management of facial appearance. This source of cultural difference can be illustrated with Klineberg's own material. Let us suppose that Williams had some reason to know that for the Orokaiva, this festive occasion was an elicitor for feelings of happiness and joy when the head man first arrived. Then would the fierce look and lack of a smile refute Darwin's claim of universality in facial expression? It would only if the further assumption were made that facial expressions are an involuntary system, not capable of being controlled, and that cultures do not prescribe the need to mask one facial expression with another. For the fierce look could be the result of a culturally required display rule for that occasion to mask any happy expression, and, if that were the case and we grant that it is possible for man to control his facial appearance, there would be no contradiction to the idea that expressions are universal. We would, however, need to add that the same facial expression will be seen across cultures only if (a) the same emotion has been elicited and in neither culture is the person interfering with or masking the expression, or (b) in both cultures the persons are simulating the same emotion, or are masking their feelings with the same emotional expression.

Klineberg himself, in his reference to Samurai women above, admitted that just such control is possible, and that cultures differ in the particular display rules they teach about controlling emotional expression. In commenting on Chinese expressions of grief, he wrote (1938) "there is an elaborate set of rules and regulations which insure that it [grief] shall be properly expressed [p.517]." And, in commenting on the Samurai women's smiles in grief, Klineberg (1940) wrote, "the smile obviously does not stand for sorrow, even though the occasions may be unhappy ones. It is rather that the sorrow may not be expressed, and that an appearance of joy must be maintained [p.195]." Thus Klineberg assumed that facial expressions of emotion can be managed and controlled, and that cultures have what we have since called display rules regarding what one should show on one's face. The fact that the mask of a smile is used to give the appearance of joy is actually evidence of universality, in that the smiling facial appearance is for this culture not a sign of anger or fear but used to simulate a joyful state. It might well be for the Orokaiva, as well, that the fierce look is a culturally determined mask.

These criticisms of Klineberg's examples, and the necessity to distinguish the question of whether the elicitors of emotion and the display rules for controlling facial expression differ cross-culturally from the question of whether the actual facial appearance for each emotion is universal will be equally applicable to our discussion of LaBarre and Birdwhistell.

The major evidence which convinced Klineberg that culture is the primary determinant of facial expression, however, was taken from a study by Foley (1935) on the ability of human beings to interpret correctly the facial expressions of a chimpanzee. Klineberg (1940) reasoned that

If expression is largely biological and innately determined, we should expect considerable similarity between these two closely related species. If on the other hand culture is largely responsible for expression we should expect marked differences since the anthropoids are presumably exposed to a culture only of the most rudimentary sort [p.179].

Klineberg described a study in which Foley used six photographs of a 5-year-old male chimpanzee, Ioni, taken by Mrs. Ladigin-Kohts of the Museum Darwinianum in Moscow. Mrs. Ladigin-Kohts thought these photographs depicted Ioni's expressions of quietude, sadness, joy, weeping, anger, and excitement. Foley showed the six photographs to 127 undergraduates at Columbia University and asked them to choose from among 16 emotions to describe Ioni's feelings. Foley concluded that the college students could not accurately interpret the chimp's facial expression because their judgments of Ioni's feelings did not coincide with how Mrs. Ladigin-Kohts thought Ioni felt when each of the pictures was taken. Klineberg (1940) accepted Foley's interpretation of his data:

. . . the great difficulty experienced by untrained human observers in recognizing the emotions of chimpanzees from their facial expressions strengthens the hypothesis of cultural or social determination of the expressions of the emotions in man. Emotional expression is analogous to language in that it functions as a means of communication, and that it must be learned, at least in part [p.200].

It is important to scrutinize Foley's experiment carefully, at least for historical reasons, since it affected Klineberg's views, and Klineberg's disagreement with Darwin was so influential in the debate over universality during the following 25 years. The first basis for challenging Foley's experiment is its very logic. Although evolutionary theory assumes that man and chimp have common ancestors, man is not a direct lineal descendant of the chimp. There is no reason to assume, as did Foley and Klineberg, that the chimp's expressions must be sufficiently similar to man's for man to recognize chimpanzee facial expression. In other words, the facial expressions of chimp and man could be dissimilar in many respects without disproving a common evolutionary basis for their facial expressions. Even if we disregard this assumption, there are other reasons for challenging Foley's results.

Foley's data would have little meaning if the six photographs of Ioni did not acutally represent the chimpanzee emotions which Mrs. Ladigin-Kohts thought they did. Were those photographs accurate depictions of the emotions ascribed to them by Foley? Not all of them. We gave the six photographs of Ioni to Suzanne Chevalier-Skolnikoff (the author of Chapter 2), and asked her to evaluate whether they actually showed the emotions claimed by Mrs. Ladigin-Kohts and Foley. In Chevalier-Skolnikoff's judgment, based upon Van Lawick-Goodall's (1968) report of expressive moments in chimpanzees, two of the six pictures actually are not good representations of the emotions they were thought to be. The one supposed to show sadness is actually more neutral than sad, and the one supposed to show anger could be joy (and half of the college students judged it as joy, which Foley considered inaccurate). If we consider only the four pictures that were good representations of the emotions Foley thought they signified, on three of them the college students did choose the corrrect emotion more often than would be expected by chance. If the observers were operating solely by chance when allowed to choose among 16 emotions, and getting no information from the photograph, only one out of 16 would choose the correct emotion—that is, 6%. In actuality, a much larger percentage of the college students identified the correct emotion on three of the pictures. Few were accurate in judging pictures of excitement, which the majority called *interest*. [In his theory of emotion, Tomkins (1962) considering excitement to be an extreme version of interest, and thus according to his theory these judgments would also be accurate.] For reasons not explained by Foley nor commented on by Klineberg, Foley failed to apply any statistical tests to determine whether his college students were accurate; that is, whether they gave the presumably correct answer more often than might be expected by uninformed guessing. When we applied a binomial statistical test, it appeared quite unlikely that Foley's college students operated on strictly a chance basis: Only once in 100 times would they have achieved that number of correct judgments if chance alone had guided their decisions.

The results, then, of Foley's experiment are as follows: With two pictures, the observers did no better than chance; one of these was an "excitement" photograph, which the majority of the observers called "interest," and the other was, in Chevalier-Skolnikoff's judgment, a neutral facial expression. For the remaining four pictures, more observers chose the correct emotion than could be expected by chance. Thus Foley's experiment shows just the opposite of what he thought it did; that human observers can accurately judge at least some chimpanzee facial expressions.

To summarize, Klineberg was the first behavioral scientist to challenge Darwin's claim that facial expressions are universal for man. His view that learning is the major determinant and that expressions vary from culture to culture was based in part on the same type of anecdotal evidence that Darwin himself had used, and we have shown how those anecdotes could be interpreted differently to support the opposite position—that facial expressions are universal. What was decisive for Klineberg was Foley's study of human judgments of a chimpanzee's facial expression, the one item of apparently "hard" or quantitative data. Examination of Foley's photographs of the chimp in light of current, more thorough information about chimpanzee facial expression and reanalysis of Foley's own data revealed that his experiment proves just the opposite of what he and Klineberg had concluded. If Klineberg had known these facts, we expect he would not have challenged Darwin, and perhaps the attitudes of subsequent scientists might have been different. However, the "zeitgeist" of the times favored the position forwarded by Klineberg: Learning and cultural relativism were more popular ideas than innate determinants and universals.

LaBarre and the Issue of Emblems

Nine years after Klineberg's initial challenge to Darwin's theory of emotional expression, LaBarre (1947) published his article on "The Cultural Basis of Emotions and Culture." An anthropologist, LaBarre cited examples from the reports of other anthropologists as well as from his own experience to document the claim in the title of his article. LaBarre's evidence, like that of Darwin and Klineberg, is vulnerable to bias or error, since it relies upon a single observer within a culture witnessing a presumably culture-specific facial expression. Even granting the accuracy of the observations he cites, they are not very damaging to a theory of universality of facial expression of emotion. LaBarre quotes from Gorer's (1935) account of Africans:

> . . . laughter is used by the Negro to express surprise, wonder, embarrassment and
> even discomforture; it is not necessarily or even often a sign of amusement; the
> significance of "black laughter" is due to a mistake of supposing that similar symbols
> have identical meanings [Gorer, 1935, p.10; LaBarre, 1947, p.52].

LaBarre then comments:

> Thus it is that even if the physiological behavior be present, its cultural and emotional
> functions may differ. Indeed, even within the same culture, the laughter of adolescent
> girls and the laughter of corporation presidents can be functionally different things;
> so too the laughter of an American Negro and that of the white he addresses [1947,
> p.52].[7]

For the African example to be proof that laughter does not universally
have something to do with pleasure or amusement, Gorer and LaBarre
must introduce evidence to eliminate two possibilities: (a) They must show
that there is nothing amusing or pleasing in the unnamed situations in which
the African experiences surprise, wonder, embarrassment, or discomforture;
certainly, in our own culture surprising events can also be pleasurable,
or we can be pleased about being surprised, or amused at our embarrassment,
etc., and (b) they must show that a look of amusement is not used to cover
or compensate for the embarrassment or discomforture of the African. In
our culture people may laugh or smile when embarrassed, either to hide
the embarrassment or to comment to others that they are amused with
themselves for being embarrassed. No such data were obtained.

LaBarre's assertion, without explication, that laughter differs in its
"function" for a corporation president and an adolescent girl may be correct,
but has no bearing on the claim of universal facial expressions of emotion.
Clearly, the social occasions when laughter is permissible by either may
differ, as may the elicitors for laughter. But to challenge universality, LaBarre
must prove that laughter occurs when there is no element of pleasure or
amusement and no attempt to appear as if one were pleased or amused.
He offers no such proof.

Emblems, Expressions, and Simulations

Few of LaBarre's examples are actually related to facial expression. Instead,
most are of bodily gestures. The failure to distinguish between gesture and
facial expression of emotion can be seen in his statement, "there is no
'natural' language of emotional gesture [1947, p.55]." Darwin may be

---

[7]From Weston LaBarre, The cultural basis of emotion and gesture. *Journal of Personality,*
1947, **16**, 49–68. Reprinted by permission of the Publisher. Copyright 1947, Duke University
Press, Durham, North Carolina.

partly responsible for confusing the two, since he was interested in showing not only that facial expressions of emotion are universal, but also that some gestures are universal. Darwin claimed such a status for the shoulder-shrug, but considered that the head-nods for "yes" and "no" and the fist-clench as a sign of aggressive intent were not universal.

The distinction between gesture and emotional expression is not an easy one, however, and in some instances the two are one and the same. Let us describe how we (Ekman & Friesen, 1969b) have distinguished them, because there are differences. LaBarre was really writing about gesture, not emotional expression, and in that sense does not contradict Darwin, who was more concerned with emotional expression. In our research, we do not use the word "gesture," but instead describe three different types of nonverbal behavior that have often been subsumed by the word gesture. *Illustrators* are movements that are tied to the speech pattern, illustrating what is being said. We distinguish among eight types of illustrators: For example, "batons" emphasize a word or phrase; "pictographs" draw a picture of what is being verbalized. *Regulators* are acts that maintain the back-and-forth rhythm of conversation. They tell the speaker to continue, repeat, elaborate, hurry up, become more interesting, stop, etc. While illustrators are interlaced with the moment-to-moment fluctuations in speech, regulators are related to the conversational flow, the pacing of the exchange. *Emblems* are those nonverbal acts which have a direct verbal translation, a dictionary definition usually consisting of a word or two or perhaps a phrase, which is known to all members of a culture or subculture. The key to detecting an emblem is whether it could replace a word or two without changing the information conveyed.

Since LaBarre was primarily concerned with what we call emblems, let us contrast emblems with emotional expressions. They differ, in some degree, in three ways—body area involved, messages, and usage. Emblems can involve any part of the body, but most involve the hands. Emotional expressions are considered by most theorists and investigators to be limited to the facial musculature, if by emotional expression we mean a patterned appearance that is distinctive for a particular momentary feeling. Many enduring feelings, or what might better be called attitudes, are seen in the body as well as the face. The body also shows the ways a person is coping with an emotion but such body movements are usually not unique to one emotion. While there may be patterns of body movement or specific body acts that are unique to a more global emotional description, such as "unhappy" or "upset," we do not believe there are unique body movements for specific emotional feelings, such as anger, fear, disgust, etc. The one exception may be the body movement which is part of the startle response.

While we suggest that the face is the chief, if not the only site for muscular movements that are unique to one or another specific emotion, we do not mean that the face shows only emotional expressions. Quite the contrary. The face is the site for *illustrators* (e.g., the brow movement as an accent mark), for *regulators* (primarily with glancing) and also for *emblems*, such as winks and tongue shows.

Any message can be conveyed by an emblem, including factual information, commands, attitudes, and—here is a complication—feelings. The message conveyed by an emotional expression is, by definition, a feeling of the moment. We agree with Tomkins (1962) that the number of feelings which have a distinctive facial appearance is probably small. Other feelings are expressed as blends of these primary feelings (e.g., the expression of smugness is a blend of the expressions of anger and happiness) or have no distinguishing facial appearance. This, however, is conjecture, not yet confirmed as fact. While there is good evidence of a distinctive facial appearance for each of seven or eight emotions, it is really not yet known whether there might be more. Similarly, the notion that blends are composed of the distinctive appearances for the primary emotions has yet to be substantiated.

The occasions for using emblems differ in major ways from those of emotional expressions. Emblems do not occur when an individual is not part of a social interaction unless he is rather crazy, because emblems are used only to send a message to another person. Emotional expressions may occur when an individual is completely alone, as, for example, while watching television. For the same reason, emblems will not occur but emotional expressions may when a person is with another but not engaged in any attempt to communicate. Although not intended to convey a message under those circumstances, they would convey information about how the person feels if they were seen. Emblems are often used when people cannot use words (because of distances, or noise, or need for silence, etc.), but they occur in conjunction with speech as well. Emotional expressions are, in some social situations, reduced in the presence of another person by the operation of display rules, but they are shown also during speech. People usually are cognizant of their emblems; they know when they are using them. A person may be quite unaware of an emotional expression until someone calls it to his attention. Yet, as with emblems, emotion expressions are subject to voluntary control; they can be stopped or masked.

Probably the greatest source of confusion between emblems and emotional expressions is that some emotional expressions may be modified and transformed into emblems. How, then, do we distinguish between an emotional expression and an emblematic expression? We need to consider both the appearance and usage of each, and we must also define a middle ground between the emblematic and emotional expression—the simulated expression. A simulated expression is a voluntary attempt to appear as if an emotion is being experienced. If it is well done, then most people who see it will be misled and think they are seeing an emotional expression, not a simulation. A simulation is used either to conceal the fact that no emotion is felt or as a mask to cover one feeling with the appearance of another.

An emblematic expression[8] resembles an actual emotional expression, but it differs sufficiently in appearance to make it evident to the beholder that the person does not feel that emotion at this moment; he is just mentioning it. The transformation of an emotional expression into an emblematic expression involves appearance changes in both muscular excursion and time duration. The emblem may be shorter or longer than the usual expression of the particular emotion in question, and it is usually stylized, showing either less muscular excursion or more than is usually seen in the emotional expression. To summarize, a simulated expression is enacted when a person wants to mislead another as to his feeling, and if performed skillfully is very similar to the expression of a felt emotion, while the emblematic expression is a stylized version of the expression, which is used to state or mention an emotion but to convey the impression that it is not being experienced at the moment. The emblematic expression is noticeably different in appearance from both the actual emotional expression and the simulation.

While any emotion can be simulated, we believe that not all emotions reach facial emblematic usage in any one culture, although it is conceivable that in some cultures all the emotions are also emblematic facial expressions. It is our impression, not yet systematically verified, that in the United States the emblematic facial expressions are the lower facial movements, associated with the emotional expression for happiness (smile), disgust (raised upper lip with or without raised lower lip), surprise (dropped open jaw, or, but not with, raised brows and open eyelids), and fear (stretched-back lips); and the wrinkled nose for disgust. In each case the emblematic version of the emotion is built out of the muscular movements that form the expression of that emotion, but it is performed in a way that distinguishes it from the expression. We have begun studies to try to document these claims, to show, for example, how the emblematic smile differs from the smile that is part of an emotional expression and, if possible, to discriminate the felt smile from the simulated smile, although that later distinction will be much more difficult, if our theory is correct.

To clarify the distinction between an emblem and an emotional expression, let us compare a facial emblem that is not an emblematic expression—the

---

[8]An emblematic expression of emotion need not be limited to the face (e.g., the fist for anger), but it is only the facial ones that concern us here, since it is only the emblematic facial expressions that can be confused with emotional expressions.

wink—with an emotional expression, a version of anger entailing the lowering and drawing together of the brows, tightening and raising the lower eyelids, and pressing lip against lip.[9] Winks do not signify any one emotion, but are used either in flirtation, or in acknowledgment, public or collusive, of a shared experience. People will not wink when alone; if they do so, it is a tic, not a wink. The anger facial expression on the other hand may be shown by the sole individual who feels angry about a memory, a TV program he is watching, etc. Prematron, middle-class women in the United States are more likely to manifest the anger facial expression when alone than when in the presence of others. Yet we should remember that most people know how to look as if they are angry and may try to do so (simulated expression) if the social occasion calls for it (e.g., scolding a young child for a wrongful but amusing act). We believe that the anger facial expression has not been transformed into an emblematic facial expression in the United States. While a person who winks knows what he does, a person who feels angry may not be aware of showing the anger face until the muscular movement becomes extreme, or until someone draws it to his attention.

We (Ekman & Friesen, 1969b) have hypothesized that all emblems are socially learned and most are culture specific. We have found a few that are multicultural in that the emblem has the same meaning in every culture where it is shown. The smile *may* be a pan-cultural emblem; at least it is multicultural. In addition to multicultural emblems derived from universal facial expressions of emotion, there may also be multicultural emblems in which the message conveyed by the emblem involves a human activity, which, because of our anatomy, must be performed in fundamentally similar ways. An example is the emblem for having had too much food. Our anatomy is such that food goes into the stomach and we do experience some sensations there if we have overeaten. If a culture has an emblem for being overfed, it is likely to involve the hands doing something to the stomach area, not to the knees or shoulders. These multicultural emblems are relatively few in number; for the most part emblems are culture specific.

The reason for elaborating here the distinction between emblem and emotional expression is that both Darwin and LaBarre failed consistently to do so. If they had, there possibly would have been less disagreement between them. Darwin was primarily concerned with emotional expressions, which he considered innately determined and thereby universal. While he mentioned a few emblems that he considered multicultural in our terms, he acknowledged that most were culture specific. LaBarre wrote almost exclusively about emblems, giving examples of different emblems in different

---

[9]This is only one of the muscular patterns unique to anger; we have accumulated some evidence that there is more than one muscular pattern of the face for each of the primary emotions (Ekman, Friesen, & Tomkins, 1971).

cultures in agreement with Darwin. If the reader does not accept the distinction between emblems and emotional expressions outlined here, the disagreement between Darwin and LaBarre can be resolved on a much simpler level: Darwin was concerned primarily with the face, LaBarre primarily with the body, and thus they were not examining the same phenomena. Let us consider now the third and last writer, who disagreed with Darwin in a more pointed and profound way.

Birdwhistell

The current leading advocate of the culture-specific view of facial expression is another anthropologist, Ray Birdwhistell. With a background in linguistics and in dance notation, Birdwhistell has attempted to prove that body movement and facial expression, what he calls *kinesics,* can best be viewed as another language, with the same types of units and organization as spoken language. Darwin's theory that emotional expressions are universal is, of course, incompatible with Birdwhistell's notion; spoken language has no universal signs. On just this point Birdwhistell (1970) writes:

> Insofar as I have been able to determine, just as there are no universal words, no sound complexes, which carry the same meaning the world over, there are no body motions, facial expressions or gestures which provoke *identical* responses the world over [p. 34].[10]

Birdwhistell claims that at first he was influenced by Darwin, but found out that Darwin was wrong.

> Early in my research on human body motion, influenced by Darwin's *The Expression of the Emotions in Man and Animals,* and by my own preoccupation with human universals, I attempted to study the human smile . . . Not only did I find that a number of my subjects "smiled" when they were subjected to what seemed to be a positive environment but some "smiled" in an aversive one. . . . It became evident that there was little constancy to the phenomenon . . . [pp. 29–30].[10]

Unfortunately, Birdwhistell did not provide information about the nature of the aversive situation in which his subjects smiled, who his subjects were, how many smiled, how often, etc., and it is difficult to evaluate his claim. Earlier, in discussing Klineberg and the example of the Orokaiva man who looked fierce when entering a supposedly festive occasion, we introduced the notion of *display rules,* socially dictated obligations which call for the management of facial appearance. Display rules may call for one facial expression to be used to cover or comment on another facial expression. It would be quite damaging to the claim of universal facial

[10]From R. L. Birdwhistell, *Kinesics and Context.* Philadelphia: University of Pennsylvania Press, 1970. Reproduced by permission of the Publisher.

expressions of emotion if there were clear evidence that, when people are in an aversive situation, experiencing pain or fear, etc., they smile to express those negative emotional experiences. Such evidence would require data to rule out the other plausible explanations for the smile: That the subject believes it is not acceptable or allowable to show negative feelings (unmanly) and covers with the simulated smile; or the smile is not a mask but is added as an emblematic comment on the negative feelings being experienced, stating to others present and to the smiler himself that it doesn't hurt that much, it's not as bad as he thought, he can manage to "grin and bear it," etc. It is a tribute to the importance of these social uses of the smile that all three authors who have claimed facial expression of emotion to be culture specific—Klineberg, LaBarre, and Birdwhistell—have emphasized smiling in the examples they cite to buttress their claim.

Birdwhistell did not consider that these social uses of the smile could answer his doubts about Darwin. He apparently has proven to his own satisfaction that smiles can signify negative feelings as well as positive ones. Again, reviewing his own development, Birdwhistell (1963) states his position:

> When I first became interested in studying body motion I was confident that it would be possible to isolate a series of expressions, postures, and movements that were denotative of primary emotional states . . . As research proceeded, and even before the development of kinesics, it became clear that this search for universals was culture bound. . . . There are probably no universal symbols of emotional state. . . . We can expect them [emotional expressions] to be learned and patterned according to the particular structures of particular societies [p.126].

Although writing many years after Klineberg and some time after LaBarre, Birdwhistell provides less evidence for his view than do they. One can only regard Birdwhistell's conclusion as the account of a person who has spent much time looking at body movement and facial expression, but who is the captive of his own linguistic model, which requires that he view nonverbal behavior as culture specific. He provides no systematic evidence to challenge Darwin, and even though we argued that Darwin's own data on universals were subject to error and bias and must be viewed as tentative or suggestive, at least Darwin attempted to document his views rather than simply assert them.[11]

Summary

The dispute over the existence of universals has not been solidly backed by firm scientific evidence on either side. Darwin's theory that emotional

[11]The reader interested in an extinsive critical evaluation of Birdwhistell's viewpoint, bringing to bear the relevant evidence of other investigators, should see Dittmann's (1971) recent review of Birdwhistell's book.

expressions are universal was a consistent outgrowth of his theory of man's evolution. Darwin's evidence was weak; the reports of those he wrote to in the field to ask if particular facial appearances signified particular emotions in their culture were open to error and vulnerable to bias, since Darwin had told these people what he hoped they would see.

Klineberg's emphasis on the learned basis of facial expressions was harmonious with psychology's almost exclusive interest in learning as the determinant of behavior. Almost all of Klineberg's evidence was anecdotal, subject to errors in reporting and open to bias. Evidence from the one systematic study, his one piece of more solid evidence—Foley's experiment on whether human subjects can accurately judge chimpanzee facial expressions—was found in our analysis to have suggested just the opposite of what Foley and Klineberg thought it proved.

LaBarre also relied on informal or anecdotal reports and failed to distinguish between facial expressions of emotion and gesture, with most of his examples relevant to the latter. Birdwhistell never revealed his data, whether from experiments, quantified observations, or anecdotal or informal impressions. Like Klineberg and LaBarre, he failed to consider that the differences he presumed across cultures in facial expressions of emotion might be due either to differences in *elicitors* of emotion or to differences in *display rules*. To note that people look sad at a funeral in our culture and happy in another culture does not prove that facial expression is culture specific. The funeral might not elicit sadness in both cultures. Or, the funeral might elicit sadness in both cultures, but there might be different display rules. The fact that in one culture people at a funeral look sad while in another they look happy might be because in one culture there is no cultural constraint on expressing or showing sadness, while in the other culture there is a display rule to mask sadness with a happy look.

The reader may well wonder at this point, with all these possibilities, how anyone could do research to settle the matter, to prove conclusively that all facial expressions of emotion are culture specific or that there are at least some which are universal. We shall explore this methodological question before examining the research that has settled this issue.

HOW TO STUDY FACIAL EXPRESSION
ACROSS CULTURES

Two quite different research approaches have been used to study the question of whether there are universal facial expressions of emotion. The first method entails systematically sampling, on film or videotape, facial behavior shown in a particular situation by people in two or more cultures, and then measuring in some fashion the facial muscular movements shown by the people in each culture to determine whether they are similar or different. We shall call this method the *components approach,* since it studies whether the actual components of facial expressions shown in two or more cultures are the same or different. The second method entails showing examples of facial expression to people in different cultures and determining whether they interpret a facial expression as signifying the same or a different emotion. This method (which we will call the *judgment approach,* since it studies whether people from different cultures will judge the same emotion when viewing the same facial appearance), was first used by Darwin, as we noted earlier, but not in his cross-cultural studies.

The components approach has been less popular than the judgment approach. There has been only one cross-cultural study using the components approach (Ekman, 1972). Although we will not discuss it until the very end of our review of the research evidence, we will now mention some of the difficulties encountered in the components approach so that the reader can understand why investigators have often avoided this methodology and instead have chosen the judgment approach.

There are four problems in a components approach experiment. First, the investigator must have some way to be sure that he has chosen a situation that not only arouses emotion in each culture, but elicits the same emotion in both cultures, for otherwise differences in facial expression might simply be due to differences in the emotion elicited. Earlier, in considering Klineberg, LaBarre, and Birdwhistell, we found that simply comparing the same eliciting event in two cultures is not itself a guarantee that the same emotion is elicited in both. Second, the investigator must be sure that the situation he has chosen does not involve the use of different display rules in the two cultures; preferably, it is a situation for which there is no rule in either culture about inhibiting or masking the facial appearance of an emotion. Otherwise, as discussed earlier, evidence of differences in facial expression might simply be due to differences in the attempts to conceal or cover an emotion, which does not bear upon whether the actual expression, when not covered or concealed, is universal or culture specific.

The third and fourth problems, new to our discussion, are the problem of recording and the problem of measuring facial expressions. The problem of recording facial expressions is threefold: the costs of film or videotape, the need to take the record unobtrusively so that the subject is not made self-conscious, and the determination of how much of the facial behavior to record. Measurement is probably the most difficult problem, as the face is a complicated expressive system, quickly changing into various appearances. Until quite recently there has been little agreement about how to measure facial expression, and the investigator has had to invent his own measurement scheme.

The judgment approach avoids the problem of measuring facial behavior. In the judgment approach, where faces are shown to observers in different cultures for their judgment, the measurement taken is of the observers' interpretation of the face, and no measurement of the actual movement of the face itself need be made. Avoiding the myriad problems of measuring facial behavior is gained at the cost of assuming a new set of problems—what should the observers be asked to say? Should they be allowed to use any word of their own choice? If so, how does the investigator solve the later problem of deciding which words are synonyms and which carry a sufficiently different meaning to represent a new category of emotion? Or should some way of describing emotion be provided? If so, what words should the investigator give; how does he know all of the words relevant to describing facial expressions of emotion, and how can he be certain that the words have the same meaning when translated into the languages of the different cultures? In all of the experiments using the judgment approach, the observers in each culture have been given some set of emotion words to use in describing facial expressions, and an attempt has been made to verify through back translation[12] that the words mean the same thing across the cultures. This becomes an especially crucial question when people who have no written language are studied, and the investigator has little or poor understanding of the people's spoken language. As we shall see, a somewhat different way of describing emotion has been used in studies of such preliterate peoples.

The problems involved in recording facial behavior—what to record, how much, and how to do it unobtrusively—have been side-stepped in most judgment studies, since rather than having people judge spontaneous facial behavior, almost all investigators have chosen to use still photographs of posed facial expression. With poses, the camera need not be hidden: The photographer simply snaps the camera shutter when the poser is ready with each expression. Judgment studies could, of course, be done with spontaneous facial behavior, and a few have been, but then some solution must be found for the usual problems involved in recording facial behavior.

The use of posed facial expressions in the judgment approach raises two questions. First, are poses the same as spontaneous facial expressions—are they at least sufficiently similar to answer the question of whether a facial expression of emotion is culture specific or universal? We shall see when discussing these experiments that the logic of these findings suggests a satis-

---

[12] A back-translation involves three steps. A word, let us say in English, is translated by translator A into another language, let us say Spanish, and then the word now in Spanish is given to another translator, B, who is asked to translate it into English. If the translation back into English yields the same word one started with, then the translation performed by A was satisfactory.

factory answer to this question. Second, does the investigator actually have good poses—do the facial expressions show the intended emotions? This parallels the problems faced by the investigator who, using the components approach, must worry about whether the situation elicits the intended emotion and whether the persons will be trying to conceal their feelings.

Most investigators using the judgment approach to study facial expression within a culture, and some of those who have done cross-cultural work, have viewed posing in too simple a light. They have assumed that if you ask someone to pose an emotion, he will do it, and if people cannot agree about what is shown, the investigator concludes that facial expression is not capable of conveying emotion rather than questioning the efficacy of the posing instructions, the suitability of the setting, or the capability of the poser. There are really two problems here, just as there were with the components approach. The first is an elicitor problem: Does the instruction "look angry," "look afraid," "look annoyed," etc., mean to the poser what the investigator intends? Probably so, except when the posers are young children or members of a preliterate culture where there are major language barriers between investigator and subjects. The difficulty may not be, however, whether the subject understands which emotion he is supposed to show, but whether he thinks he is to show an emblematic expression or a simulated expression of the emotion. No other investigators have actually made the distinction between the two, and it may well be that some subjects pose emblematic expressions, some attempt simulations, and some do both. Emblematic expressions may be culture specific, unlike actual and simulated emotional expressions. There is no reason why every culture must develop the same emblematic abstraction of an emotional expression, and thus an emblematic expression of a particular emotion might be understandable in one culture but not in another.

Another source of difficulty in posing is the operation of display rules. When attempting to simulate an emotional expression, posers may be generally embarrassed about showing emotions. Or there may be cultural rules against showing certain emotions. We (Ekman & Friesen, 1971b) have suggested, and have some partial evidence for the notion that among middle-class, white, urban United States college-age subjects, females have a more difficult time than males in posing anger, while males have a more difficult time in posing fear. We have also found some evidence to suggest that the ability to pose specific emotions is related to personality; that is, people with certain types of personalities may be better or worse in posing one or another emotion. We have further found that anatomical differences make some persons unable to pose the complete facial appearance of certain emotions.

Thus posing is not as easy a way to obtain representations of emotion as it may at first seem. Some persons may pose emblematic expressions;

others may attempt simulated expressions. The poser may not be able to simulate all emotions because of cultural display rules, personality factors, or anatomical limitations. It is necessary therefore that the investigator take some step to insure that he has obtained reasonably good simulated expressions for each emotion. He could ask the poser whether he was attempting to simulate an actual expression as it would occur, or an emblematic expression. He could ask people within a culture not only whether the expression is of happiness or anger, etc., but whether it is convincing, whether the person photographed feels what he appears to show. Or, he could measure the posed facial expression to see if it contains the particular muscular movement or configuration he wishes to represent. We will see that those investigators who did take one or more such steps in selecting their poses obtained much more clear-cut results. A further precaution is to utilize more than one or two posers to avoid idiosyncracies due to personality or anatomical limitations. Again, we will see that those investigators who used many posers obtained more clear-cut results in their cross-cultural experiments than those who used one or two posers.

THE EVIDENCE[13]

All but one of the studies of facial expression in different cultures have, as mentioned earlier, used the judgment rather than the components approach. The judgment approach presumes that people can recognize emotion when they view facial expression totally out of context, with no other information available. Such judgments must be based upon the observer's past experience of that particular facial expression, either of his own face in conjunction with a particular feeling, or of someone else's in conjunction with other revealing verbal or nonverbal behavior. If the emotional meaning of facial expressions is largely or totally determined by culture, then the observers of a facial expression in one culture will draw upon different experiences with that facial expression and will judge it as a different emotion than will observers from another culture. If Darwin was correct, however, if at least some facial expressions of emotion are universal, then all people will have at least some common experiences associated with these facial expressions of emotion. When observers are shown a facial photograph, they will judge it as showing the same emotion regardless of their culture or language. (Figure 1 illustrates, with an example, the reasoning that underlies a judgment study.) Thus investigators using a judgment approach can determine, on the basis of what observers in different cultures *say* about photographs of the face, and without measuring

---

[13]The order in which the evidence is presented was dictated by interrelationships among the studies and by methodological and theoretical concerns rather than by chronology.

FIG. 1. *Logic of a Judgment Study.* If facial expressions of emotion were unrelated to emotion, then this picture might be judged as anger by one reader, as sadness by another reader, as surprise by another, etc. Within the United States, 90% of those shown this picture judged it as surprise. Such agreement must mean that these judges had common experiences with this particular facial appearance, so that they could agree about what it means without hearing the person's voice or words, without any knowledge of the context, and without knowledge of what went before or came after this facial expression. Such experiences with particular facial expressions must differ substantially across cultures, if indeed Klineberg, LaBarre, and Birdwhistell are right. From their viewpoint we would expect that people in one culture may have seen this "surprise" face most often when someone is about to fight, or right after a sick loved one dies, rather than when something unexpected suddenly occurs; or perhaps they would have never seen this facial expression. If Darwin was right, however, we need not use quotation marks around the word *surprise*. This is a surprise face for all peoples; they all will have had certain common experinces which tell them when this expression is shown—presumably at the onset of a sudden unexpected event which, at the moment of this expression, is not evaluated as threatening or unpleasant.

actual facial expressions, whether there are any facial expressions of emotion that are universal.

ATTEMPTS TO PROVE THE
CULTURE-SPECIFIC HYPOTHESIS

The first five studies we will discuss were conducted by investigators who were attempting to prove that facial expressions are either partly or totally culture specific. While each found some evidence for culture-specific facial expressions, each also found evidence of universals. All five studies have major flaws in their methods of research, which limit the conclusiveness of their evidence both for universal and for culture-specific facial expressions. After discussing each and summarizing the group of five studies, we will turn to the research by our own team and by Izard. Both overcame these methodological problems and provided more conclusive evidence on the universality of facial expression.

Triandis and Lambert

Triandis and Lambert (1958) showed photographs of a professional actress to college students at Brown University in the United States, college students in Athens, Greece, and villagers from Sfakera on the Island of Corfu in Greece. All observers rated the actress' pictures on three nine-point scales, from pleasant to unpleasant, from attention to rejection, and from sleep to tension. Figure 2 shows one of the pictures used in this experiment. The investigators compared the judgments made by the three groups of observers on each of the three scales and found ``... there is little doubt that Greek subjects, even when they come from very different populations, rate emotional expressions in the same way as American college students [p.323].''[14]

Within this overall similarity among the three groups, Triandis and Lambert did find that the two groups of college students (in the U.S. and Greece) were more similar to each other than were either to the villagers. The investigators attributed this to the college students having seen more movies than the villagers, and thus having been exposed to the same stereotyped facial expressions. The greater similarity among college students may have

[14]From Triandis, H. C. & Lambert, W. W. A restatement and test of Schlosberg's theory of emotion with two kinds of subjects from Greece. *Journal of Abnormal and Social Psychology,* 1958, **56**, 321–328. Copyright 1958 by the American Psychological Association and reproduced by permission.

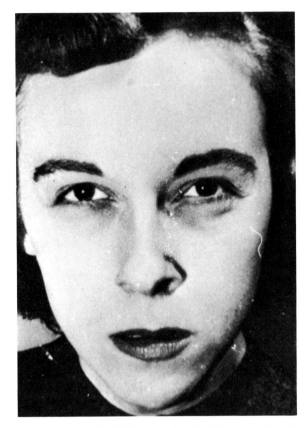

FIG. 2. Photograph of the actress M. Lightfoot used in the Triandis and Lambert experiment.

been due to other, more simple similarities among them. Because of the college students' intellectual skills and familiarity with psychological research, Triandis and Lambert had administered the experiment identically to the U.S. and Greek college students, but quite differently to the villagers (as a game rather than as a test of ability to recognize emotions).

Triandis and Lambert (1958) also found some differences between college students and villagers in judgment of particular pictures.

It is the custom in the Greek village studied to engage in verbal aggression as a means of entertainment—a kind of aggressive play that may function to express anger but also provide practice in control of aggression. Loud and angry debates are a favorite pasttime in Sfakera. It is interesting therefore to note that there are significant differences in judging the picture [see Figure 2] described by Schlosberg [the psychologist who obtained the photographs of this actress] as "intense anger in argument." Compared to either the Athens or Brown groups, the villagers see the picture as more pleasant and less tense . . . The hypothesis emerges, then, that to the degree that anger is displayed under pleasurable circumstances pictures of that state are viewed as more pleasurable and less tense. Such a hypothesis seems applicable to individual differences as well as to group or cultural differences [p.326].[15]

Their result on this picture does not challenge Darwin's theory of universal expressions of emotion. Instead, it shows how cultures may differ in the particular *elicitor* of a facial expression (in this case, the verbal play being a high-frequency elicitor for a type of anger) and also in the typical *consequences* of particular facial expressions, a consideration we have not yet introduced.

When an emotion is experienced, one consequence is a change in facial expression (if a display rule to maintain a neutral expression does not intervene). There are, however, other possible consequences including physical sensations, verbal statements, body movements, autonomic activity, and various attempts to cope with the emotion. We (Ekman & Friesen, 1969b; Ekman, 1972; Ekman, Friesen, & Ellsworth, 1972) believe that many of these consequences are not universal, but socially learned and culturally variable. When anger is aroused in a particular social context, for example, one person may have learned to attack verbally, another to attack bodily, another to make snide jokes, another to withdraw, and still another to feel depressed and guilty. In these terms, the Triandis and Lambert experiment has shown that one consequence of anger for the villagers differs from that for the urbanites; rather than leading to a serious fight, this particular angry facial expression is associated with entertaining, play-like anger.

The other difference between cultures found by Triandis and Lambert was, they acknowledged, difficult to interpret. Greeks (college students and villagers) tended to rate pictures they had judged as unpleasant as more towards attention and tension on the other two scales, while American college students gave ratings more towards attention and tension for pictures they judged as pleasant. We agree that this is difficult to interpret; it may reflect differences in attitudes about emotions.

This finding, however, like some of their other data must be questioned because only *one* person's facial expressions were used in the experiment. The requirements regarding the number of different persons shown in an experiment are stricter if the investigator is attempting to find evidence of cultural differences than if he is seeking evidence of universality. The strictness of the requirements regarding observers is just the reverse; here the investigator who thinks he has obtained proof of universals must meet a stricter requirement than the investigator whose results show culture-

[15]See footnote 14.

specific facial expressions. Let us explain each of these points, applying them to the Triandis and Lambert experiment.

If only one person's facial expressions are interpreted as showing the same emotion across cultures, we know that these facial expressions have a common meaning in these cultures, no matter how special that person might be. For unless divine, how could that person imagine an expression that people would understand across the cultures compared? Even if the one person was a marvelously gifted actress, the same argument would hold. For an actress' various facial expressions of emotion to be understood as signifying the same emotion in a number of cultures, the emotional meaning of the facial expressions must be shared across those cultures. Note that we say *shared*, not universal. A second requirement, discussed a few paragraphs below, which has to do with the amount of visual contact among the cultures studied, must be met before evidence for shared facial expressions can be interpreted as proving that they are shared by all cultures and are thus universal.

If cultures differ in their interpretation of the facial expressions of one person, can we conclude that all facial expressions of emotion are culture specific? No, since there may be peculiarities in that one person. Anatomical peculiarities could limit her expression so that no one even in her own culture understands her very well. Or, she may have psychological blocks which inhibit her expression of particular emotions, and the evidence of these blocks (strange, interrupted, or incomplete facial expressions) might be interpretable by her fellow countrymen or women, but not by people from another culture. Or, she may use culture-specific facial gestures or emblems, not emotional expressions, and these emblems could be under-standable in one culture but not another. (For example, an actress could wink in one pose and stick out her tongue in another, and if observers had to choose from a list of emotion words such as happiness, sadness, anger, fear, surprise, disgust, they would be likely to choose happiness for the wink, and anger for the tongue show, even though these are facial emblems, not emotional expressions.) Or, she may, when posing one emotion, unwittingly show a blend of two or more emotions, which may be interpreted differently in different cultures.

Interpreting the data in the Triandis and Lambert experiment in the light of these considerations, we cannot know whether the differences they found between Greeks and Americans were peculiar to this one lady's photographs. We should question not only Triandis and Lambert's evidence of culture-specific facial expressions of emotion, but also that part of their evidence which points to universal facial expressions. Remember, Triandis and Lambert found that, by and large, the observers in Greece, even the villagers, judged the faces to be showing the same emotions as did the American observers, despite some differences. Can we say that this constitutes proof for our contention of universal facial expressions of emotion? Not necessarily, for here we encounter the requirement which is more strict for demonstrating the universality hypothesis than the culture-specific hypothesis. This require-ment derives from the possibility that visual contact between peoples from two different cultures may provide them with the opportunity to learn each other's culturally determined different facial expressions. If people in two cultures are exposed to each other or to the same visual sources, such as television, motion picture films, photographic magazines, art, and illus-trated children's books, they may learn the same facial expressions by imita-tion of these shared models. John Wayne's look of anger on the TV set—not man's evolutionary history—may be responsible for people's ability to recog-nize the same anger expression across cultures! Facial expressions, in that case, would not be universal but shared only among those who have com-mon visual sources; cultures that are visually isolated would have a different set. Triandis and Lambert's Greek subjects, even the villagers, were not sufficiently visually isolated to establish universality. We shall see that this problem emerges in *almost* all of the research we will review.

Cüceloglu

Cüceloglu's (1970) use of drawings of the face may appear to circumvent problems associated with any one person's facial expression, but drawings present problems of their own. He showed 60 line drawings of facial expres-sion composed from four eyebrow types, three eye types and five mouth types to college students in the U.S., Japan, and Turkey. Figure 3 shows the elements he used to create his 60 faces. The subjects in each culture were asked to judge the faces by rating on a seven-point scale whether each of 40 emotion words was applicable to the drawn facial appearance. Cüceloglu (1970) concludes that

> ... some static facial features are regarded as distinctive in the expression of a
> given emotion and some are not. Some of these distinctive features are shared across
> cultures reflecting what seem to be universals in facial communication, others seem
> to be peculiar to particular racial or cultural groups. In other words there seems
> to be a facial code employed in the communication of affective meaning which
> is to a great extent, although not wholly, common to different cultures [p.99].[16]

While drawings of the face are certainly free of the idiosyncrasies of any one person, they are not necessarily relevant to facial expressions of emotion. The question is whether they represent most or some of the facial

[16]From Cüceloglu, D. M. Perception of facial expressions in three cultures. *Ergonomics,* 1970, **13**, 93–100. Reproduced by permission of the Publisher.

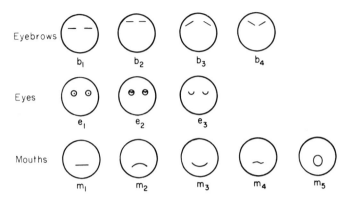

FIG. 3. Facial elements used to create the stimuli for Cüceloglu's experiment.

appearances that occur when there is muscular movement in the human face or instead depict an artist's fancy? Do they show facial expressions that are anatomically impossible to perform, or which occur very rarely?

Comparing the facial appearances in Cüceloglu's drawings with those represented in the works of investigators who have attempted to describe either all of the possible appearances of the face, or those relevant to emotion (Birdwhistell, 1970; Blurton Jones, 1972; Ekman, 1972; Ekman, Friesen, & Tomkins, 1971; Hjortsjö, 1970; Grant, 1969) shows that Cüceloglu's group of 60 faces includes but a very small proportion of what the face can show. Furthermore, by combining every brow with every eye with every mouth, Cüceloglu derived some facial appearances that are anatomically impossible. We estimate that between a fourth and a third of Cüceloglu's faces can never occur in life. These may well be the ones which his observers, presumably in all three cultures, failed to agree about—for they would never have encountered such facial appearances before.

Many of the anatomically possible expressions depict blends of emotion rather than single emotions. The face can show muscular movements relevant to but one emotion in the brows, eyes, and lower face, or it can show a blend of two or more emotions simultaneously, combining elements of one emotion in the brow/forehead or eyes, with those of a different emotion in the lower face. (Figure 4 shows an example of two single emotions and of blends.) While the single emotions are universal, we contend that cultures do vary in the particular blends of emotion that frequently occur. This reasoning could explain Cüceloglu's findings: Some expressions would have been interpreted the same across cultures and others differently if the former were single emotion and the latter blend expressions.

Our last comment on Cüceloglu's study is that, like almost all of the other recognition studies, it suffers from a lack of visual isolation among

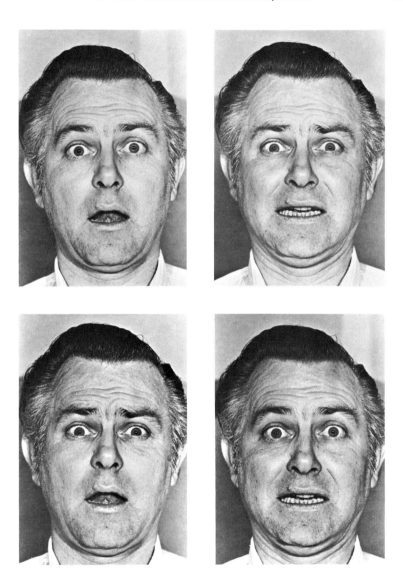

FIG. 4. *Example of single emotion and blend facial expression.* The photograph on the top left shows a single-emotion surprise expression; the photograph on the top right shows a single-emotion fear expression. The two bottom photographs are fear-surprise blend facial expressions. On the bottom left, the expression combines the surprise mouth with the fear brows-forehead and eyes. On the bottom right, the expression combines the surprise brows-forehead and eyes with the fear mouth. Copyright © 1973 by Paul Ekman.

the different cultures compared. His evidence of universality must be regarded as tentative, not conclusive.

Dickey and Knower

Dickey and Knower (1941) conducted the first judgment study of facial expression in which the judgments of observers from different cultures were compared. They expected to find cultural differences, and reported that Mexican school children interpreted the posed facial expressions of emotion of two American actors more accurately than did American school children. Accuracy in their experiment entailed judging the emotion intended by the actor and they found that in most instances more Mexicans than Americans correctly guessed the actor's pose. They explained the superiority of the Mexican children as resulting from their being exposed to more expressiveness within their culture. They did not take a position regarding the possible universality of some facial expressions, although other investigators (for example, Vinacke, whom we will discuss shortly) have interpreted their findings in this fashion. We believe that in our analysis of their data, we found their evidence of cultural differences to be more limited than they or others have considered it. Let us look at their study.

Dickey and Knower presented photographs of eleven emotion poses by a male actor and eleven poses of the same emotions by an actress to school children in the U.S and Mexico, who were given a list of eleven emotion categories and asked to choose the correct category for each picture. Their results show two things. (1) In almost all instances the most frequent judgment of each facial expression was the same for Mexicans as for Americans. (2) In a number of instances more Mexicans than Americans gave the correct answer, if the correct answer is defined as being the emotion the actor attempted to convey. For example, on the anger pictures, 69% of the Americans chose anger, while 86% of the Mexicans chose anger.

Thus, in both cultures the most frequent judgment was the same, but more of the Mexicans gave the correct judgment. While Dickey and Knower emphasized the latter finding, we want to emphasize the former finding, for it suggests that the facial expressions have the same meaning in the two cultures. The fact that more of the Mexicans than Americans were accurate could well be due, as they suggest, to a cultural difference: If Mexicans are more expressive they might be also more attentive and accustomed to seeing facial expression. While any two cultures might differ in the extent to which people are accurate in interpreting facial expression, nevertheless to those who do understand the expression, it has the same meaning in both cultures. Damaging evidence to the notion of universals would have been results showing that facial expressions judged as anger by the majority of the Mexicans were judged as sadness, fear, or some other emotion by the majority of Americans. But that they did not find.

Dickey and Knower's finding of a cultural difference between Mexicans and Americans in the extent of accurate judgments should be questioned for two reasons. (1) Their results were based on the facial expressions of only two persons and, as already explained, there must be a broader sampling of persons if we are to have confidence in a finding of culture-specific facial expressions. (2) The differences in accuracy may not pertain to emotion. The study's 11 facial expressions include six that have been commonly considered to be emotion expressions by other investigators, and that have been found to be so by all other investigators who have sought to determine what emotions can be judged from the face (cf. Ekman, Friesen, & Ellsworth, Chap. 13, 1972). These six are happiness, sadness, anger, fear, surprise, and disgust. Dickey and Knower also included categories which almost no other investigator has considered to be emotion categories, such as religious love, firmness, questioning, etc. When we analyzed their results separately for the six emotions and for what might better be called attitudes, we found more difference between the Mexicans and Americans in judging the attitudes than the emotions.[17]

Winkelmayer *et al.*

Winkelmayer, Exline, Gottheil, and Paredes (1971) recently conducted an experiment in which they attempted to prove that Mexicans are less accurate than Americans in judging the facial expressions of Americans— although they failed to cite Dickey and Knower's finding to the contrary. Winkelmayer *et al.* knew some of the evidence of universality (which we will discuss shortly), but they interpreted our findings and those of Izard as being limited to very special cases. Only "striking, stereotyped expressions" are universal, they said. If spontaneous, more usual facial expressions were shown, observers from different cultures would differ in their judgment. Winkelmayer *et al.* also considered their use of motion picture filmed presentations of facial expressions to be more likely to lead to cultural differences than the use of still photographs of facial expression. For reasons they failed to explain, they thought that records showing the sequence or unfolding of an expression, such as a motion picture film, would elicit greater differences in judgment across cultures than would still photographs of the apex of an expression.

In their study, 13 psychology students in the United States, 31 British psychology students, and 36 Mexican medical students viewed silent motion

---

[17]A chi-square test applied to Dickey and Knower's data showed a significant difference between Mexicans and Americans on the attitudes ($\chi^2 = 7.50$, $df = 1$) but not on the emotions ($\chi^2 = 2.94$, $df = 1$).

pictures of 10 normal and 10 schizophrenic American women, as each told about one happy, one sad, and one anger-related personal experience. Their results were mixed, only partly supporting their expectation of a difference between cultures in the judgment of facial expressions.

Disregarding whether the person judged was normal or schizophrenic, no difference was found among the U.S., British, and Mexican observers. When they considered only the judgments made of the schizophrenic women, again no difference was found among the three cultures. In judgments of the normal people, no difference was found between U.S. and British observers, but both these groups were more accurate than the Mexicans. One must ask, however, whether this last finding was due to cultural differences, as the authors claimed, or to the strong possibility that psychology students are better judges of emotion than medical students.

While the Winkelmayer et al. experiment is not flawed by being limited to judgments of only one or two people, it is problematic in terms of how the observers' judgments were analyzed. The observers had a choice among only three emotions—happiness, sadness, and anger. The discrimination of happiness from all other emotions has repeatedly been found to be such an easy judgment (cf. Ekman, Friesen, & Ellsworth, Chap. 15, 1972) that meaningful results require more than this simple distinction. The way in which Winkelmayer et al. reported their data makes it impossible to know whether the difference between the Mexicans, British, or Americans was in making the easy discrimination of happiness from either sadness or anger, or the more difficult discrimination of anger from sadness. A further problem with the report of their data is that it does not show whether the cultural difference was in regard to the extent of accuracy (it might be, for example, that more Americans were accurate than Mexicans, but in both groups a particular facial expression was judged by most observers as showing the same emotion) or in the type of emotion judged. As we pointed out in discussing Dickey and Knower's findings, only the latter result—where, for example, a face interpreted in one culture as anger is seen by another culture as fear—would be damaging to the claim that some facial expressions are universal.

One must conclude that, because of inconsistency in results and failure to analyze the data in a sufficiently informative fashion, the Winkelmayer et al. study is ambiguous.

Vinacke

The last investigator for us to consider is Vinacke, who believed that facial expressions are culture specific, but acknowledged his failure to prove it. He was influenced by Klineberg and by the Dickey and Knower study.

Furthermore, he thought that racial differences in facial appearance are related to differences in facial expressiveness. He (Vinacke, 1949; Vinacke & Fong, 1955) obtained judgments on what he thought were spontaneous facial expressions of emotion (candid shots of Caucasians and Orientals taken from magazines) and from groups of Caucasians, Chinese, and Japanese students at the University of Hawaii. His findings (1955) showed that

> ... the differences between the three national-racial groups, both in the judgment of Caucasian faces and of Oriental faces, are so slight that no *practical* difference exists. Thus, all the groups of subjects usually agree upon the same term to describe the facial expression, although in different degrees [p.193].[18]

Vinacke explained his failure to find cultural differences as due to his subjects all having had sufficient contact with each other to obliterate cultural differences. He also thought that his mistake could have been in using spontaneous facial expressions—that if he had used posed faces perhaps he would have found cultural differences. This is paradoxical, since Winkelmayer *et al.* used just the opposite argument, advocating the use of spontaneous facial expression to prove cultural differences in the judgment of emotion. (When we have completed our discussion of the judgment studies, we will deal with this slippery issue of posed versus spontaneous facial expression and its possible effect on cross-cultural studies of the judgment of emotion.)

Summary

All five of these studies found evidence of universals, and four of them also found evidence of cultural differences in the judgment of facial expressions. We saw that the evidence of cultural differences was not of the type which would contradict the idea that there are universal facial expressions of emotion. No one reported evidence that facial expressions interpreted as one emotion by the majority of observers in one culture were interpreted as other emotions by the majority of observers in another culture. Instead, the evidence of cultural differences in the interpretation of facial expressions of emotion was that, within a more general finding that facial expressions are interpreted similarly across cultures, the *context* of facial expressions of emotion, the *consequences* of emotional expressions, the judgments of emotion *blends,* and the *extent of accuracy* in judgment may differ among cultures.

[18]From Vinacke, W. E. & Fong, R. W. The judgment of facial expression by three national-racial groups in Hawaii: II. Oriental faces. *Journal of Social Psychology,* 1955, **41**, 185–195. Reproduced by permission of the Publisher.

While these studies tend to support more than refute Darwin, they are not conclusive in establishing either universals or cultural differences in facial expression. They could not establish universals, because none of the observers represented cultures which are visually isolated from each other. The observers in these experiments might have learned each other's different facial expressions, or all might have learned some common set of facial expressions from a shared visual source, such as movies. The experiments failed to establish cultural differences because of the limited number of people whose faces were shown, or because of contradictions in the findings within or across studies, or because of the possible presence of blends of two or more emotions in the stimuli.

ATTEMPTS TO DEMONSTRATE UNIVERSALITY

We turn now to the recent judgment studies conducted in literate cultures by our own research team and by Izard. Our team and Izard's worked independently, conducting research at the same time, but unaware of each other's work until very near the end of the studies. Both were influenced by Tomkins' (1962, 1963) theories of facial expression. Both made some methodological improvements over the previous studies: many different persons' facial expressions were included, many cultures were compared, and the facial expressions were screened in advance to eliminate blends or non-affect faces. While, as we shall see, the evidence is consistent and strongly suggestive of universal facial expressions, it too is inconclusive because visually isolated cultures were not studied. This problem was finally met by a set of judgment studies, conducted by our own research group and replicated by an independent research team, on the judgment of facial expressions among visually isolated, preliterate peoples in New Guinea.

Ekman and Friesen: Literate Cultures Study

We (Ekman, 1968; Ekman, Sorenson, & Friesen, 1969; Ekman, 1972) conducted an experiment in which photographs of facial expressions were shown to college students in five literate cultures, crossing four language groups—Japan, the United States, Brazil, Chile, and Argentina. In designing our research, we thought that the crucial question was how to select the faces to be shown.

We rejected the selection procedures of past investigators. We thought that a collection comprised simply of an actor's poses (as were Triandis and Lambert's, and Dickey and Knower's) or of spontaneous facial expressions (as were Winkelmayer's et al. and Vinacke's) would be likely to include many blends of emotional expression. This expectation was based on our theory (Ekman & Friesen, 1967, 1969a, b) that blend expressions occur more frequently than single emotion expressions, whether a person poses or shows emotions spontaneously, and that the interpretation of blends may vary with culture. Another procedure for selecting photographs, that used by Izard, is to present to people in other cultures only those faces which observers in the United States have clearly agreed upon. We rejected this procedure because of the possibility that the collection might still include blends, and if so, that observers in one culture might respond more to one of the emotions in the blend, while observers in another culture might pay more attention or give more weight to the other blended emotion. The other reason for not selecting pictures on the basis of judgments made within a single culture is that such a procedure might allow the inclusion of emblematic expressions interpretable within one culture, but not within another. It was important to use a selection procedure that would include only emotional expressions or good simulated expressions and exclude blends and emblematic expressions.

The novel element in the selection procedure we adopted was that we *looked* at facial expressions and based our selection on our theory of the facial muscular movements associated with each emotion. Although we did not publish this theory until some years later (Ekman, Friesen & Tomkins, 1971), at the time we had already developed a complete theoretical description of the universal facial appearance of each primary emotion.

We examined over 3000 still photographs, checking each one to see if it contained all of the muscular movements and wrinkles that we postulated as showing a particular emotion. The photographs included almost all those which had been used in studies of the face from 1930 to 1966, the time at which we made our selection (Engen, Levy, & Schlosberg, 1957;[19] Frois-Wittmann, 1930; Tomkins & McCarter, 1964), as well as our photographs of mental patients (Ekman & Friesen, 1968). These were both posed and spontaneous facial expressions of adults and of children. To determine what emotion, if any, each expressed, we did not consider the poser's intent if it was a posed expression, nor the circumstance if it was a spontaneous expression, nor what observers had previously judged the picture to show. Instead we compared each photograph with a description of the muscular movements we hypothesized as relevant to each emotion. We found many photographs for happiness, sadness, disgust, and anger, but only a few for surprise and fear; most of those pictures showed fear-surprise blends. Our selection yielded 30 pictures of 14 different persons, with pictures for each of six emotions.

We chose to study the six emotions (happiness, sadness, anger, fear, surprise, and disgust) that had been previously found by all investigators who sought to determine what emotions can be judged from the face

---

[19]These are the pictures used in the Triandis and Lambert experiment, an example of which is shown in Figure 2.

(Woodworth, 1938; Plutchik, 1962; Tomkins & McCarter, 1964; Osgood, 1966; Frijda, 1968; as reevaluated by Ekman, Friesen, & Ellsworth, Chap. 13, 1972). The logic of our experiment did not require any final decision on our part as to whether there are six, or four, or nine universal expressions of emotion. Our purpose was to show that there are the same facial expressions for the same emotions regardless of culture; and, that this was so for more than just the simple distinction between happiness and unhappiness. In every culture we studied, the observers were given the words for these emotions in their own language and were required to choose one word for each picture (the only exception was that for disgust both the words ''contempt'' and ''disgust'' were used).

If facial expressions of emotion are entirely specific to each culture, or if our theory as to the appearance of the face for each emotion were wrong, then these faces would be judged as showing different emotions by people from the different cultures. The results shown in Table I provided strong evidence in support of universal facial expressions. The Table shows that the expressions interpreted as conveying a particular emotion by the majority of observers in one culture were interpreted the same way by the majority of observers in other cultures.[20] The Table also shows a very high level of agreement within each culture. Figure 5 shows some of the faces included in this study, and how these faces were judged in each of the five cultures.

TABLE I
Judgments of Emotion by Observers in Five Literate Cultures[a,b]

	Japan	Brazil	Chile	Argentina	United States
Happiness	87	97	90	94	97
Fear	71	77	78	68	88
Surprise	87	82	88	93	91
Anger	63	82	76	72	69
Disgust/Contempt	82	86	85	79	82
Sadness	74	82	90	85	73
Number of Observers	29	40	119	168	99

[a]From Ekman and Friesen (1971b).

[b]The Table is organized so that one may examine any row, or set of photographs which Ekman and Friesen had assumed to represent a particular emotion, and compare the percentage of observers in each culture which identified those faces as showing the expected emotion.

[20]The statistical test used to test the culture-specific hypothesis (analysis of variance) failed to show any significant difference between cultures across all emotions, or on particular emotions.

FIGURE 5. Judgments of emotion in five literate cultures.

	Percentage Agreement in How Photograph Was Judged Across Cultures				
	United States (N=99)	Brazil (N=40)	Chile (N=119)	Argentina (N=168)	Japan (N=29)
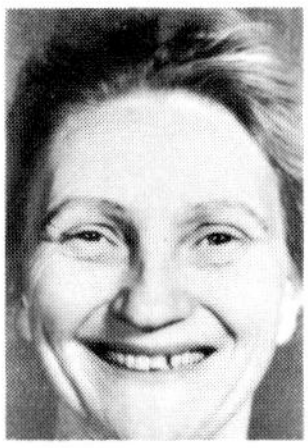	97% Happiness	95% Happiness	95% Happiness	98% Happiness	100% Happiness
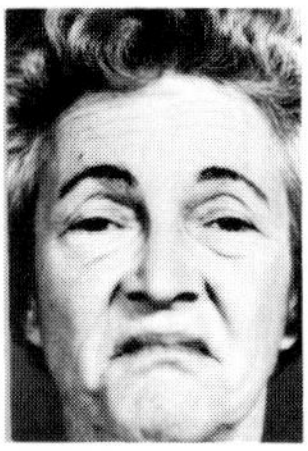	92% Disgust	97% Disgust	92% Disgust	92% Disgust	90% Disgust
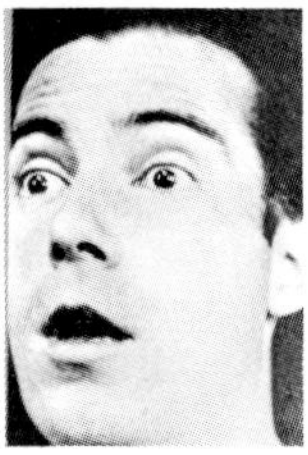	95% Surprise	87% Surprise	93% Surprise	95% Surprise	100% Surprise
	84% Sadness	59% Sadness	88% Sadness	78% Sadness	62% Sadness
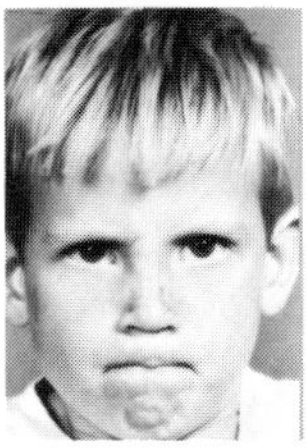	67% Anger	90% Anger	94% Anger	90% Anger	90% Anger
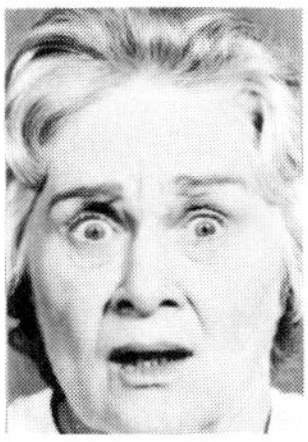	85% Fear	67% Fear	68% Fear	54% Fear	66% Fear

In this experiment, we were concerned with a second question, namely, whether the judgment of the intensity of emotion varies with cultures. We reasoned that, while the type of emotion is universally evident (whether fear, anger, disgust, etc.), judgments of intensity could vary with culture (whether the anger, etc., is slight, moderate, or extreme). Such variations might be expected if cultures differ in the customary level of overt emotional expression. For example, if the stereotype is accurate that in Latin cultures there is less constraint in showing emotion than in the United States then what appears as extreme emotion to Americans might be seen as moderate to Latins. To check this possibility, we asked observers in four of the cultures (all but Japan) to rate each facial expression on a seven-point intensity scale (slight to extreme). We found no significant differences in the intensity ratings from one culture to another. Instead, the intensity ratings were almost identical across cultures. The correlations between the United States and the Latin cultures were close to perfect: .93 for Chile–United States, .96 for Brazil–United States and for Argentina–United States.[21] Among South American countries the correlations were equally high.

Izard: Literate Culture Study

Izard's experiment (1968; 1971) on the judgment of emotion across cultures was almost identical with ours, except that he selected his faces by showing pictures to American observers and used only those pictures that elicited high agreement. He used posed facial expressions of adult males and females showing what had been judged within the United States as interest–excitement, enjoyment–joy, surprise–startle, distress–anguish, disgust–contempt, anger–rage, shame–humiliation, fear–terror. This list of eight emotions was based on Tomkin's (1962) theory of primary affects. In each culture college students were given the list of eight pairs of emotion words, each pair containing a word in their own language for a low and a high-intensity version of the emotion, and were requested to select the word pair that best described the facial expression. Table 2 shows that in all nine literate cultures the emotion judged by the majority in one culture was almost always the same in the others—quite strong evidence that facial expressions are interpreted similarly regardless of culture or language.

Table 2 also shows that for the African observers and for the Japanese observers, a significantly lower percentage of agreement was found than for the other cultural groups. These differences were probably due to prob-

---

[21] A correlation coefficient would have a value of 0 if two sets of scores were totally unrelated, and a value of 1.0 if the intensity judgments in one culture perfectly corresponded with those in another culture.

TABLE 2

Judgments of Emotion in Nine Literate Cultures[a,b]

	United States	English	German	Swedish	French	Swiss	Greek	Japanese	African
Interest–Excitement	84	79	82	83	77	77	66	71	52
Enjoyment–Joy	97	96	98	96	94	97	93	94	68
Surprise–Startle	90	81	85	81	84	85	80	79	49
Distress–Anguish	74	74	67	71	70	70	54	67	32
Disgust–Contempt	83	84	73	88	78	78	87	56	55
Anger–Rage	89	81	83	82	91	92	80	57	51
Shame–Humiliation	73	59	72	76	77	70	71	41	43
Fear–Terror	76	67	84	89	83	67	68	58	49
Numbers of Observers	89	62	158	41	67	36	50	60	29

[a]From Izard (1971).
[b]See Table 1 for explanation of how this table is organized.

lems within the experiment rather than to any cultural difference. The Africans were the only group who were not tested in their native country and in their native tongue. They were citizens of many different African nations, speaking many different languages, studying in Paris, where they judged the faces in French. The lower percentage of agreement among the Japanese observers may also have been due to a language problem. Our own Japanese translators considered some of Izard's Japanese translations of the emotion words to be awkward and dated, and when we utilized Izard's own photographs with our Japanese translations, the agreement among Japanese observers was much higher than that obtained by Izard.

Regardless whether the lower agreement among the Japanese and the Africans is considered to be of import, Izard's main finding is positive and is consistent with ours. Across literate cultures facial expressions convey the same emotion; if a facial expression is judged by most people within one culture as anger, it will be judged by most people within any other literate culture as anger, and so on for the other emotions studied by Izard and by ourselves.

As we have repeatedly mentioned, one loophole remains—visual contact. While wishing to interpret our results as conclusive evidence that facial expressions are universal, we, like Izard, recognized that our findings may be limited to showing that among peoples who share visual contact, facial expressions are common, but among peoples who have not had the chance to view mass media portrayals of facial expressions of emotion, facial expression might vary considerably. While this seemed improbable, the argument was made presumably with some seriousness by one of the advocates of the view that there are no universal facial expressions of emotion—Bird-whistell (1967).[22] The only way to establish conclusively the existence of universal facial expressions of emotion was to show that visually isolated people interpret facial expressions in the same way as people from literate cultures. This would establish that exposure to a common source is not responsible for common facial expressions, and that Darwin must have been correct in claiming that human facial expressions of emotion are universal.

Ekman and Friesen: Preliterate Culture Study

Four experiments were conducted. In our first study conducted in 1967 (Ekman, Sorenson, & Friesen, 1969), we showed photographs of facial expression to people in two preliterate cultures, in Borneo and in New Guinea. We encountered difficulty with the judgment procedure, in which an observer is shown a photograph and asked to choose an emotion word or category from a list. These people could not read any language, and asking them to remember a list of emotion words repeatedly read to them after each photograph seemed awkward, tiresome, and by no means easy for the subject. Further, there was some question as to whether we really knew the languages of these people well enough to convey an emotion with a single word in their language.

Our results, while similar to those found for literate cultures, were much weaker; agreement among members of these preliterate cultures was low on most emotions and totally absent on some. Was this because of the difficulty with the judgment procedure? *Or,* was it because, having finally studied visually isolated cultures, we had now encountered fundamental cultural differences in facial expressions of emotion? It became crucial to settle this question, particularly since in another decade there would be few people left who remain visually isolated from literate cultures. This was one of the last chances to use the study of visually isolated people to settle a question first raised by Darwin.

Convinced that defects in the judgment task were responsible for our weak results, we returned to New Guinea a year later, with a judgment task that we thought would overcome the problems experienced the previous year. The procedure was based on a task first used by Dashiell (1927) for his studies of the ability of young children to judge facial expression. Instead of a single photograph of a face and instructions to select an emotion word, the observer was given either two or three photographs and asked to select the face that fit an emotion story. Simple stories, likely to connote

---

[22]Birdwhistell had occasion to see these results prior to their publication, and made this argument in disputing our claim to have established that there are some universal facial expressions of emotion.

| *Fear* | *Happy* | *Anger* |

FIG. 6. In presenting this task to a particular person, all three photographs would be shown. Only one of the stories would be read and the person would be asked to select the photograph which fits·the story.

Fear—She is sitting in her house all alone and there is no one else in the village; and there is no knife, ax, or bow and arrow in the house. A wild pig is standing in the door of the house and the woman is looking at the pig and is very afraid of it. The pig has been standing in the doorway for a few minutes and the person is looking at it very afraid and the pig won't move away from the door and she is afraid the pig will bite her.

Happy—Her friends have come and she is happy.

Anger—She is angry and is about to fight.

only one emotion (not a blend), were developed on the basis of the first study of these New Guinea people. Figure 6 shows one of the sets of three pictures and the three different stories that were used with them.

In this second experiment, we (Ekman & Friesen, 1971a) worked only with people in New Guinea, not in Borneo. The subjects were from the Fore linguistic-cultural group of the South East Highlands of New Guinea. Until 14 years ago this was an isolated, Neolithic, material culture. By the time of the second study, many of these people had had extensive contact with missionaries, government workers, traders and United States scientists but some had not. We were most interested, of course, in the latter persons. Subjects who were selected for the experiment met criteria intended to ensure, as much as possible, that they were not influenced by exposure to other cultures. They had seen no movies, neither spoke nor understood English or Pidgin, had not lived in any of the Western settlement or government towns, and had never worked for a Caucasian. The judgment task was administered individually with three photographs for each emotion story to 189 male and female adults, and with two photographs for each story to 130 male and female children.

Table 3 shows how often the New Guineans chose the facial expression for a particular emotion that members of literate cultures had chosen. For example, in the first row, the figure of 92% for the adults signifies that

TABLE 3

Judgments of Emotion by Observers in a Preliterate Culture,
the Fore of New Guinea[a]

Emotion described in the story	Percent choice of the emotion expected, which would agree with judgments by members of literate cultures	
	Adults	Children[b]
Happiness	92	92
Sadness	79	81
Anger	84	90
Disgust	81	85
Surprise	68	98
Fear from anger, disgust or sadness	80	93
Fear from surprise	43	— [c]
Number of Observers	189	130

[a]From Ekman and Friesen (1971a).

[b]The higher figures for the children probably reflect the fact that they were asked to choose from a pair of photographs rather than sets of three.

[c]Through an oversight, this discrimination was not tried with the children.

when the Fore adults were read a happiness story ("His friends have come and he is happy") and were shown a facial expression previously judged by persons in literate cultures as happy with two others judged as surprise, anger, sadness, or disgust, 92% of their choices were of the happiness face. For anger, happiness, sadness, disgust, and surprise (except in relation to fear), the faces chosen for the emotion were the same as in literate cultures. The Fore failed to distinguish fear from surprise , perhaps because in this culture fearful events are usually also surprising. Even so, these results strongly support the contention that there are universal facial expressions of emotions.

In the third experiment, we (Ekman & Friesen, 1971a; Ekman, 1972) asked other members of this New Guinea culture, who had not been in the prior experiment, to show how their own faces would look if they were the person in an emotion story. Unedited videotapes of nine of these New Guineans were shown to a group of college students in the United States. These American college students, who had never seen New Guineans, had little trouble accurately judging the emotion intended by the New Guineans for anger, disgust, happiness, and sadness. The fear pose was often judged as surprise, and vice versa, (as happened when the Fore themselves attempted this discrimination in judging Caucasian facial expressions). Figure 7 shows some examples of the New Guineans' posed facial expressions.

FIG. 7. Video frames of attempts to pose emotion by subjects from the Fore of New Guinea. The instructions for the top left photograph was "your friend has come and you are happy"; for the top right "your child has died"; for the bottom left "you are angry and about to fight"; and for the bottom right "you see a dead pig that has been lying there for a long time." Copyright © 1972 by Paul Ekman.

In discussing the findings of our second and third studies (1971a), we wrote:

> The only way to dismiss the evidence for both the judgment and posing studies would be to claim that even those New Guineans who had not seen movies, who did not speak or understand English or Pidgin, who had never worked for a Caucasian, still had *some* contact with Westerners, sufficient contact for them to learn to recognize and simulate culture-specific, uniquely Western facial behaviors associated with each emotion. While these subjects had some contact with Westerners, this argument seems implausible for three reasons. First, the criteria for selecting these subjects make it highly improbable that they had learned a "foreign" set of facial behaviors to such a degree that they could not only recognize them, but also display them as well as did those to whom the behaviors were native. Second, contact with Caucasians did not seem to have much influence on the judgment of emotion,

since the most Westernized subjects [we had also studied subjects who had been to mission school and read and spoke English] did no better than the least Westernized and, like the latter, failed to distinguish fear from surprise. Third, the women, who commonly have even less contact with Westerners than the men, did as well in recognizing emotions [p.128].[23]

The best way to dispel any lingering doubts, of course, would be to repeat the experiment with another visually isolated group of people, preferably a group who had even less contact with literate cultures. Just this was done by investigators who were not committed to the notion that there are universals in facial expression. This made the replication especially useful, since a scientist may unwittingly bias his own results. In a judgment experiment, the investigator might, for example, unwittingly give cues to the subject to indicate the right response. We had taken a number of precautions to prevent such biasing, but the best assurance is to have other investigators who do not hold the same hypothesis repeat the study.

Karl and Eleanor Heider, an anthropologist and a psychologist, were skeptical of our claim that at least some facial expressions of emotion are universal. At the time we met, Karl had already worked with the Grand Valley Dani. These people live in the Central Highlands of New Guinea and speak a Papuan language that perhaps is remotely related to the language of the Fore. They live some 500 miles to the West of the Fore, in West Irian, the Indonesian half of New Guinea. Only during the 1960s did they give up stone axes and intertribal warfare. Karl and Eleanor Heider were doubtful that the Dani people would judge our photographs of facial expressions of emotion in the same way as did members of other cultures, particularly in view of the fact that the Dani do not have words for all six emotions studied.

The Heiders spent a few months working with us, learning our methods of studying facial expression within a preliterate culture. They returned to New Guinea in 1970 and conducted an experiment with the Grand Valley Dani that was almost identical to ours with the Fore. Their results (Ekman, 1972; Ekman, Heider, Friesen, & Heider, in preparation) were very similar, again showing that a preliterate, visually isolated people interpret almost all of the basic facial expressions of emotion in the same way as do members of literate cultures. Furthermore, Eibl-Eibesfeldt (1970) using nonquantitative ethological methods has collected many examples of seemingly similar facial expressions of emotions in a number of visually isolated cultures.

Ekman and Friesen: Study of Spontaneous Expression

Before considering this last set of experiments, let us discuss the differences between posed and spontaneous facial expression. While a few investigators

[23]From Ekman, P. & Friesen, W. V. Constants across cultures in the face and emotion. *Journal of Personality and Social Psychology*, 1971, **17**, 124–129. Copyright 1971 by the American Psychological Association and reproduced by permission.

did use photographs of spontaneous facial expression and did find evidence of universals (Winkelmayer *et al.*, 1971; Vinacke, 1949), most used photographs of posed faces. Does this invalidate or limit the finding of universals? Landis (1924) and later Hunt (1941) argued that posed facial expressions are a conventional language, socially learned and unrelated to emotion. If they are right, it would be logical to expect (as they did) that poses of facial expression of emotion would be both performed and judged differently across cultures. The fact that posed facial expressions are similarly judged across cultures, and that not only are Western poses understood by New Guineans but New Guinean poses understood by Westerners requires either that these supposedly conventional, arbitrary facial expressions are for some inexplicable reason learned the same way in all cultures, or that Landis and Hunt were wrong—that posed facial behavior resembles and grows out of spontaneous facial behavior. Although not designed for that purpose, these cross-cultural studies of the judgment of posed facial behavior provide the logical basis for concluding that posed behavior must resemble spontaneous facial behavior. Ekman, Friesen, and Ellsworth (1972), in reviewing this evidence, have suggested that

> posed facial behavior is similar to, if perhaps an exaggeration of, those spontaneous facial behaviors which are shown when the display rules to deintensify or mask emotion are not applied. Posed behavior is thus an approximation of the facial behavior which spontaneously occurs when people are making little attempt to manage the facial appearance associated with intense emotion [p.167].

Our most recent observations would suggest that the extent of similarity between posed and spontaneous emotional expression depends upon whether the poser attempts an emblematic or simulated expression, and, if simulating, whether a slight or extreme expression is attempted.

The following set of experiments should resolve any question about whether the universality of facial expression could be limited to poses, since it used spontaneous facial behavior. It was undertaken at the same time as the studies reported here, but the analysis of the results was not completed until quite recently. We had three objectives: first, to complement our other cross-cultural studies by using spontaneous rather than posed facial behavior; second, to use a components approach, directly measuring the movements of the face in two different cultures rather than measuring observers' judgments of emotion, as was done in other studies. Third, we wished to lend credence to our concept of display rules and to our interpretation of the results of those investigators whose studies showed culture differences. Our aim was to substantiate our notion that their results were due to display rules by showing in this experiment culture-specific facial expressions when we expected display rules to be operable and evidence of similar facial expressions when we did not expect display rules to operate.

We compared the facial behavior of Japanese and American subjects in two social contexts, when alone and when in the presence of another person. We were intrigued by the idea of studying Japanese subjects because of the popular notion that the Japanese are inscrutable to the Westerner. In our terms this should be due to the operation of display rules, and would be evident when a Japanese subject was in the presence of others; when he was alone, he could be expected to show the same facial expression for a particular emotion as anyone else. In addition to requiring that one of the situations would be such that display rules would operate minimally, our theory also suggested the need to ensure that the same emotion was elicited in both Japanese and American subjects, and that consequential actions that might obscure the expressions would be unlikely.

We chose a situation in which a subject sat alone watching stressful and neutral films. Lazarus, Opton, Tomita, & Kodama (1966) had obtained evidence that these stressful films elicit a comparable verbal report of emotional arousal, suggesting that this situation would elicit the same emotion in both cultures. Watching a stress film is the type of arousal situation that could be expected to produce little in the way of consequential actions to obscure the expressions. There is little an individual can do to cope with the unpleasant emotions; unless he turns away from the screen, his face remains visible; and the movements of the facial muscles are not distorted by speech.

Twenty-five subjects from Waseda University in Tokyo and 25 from the University of California in Berkeley participated in the study. An investigator from their own culture explained the experiment as a study of physiological response to stress and connected wires for the measurement of heart rate and galvanic skin response, and then left the subject alone in the room. With a concealed camera, videotape records were made of the subject's facial behavior while he watched both neutral and stress films. An investigator from his own culture then entered the room and interviewed him about his feelings, and continued to interview him while additional stress film material was shown. Two studies were performed, one with the videotape made while the subject was alone, the other with the videotape made when the subject was with the interviewer.

Three minutes of each subject's reactions to a neutral film while alone, and three minutes of reaction to a stress film were measured with FAST, our Facial Affect Scoring Technique (Ekman, Friesen, & Tomkins, 1971). In essence, FAST entails isolating each observable movement of the face, examining separately each part of the face that can move independently, and measuring the exact duration of each such facial movement. (The reader interested in how the measurement procedure was applied to these records is referred to Ekman, 1972.)

The correlations between the facial behavior shown by Japanese and American subjects in relation to the stress film were extremely high, ranging

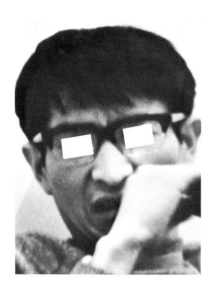

FIG. 8. Video frames of facial behavior scored by FAST as showing disgust; a Japanese subject on the left, and an American subject on the right. Copyright © 1972 by Paul Ekman.

from .72 to .96, depending upon whether a particualr facial area was compared (such as eyes and lids) or the movement of the entire face. Figure 8 shows an example from the videotapes. This experiment, using a components approach to measure directly the movements of the facial muscles, provides strong evidence that there are universal facial expressions of emotion. There were strikingly similar facial responses to a stress film by Japanese and American subjects when they were alone.

In the second study, we measured the facial behavior shown when each subject, in the presence of another person from his own culture, answered questions about his feelings as he watched more stress film material. Here, we expected from our theory about display rules that the Japanese more than the Americans would mask negative emotions with polite smiles. We found such a difference between cultures. The Japanese showed more positive emotions than the Americans and less negative emotions (Friesen, 1972).

Thus, in this one experiment with the same two groups of subjects, we found evidence both of universal facial expressions and culture-specific differences in facial expression. When the subjects were alone, we found the same facial expressions in response to a stress film for Japanese as for American subjects. There was also evidence that display rules can produce an overlay of cultural differences. In the presence of another person the Japanese subjects (presumably masking negative facial expressions) showed more positive facial behavior than did the Americans.

This experiment met the three objectives it was designed to achieve. Universal facial expressions were found when we measured spontaneous behavior, adding evidence consistent to that found in the previous studies of posed behavior. Universal facial expressions were found by direct measurement of facial behavior rather than by measuring observers' judgments of facial expression.[24] And, the utility of our concept of display rules was demonstrated, for, in an experimental context where we predicted cultural difference due to attempts to mask facial expression, that is exactly what we found.

CONCLUSION

The evidence is remarkably consistent from all of the experiments we have reviewed:

From experiments conducted by investigators primarily interested in culture-specific facial expressions or committed to the theory that there are no universal facial expressions, as well as from experiments by those who sought to prove universals in facial expressions,

From experiments that used a judgment approach, as well as from the one study that actually measured the components of facial behavior,

From experiments that dealt with spontaneous facial behavior as well as from those which dealt with posed facial behavior.

Comparable results were found in studies conducted in 13 literate cultures (in many of which subjects were studied by more than one investigator):

African nations	Greece (2 investigations)
Argentina	Hawaii
Brazil	Japan (4 investigations)
Chile	Sweden
England (2 investigations)	Turkey
France	United States (7 investigations)
Germany	

and in two visually isolated, preliterate cultures:

the Fore of New Guinea
the Grand Valley Dani of West Irian (New Guinea).

---

[24]We also did a judgment study with the materials from this experiment, presenting the facial behavior that spontaneously occurred when the subjects were alone to observers in each culture, who were required to judge whether the facial expressions had occurred in response to a stress or neutral film. As predicted, both Japanese and American observers were able to judge accurately the facial expressions of members of their own and members of the other culture. Neither group of observers was more accurate in judging their own than the other culture. Also, the judgments of the Japanese and Americans were highly correlated, between .79 and .86.

The same facial expressions are associated with the same emotions, regardless of culture or language. One hundred years after Darwin wrote his book on emotional expression, a conclusion is possible. There are some facial expressions of emotion that are universally characteristic of the human species. This evidence raises two questions about the origins of these universal facial expressions. How does it happen that there are the same muscular movements of the face for all people, regardless of culture? And why does a particular muscular movement of the face come to be associated with a particular emotion? For example, why do we not press our lips tightly together when happy and curve the corners up when angry, rather than the reverse? Evidence of universality cannot answer these questions, but it does increase the likelihood of certain answers. Darwin thought the answer to the first question was that facial expression is innately determined. In the introduction, we pointed out that universal facial expression could alternatively arise from species-constant learning experiences and explained our own view that some universal expressions may be so derived, but that some must be genetically determined. The question awaits further research for a final answer.

Darwin thought the second question could be answered by looking at the evolution of facial expression, the similarities between man's expressions and those of other primates. He suggested three explanatory principles, which other authors in this book have described in detail. We refer the reader to Chevalier-Skolnikoff's chapter in particular for an answer to the question of the similarity between human and other primate facial expression.

We have established in this chapter a conclusive answer to one of Darwin's questions, and an answer in agreement with Darwin's own conviction: There are some facial expressions of emotion that are universal.

We will close by quoting from our report (Ekman, 1972) on all our cross-cultural studies, in which we presented what we have called a neurocultural theory of facial expression that attempts to account for both the universal elements (neurally determined) and the culture-specific (learned) elements in facial expression.

> We believe, then, that we have isolated and demonstrated a basic set of universal facial expressions of emotion. They are not a language which varies from one place to another; one need not be taught a totally new set of muscular movements and a totally new set of rules for interpreting facial behavior if one travels from one culture to another. While facial expressions of emotion will often be culture-specific because of differences in elicitors, display rules, and consequences, there is also a pancultural set of facial expressions of emotion . . . Our findings, supported by those of others, now provide the basis for settling the old dispute as to whether facial expressions are completely specific to each culture or totally universal. Our neuro-cultural theory maintains there are both universal and culture-specific expressions. The evidence now proves the existence of universal facial expressions. These findings require the postulation of some mechanism to explain why the same facial

behavior is associated with the same emotion for all peoples. Why are observers in all these cultures familiar with a particular set of facial expressions (a set which is only a fraction of the anatomically possible facial muscular configurations)? But they are not merely familiar with these facial expressions. Regardless of the language, of whether the culture is Western or Eastern, industrialized or preliterate, these facial expressions are labelled with the same emotion terms: happiness, sadness, anger, fear, disgust, and surprise. And it is not simply the recognition of emotion that is universal, but the expression of emotion as well. How do we explain that the same facial muscular movements occur in Japanese and Americans in response to a stress film, or that the same facial muscular movements occur whether a New Guinean or an American is asked to show what his face would look like if his child had died, or if he were angry and about to fight, etc.?

We must abandon the notion that facial expressions are a language, where arbitrary facial muscular movements have a different meaning in each culture; but we must also attempt to explain the basis for the demonstrated pancultural facial expressions of emotion. Our neuro-cultural theory postulates a facial affect program, located within the nervous system of all human beings, linking particular facial muscular movements with particular emotions. It offers alternative nonexclusive explanations of the possible origin of the linkages in the affect program between the felt emotion and the movement of the facial muscles. Our theory holds that the elicitors, the particular events which activate the affect program, are in largest part socially learned and culturally variable, and that many of the consequences of an aroused emotion also are culturally variable, but that the facial muscular movement which will occur for a particular emotion (if not interfered with by display rules) is dictated by this affect program and is universal [pp. 277–279].[25]

REFERENCES

Beach, F. A. The descent of instinct. *The Psychological Review*, 1955, **62**, 401–410.

Birdwhistell, R. L. The kinesic level in the investigation of emotions. In P. H. Knapp (Ed.), *Expression of the emotions in man*. New York: International Universities Press, 1963.

Birdwhistell, R. L. Personal communication, 1967.

Birdwhistell, R. L. *Kinesics and context*. Philadelphia: University of Pennsylvania Press, 1970.

Blurton Jones, N. G. Criteria used in describing facial expressions. In N. G. Blurton Jones (Ed.), *Ethological studies of child behavior*. London: Cambridge University Press, 1972.

Cüceloglu, D. M. Perception of facial expressions in three cultures. *Ergonomics*, 1970, **13**(1), 93–100.

Darwin, C. *The expression of the emotions in man and animals*. Chicago: University of Chicago Press, 1965.

Dashiell, J. F. A new method of measuring reactions to facial expression of emotion. *Psychology Bulletin*, 1927, **24**, 174–175.

Dickey, E. C., & Knower, F. H. A note on some ethnological differences in recognition of simulated expressions of the emotions. *American Journal of Sociology*, 1941, **47**, 190–193.

Dittmann, A. T. Review of Ray L. Birdwhistell, *Kinesics and context*. *Psychitry*, 1971, **34**(4). 334–342.

Eibl-Eibesfeldt, I. *Ethology: The biology of behavior*. New York: Holt, Rinehart and Winston, 1970.

[25]From Ekman, P. Universals and cultural differences in facial expressions of emotion. In J. K. Cole (Ed.), *Nebraska symposium on motivation*, 1971. Nebraska Press, 1972. Reproduced by permission of the Publisher.

Ekman, P. The recognition and display of facial behavior in literate and non-literate cultures. Paper presented at the symposium Universality of Emotions of the American Psychological Association, September, 1968.

Ekman, P. Universals and cultural differences in facial expressions of emotion. In J. K. Cole (Ed.), *Nebraska symposium on motivation, 1971.* Lincoln, Nebraska: University of Nebraska Press, 1972.

Ekman, P. & Friesen, W. V. Origin, usage and coding: The basis for five categories of nonverbal behavior. Paper presented at the Symposium on Communication Theory and Linguistic Models, Buenos Aries, October, 1967.

Ekman, P., & Friesen, W. V. Nonverbal behavior in psychotherapy research. In J. Shlien (Ed.), *Research in psychotherapy,* Vol. III, American Psycological Association, 1968.

Ekman, P., & Friesen, W. V. Nonverbal leakage and clues to deception. *Psychiatry,* 1969, **32**(1), 88–105. (a)

Ekman, P., & Friesen, W. V. The repertoire of nonverbal behavior: Categories, origins, usage, and coding. *Semiotica,* 1969, **1**(1), 49–98. (b)

Ekman, P., & Friesen, W. V. Constants across cultures in the face and emotion. *Journal of Personality and Social Psychology,* 1971, **17**(2), 124–129. (a)

Ekman, P., & Friesen, W. V. Communication through nonverbal behavior. Progress report to the National Institute of Mental Health. Unpublished, 1971. (b)

Ekman, P., Friesen, W. V., & Ellsworth, P. *Emotion in the human face: Guidelines for research and an integration of findings.* New York: Pergamon Press, 1972.

Ekman, P., Friesen, W. V., & Tomkins, S. S. Facial Affect Scoring Technique: A first validity study. *Semiotica,* 1971, **3**(1), 37–38.

Ekman, P., Heider, E., Friesen, W. V., & Heider, K. Facial expression in a preliterate culture. Manuscript in preparation.

Ekman, P., Sorenson, E. R., & Friesen, W. V. Pan-cultural elements in facial displays of emotion. *Science,* 1969, **164**(3875), 86–88.

Engen, T., Levy, N., & Schlosberg, H. A new series of facial expressions. *American Psychologist,* 1957, **12**, 264–266.

Foley, J. P., Jr. Judgment of facial expression of emotion in the chimpanzee. *Journal of Social Psychology,* 1935, **VI**(1), 31–54.

Friesen, W. V. Cultural differences in facial expressions in a social situation: An experimental test of the concept of display rules. Unpublished doctoral dissertation, University of California, San Francisco, 1972.

Frijda, N. H. Recognition of emotion. In L. Berkowitz (Ed.), *Advances in experimental social psychology.* Vol. 4. New York: Academic Press, 1968.

Frois-Wittmann, J. The judgment of facial expression. *Journal of Experimental Psychology,* 1930, **13**, 113–151.

Gorer, G. *African dances.* New York: Norton, W. W. & Co., Inc., 1935. Cited by W. LaBarre, The cultural basis of emotions and gestures. *Journal of Personality,* 1947, **16**, 49–68. P.52.

Grant, N. G. Human facial expression. *Man,* 1969, **4**, 525–536.

Hearn, L. *Japan: An attempt at interpretation.* New York: Grosset & Dunlap, 1904. Cited by O. Klineberg, *Social psychology.* New York: Henry Holt, 1940, Pp.194–195.

Hjortsjö, C. H. *Man's face and mimic language.* Lund, Sweden: Studentlitteratur, 1970.

Hunt, W. A. Recent developments in the field of emotion. *Psychological Bulletin,* 1941, **38**(5), 249–276.

Izard, C. E. The emotions and emotion constructs in personality and culture research. In R. B. Cattell (Ed.), *Handbook of modern personality theory.* Chicago: Aldine, 1968.

Izard, C. E. *The face of emotion.* New York: Appleton, 1971.

Klineberg, O. Emotional expression in Chinese literature. *Journal of Abnormal and Social Psychology,* 1938, **33**, 517–520.

Klineberg, O. *Social psychology*. New York: Holt, 1940.

LaBarre, W. The cultural basis of emotions and gestures. *Journal of Personality*, 1947, **16**, 49–68.

Landis, C. Studies of emotional reactions: II. General behavior and facial expression. *Journal of Comparative Psychology*, 1924, **4**, 447–509.

Lazarus, R. S., Opton, E., Jr., Tomita, M., & Kodama, M. A cross-cultural study of stress-reaction patterns in Japan. *Journal of Personality and Social Psychology*, 1966, **4**(6), 622–633

Lehrman, D. S. A critique of Konrad Lorenz's theory of instinctive behavior. *Quarterly Review of Biology*, 1953, **28**(4), 337–363.

Lorenz, K. *Evolution and modification of behavior*. Chicago: University of Chicago Press, 1965.

Osgood, C. E. Dimensionality of the semantic space for communication via facial expressions. *Scandinavian Journal of Psychology*, 1966, **7**, 1–30.

Plutchik, R. *The emotions: Facts, theories, and a new model*. New York: Random House, 1962.

Tomkins, S. S. *Affect, imagery, consciousness*. Vol. 1. *The positive affects*. New York: Springer, 1962.

Tomkins, S. S. *Affect, Imagery, consciousness*. Vol. II. *The negative affects*. New York: Springer, 1963.

Tomkins, S. S., & McCarter, R. What and where are the primary affects? Some evidence for a theory. *Perceptual and Motor Skills*, 1964, **18**, 119–158.

Triandis, H. C., & Lambert, W. W. A restatement and test of Schlosberg's theory of emotion with two kinds of subjects from Greece. *Journal of Abnormal and Social Psychology*, 1958, **56**(3), 321–328.

Van Lawick-Goodall, J. A preliminary report on expressive movements and communication in the Gombe Stream chimpanzee. In P. C. Jay (Ed.), *Primates: Studies in adaptation and variability*. New York: Holt, 1968.

Vinacke, W. E. The judgment of facial expressions by three national-racial groups in Hawaii: I. Caucasian faces. *Journal of Personality*, 1949, **17**(4), 407–429.

Vinacke, W. E., & Fong, R. W. The judgment of facial expressions by three national-racial groups in Hawaii: II. Oriental faces. *Journal of Social Psychology*, 1955, **41**, 185–195.

Williams, F. E. *Orokaiva society*. Oxford: Clarendon Press, 1930. Cited by O. Klineberg, *Social psychology*. New York: Henry Holt, 1940. P.194.

Winkelmayer, R., Exline, R. V., Gottheil, E., & Paredes, A. Cross-cultural differences in judging emotions. Unpublished work, 1971.

Woodworth, R. S. *Experimental psychology*. New York: Henry Holt, 1938.

5

Darwin and the Representative Expression of Reality[1]

Lewis Petrinovich
University of California at Riverside

... but with organic beings we should bear in mind that the form of each depends
on an infinity of complex relations ... on the nature of the variations preserved,
these depending on the physical conditions, and still more on the surrounding organisms which compete with each—and, lastly, on inheritance (in itself a fluctuating
element) from innumerable progenitors, all of which have had their forms determined
through equally complex relations [Darwin, 1871, p.538–539].

To learn of the facts, one reads the latest journals. To understand biology, one
reads Darwin [Ghiselin, 1969, p.232].

On its way to becoming a science, psychology had to face certain requirements
of ... general methodology ... A ... set of problems arises in connection with
efforts not to lose sight of the specific tasks of psychology in the process of objectifying
it but to establish exact study on an adequate level of complexity, sometimes called
"molar" or "functional" [Brunswik, 1952, p.1].

Charles Darwin is one of those exceptional individuals who molded our
current conceptions of the nature of man and his universe. Darwin provoked
one of the major revolutions in the history of ideas; the idea that there
is a continuity of species. His presentation of voluminous evidence supporting
the doctrine of evolution of species in *The Origin of Species by Means*

[1]The preparation of this paper was done with the support of Grant HD–04343 from the
National Institutes of Child Health and Human Development and a University of California
Intramural Research Grant.

of Natural Selection, published in 1859, created an overnight revolution in biological thinking. He is, accordingly, ranked along with other revolutionaries such as Copernicus, who dethroned man's planet as the center of the universe, and Freud, who dethroned man as even being the conscious master of his own desires. Darwin dethroned man as being a unique entity within the animal kingdom. True, Darwin placed man at the pinnacle of descent, but he convincingly argued against any unique emergent status for man among living beings.

NATURAL PHILOSOPHY PRIOR TO DARWIN

The significance of Darwin's contributions can perhaps be better understood if they are placed in the context of the earlier biological conceptions that he faced. The dominant philosophical view of the time regarding the descent of man was the doctrine of special creation. This doctrine gained ascendancy with the rise of Christianity in the Early and Middle Ages and was accompanied by a decline in natural science. In the words of Carl Warden (1927),

> Man and his redemption became the one problem of supreme importance, and the animal was degraded and despised in common with the physical world. A sharp dichotomy was drawn on theological grounds, between mankind and the beasts that perish, by placing undue stress upon the superiority of the one and upon the inferiority of the other [p. 79–80].

The doctrine of special creation, in addition to insisting on the existence of an impassable discontinuity between the various animal species (and especially between man and the "lower" animals), strenuously insisted on the immutability of species: that all species are unchangeable, and that they were created during the six days of Genesis when they were endowed by a munificent creator with their essential physical structure and mental abilities. The mental life of animals was held to be entirely instinctive, and only man had the faculty of reason. While some theologians were puzzling over the problem of how a pair of all of the known species could fit into the Ark, Darwin was collecting and organizing evidence to establish the doctrine of evolution.

Of course, Darwin did not arrive at the idea of the evolution of species *de novo.* Goethe espoused a theory of the metamorphosis of homologous parts in 1790. This theory maintained that the various parts of different kinds of organisms correspond; that different forms can be created by the change of one part into another. For example, he considered the skull essentially to be a modified and developed vertebra. Charles Darwin's grandfather, Erasmus Darwin, independently formulated the notion of evolution of species and spoke of heredity, adaptation to the environment, and sexual selection. Erasmus Darwin's arguments tended to be obscure, however. Charles Darwin

(1887) disclaimed any influence of his grandfather's views on his own because of the "proportion of speculation being so large to the facts given [p.49]"—a typical Darwinian attitude.

Charles Darwin does, however, acknowledge that knowing the views of his grandfather and hearing them praised rather early in life may have favored his upholding them under a different form in *The Origin of Species.*

The most influential figure of the day in the history of evolution was the French naturalist Lamarck, who developed the theory of the inheritance of acquired characteristics. The essential points in this theory are: (1) in confronting the physical environment, the organism has needs and must adapt to the environment to satisfy them; (2) these demands cause the animal to exercise certain parts of its body; (3) the exercise of a part of the body makes that part develop and causes the resulting change to appear in the offspring as an acquired characteristic. The classic example offered of the inheritance of such an acquired characteristic is the development of the long neck of the giraffe. Assuming that the giraffe had a limited environment in which to forage so that there was a scarcity of low foliage, it would be forced to stretch its neck to reach foliage on the higher branches. According to Lamarck, this stretching would cause the giraffe's neck to lengthen, and the effect of this stretching would be inherited by the giraffe's offspring. If this tendency continued for generation after generation, the result would be the characteristic long neck.

One of the leading philosophers of the day who wrote on evolution as early as 1850 was Herbert Spencer. Spencer formulated an evolutionary associationism in which the association of ideas operated phylogenetically. If such associations are repeated often enough, the cumulative effects are inherited by successive generations. Thus, there is an inheritance of acquired traits; by this process associations become instincts. He was among the first to elaborate the conception that the mind is what it is because it has had to cope with particular environments. Spencer had a strong impact on psychology through his influential *Principles of Psychology* (1855), but Darwin (1887) denied that he derived any conscious profit as a consequence of Spencer's writings because the philosophical methods employed lacked an empirical base and were, therefore, of no scientific use. "They partake more of the nature of definition than of laws of nature. They do not aid one in predicting what will happen in any particular case. Anyhow they have not been of any use to me [p.109]."

DARWIN'S WRITINGS

Against this background, Charles Darwin developed the fabric of the theory of natural selection. Darwin was born to an eminent family: Erasmus Darwin, his grandfather; his father, Robert Darwin, a physician; and the brilliant Francis Galton, his cousin. In addition to his family, his circle of acquaintances included such notables as Thomas Henry Huxley and Charles Lyell. Darwin studied to be a physician at Edinburgh University but found it dull. He then studied for the ministry at Cambridge for three years but found this also not to his liking. In fact, he considered his time there to be wasted as far as the academic studies were concerned, with the exception of geometry—Euclid "gave me much pleasure." During this time he considered his passion for collecting beetles to be his most important intellectual acquisition. Shortly after Darwin abandoned his studies at Cambridge, he signed on as naturalist to the voyage of the Beagle and toured the South Seas—a voyage from December 27, 1831 to October 2, 1836. During the voyage he made copious notes regarding the flora, fauna, and geological strata of the various places he visited. Ironically, one of the reasons the captain of the Beagle, an ardent anti-evolution religionist, invited a naturalist on the voyage was to obtain geological evidence to refute such evolutionary views as those of Lamarck.

At the outset of the voyage, Darwin was a believer in the Biblical story of the Creation. However, during the voyage he read Charles Lyell's Principles of Geology, which then argued against the current cataclysmic theory of geology. Lyell, on the basis of his study of rock strata, argued that the past could be interpreted in terms of orderly changes in the earth in which a chaos of elements were gradually differentiated, separated into those forms of rocks we know, and that this occurred as a result of processes known to occur at present. The alternative—cataclysmic theory—argued that each geological epoch was marked by a cataclysm which swept away all existing life and was replaced by the creation of improved life forms. Lyell rejected the idea that one should invoke such extraordinary causes as universal deluges if a current explanation fails; he argued that science would be better advanced if one questioned a premise of a current theory instead of evoking such extraordinary causes to explain the inexplicable.

After Darwin published The Voyage of the Beagle (1839), he turned his major efforts to developing an irrefutable amount of documentation; the case for the doctrine of evolution. The basic fabric of this doctrine and of the principle of natural selection was essentially complete upon a reading, in 1838, of the Essay on Population by the economist, Malthus. This essay, written in 1798, was concerned with the relationship between the death rate and the birthrate in human societies. Malthus argued that the food supply would follow an arithmetic progression while the population level would follow a geometric progression. Thus disease and famine would be inevitable, and a struggle for existence would ensue in which some individuals would be eliminated and some preserved. This biological view of human society led Darwin, in 1839, to the theory of natural selection. Darwin wrote a 35-page abstract in 1842 and a 230-page version in 1844.

The essential argument is that for most species the population level is stationary, yet there are typically more offspring than parents. Many offspring must not survive, then, and Darwin arrived at the conclusion that those animals which survive and reproduce are the fittest in terms of being best able to get food and to ward off enemies. Thus we have survival of the fittest in the particular environment to which the animals must adapt. If the environment changes, and if there is some basic variability in the instincts the individual animals inherit, then it is possible to develop new species. The effects of this natural selection are transmitted to succeeding generations, and these generations will continue to improve. In 1856 Lyell advised Darwin to develop the theory fully, and Darwin set about preparing a work that was planned to be three or four times the size of the eventual *Origin of Species.*

Alfred Russell Wallace read *Malthus,* came to the same basic conclusion as did Darwin (although without the empirical documentation) and sent the manuscript outlining his ideas along with a request that Darwin send it to Lyell if he thought it worthy. Darwin sent his own manuscript with its detailed observational support as well as Wallace's manuscript to Lyell. Lyell advised Darwin to submit Wallace's manuscript and an abstract of his own to the *Linnaean Society Journal,* where both appeared in 1858 with little attention being occasioned to the two papers. When *The Origin of Species* appeared in 1859, however, it was highly successful; the first edition of 1250 copies was sold on the day of publication, and a second edition of 3000 copies was exhausted soon afterward.

Darwin (1887) attributed the success of *The Origin of Species* not to the fact "that the subject was in the air" or "that men's minds were prepared for it," but rather to the fact "that innumerable well-observed facts were stored in the minds of naturalists ready to take their proper places as soon as any theory which would receive them was sufficiently explained [p. 124]." It is clear, however, that evolution was part of the *Zeitgeist* and that the significance of *The Origin* was the clear, concise exposition of the theory accompanied by a compelling mass of empirical support.

"The Descent of Man"

The Descent of Man (1871) is of particular interest to psychologists, since it is here that Darwin applied the theory to man and here that he argued extensively for the continuity of mental faculties between man and the "lower" animals. This doctrine of mental continuity was repugnant to many authorities and was the storm center of controversy in the scientific sphere. The doctrine of mental continuity maintained that the mental faculties of man and the "lower" animals do not differ in kind, though they might differ immensely in degree. Darwin believed it absurd to deny at least a low order of intelligence to the higher animals, and it was in the interest of establishing this point that the anecdotal school flourished. This school, most ably represented by George John Romanes, produced collections of stories emphasizing the human-like behavior of the higher animals, especially in regards to reasoning ability, social behavior of a high order, and characteristic human emotions such as a sympathy, shame, courage, curiosity, and the like.

The other major contribution in *The Descent of Man* is the principle of sexual selection. This principle provides a behavioral mechanism that ethologists have found to be of paramount importance in animal behavior. Part of the importance of this principle is the degree of flexibility it imparts to the overall system. About half of *The Descent of Man* is concerned with marshaling both behavioral and structural evidence on behalf of the doctrine of mental continuity. The latter half of the book is concerned with establishing the importance of the principle of sexual selection across the phyla—including man.

The essential point of the principle of sexual selection is that the largest number of vigorous offspring are reared from the pairing of the strongest and best-armed males, since these are victorious in contests over other males. These ''fittest'' males breed with the most vigorous, best-nourished, and most attractive females (in terms of displays), since it is these females which breed first in the season. If these more vigorous females select the more attractive and at the same time the more vigorous males, they will rear a larger number of offspring than will the less vigorous females, which must pair with the less vigorous and less attractive males. This will produce a substantial reproductive advantage in terms of both fertility and fecundity, an advantage that will be sufficient to render sexual selection an efficient mechanism in the process of evolution. In fact Darwin (1871) suggests ''that the power to charm the female has sometimes been more important than the power to conquer other males in battle [p.583].''

"The Expression of the Emotions
in Man and Animals"

Darwin had originally intended *The Expression of the Emotions in Man and Animals* (1872) to be a chapter in *The Descent*, but the length became so extensive as he compiled his notes that he published *The Expression* as a separate volume the year following the publication of *The Descent*. The aim of *The Expression* was to describe the chief expressive actions in man and the lower animals and to explain the origin and development of these actions. Darwin (1872) delineated three general principles which ''account for most of the expressions and gestures involuntarily used by man and the lower animals, under the influence of various emotions and sensations [p. 27]."

The three universal principles are as follows:

1. *The principle of serviceable associated habits.* "Certain complex actions are of direct or indirect service under certain states of the mind, in order to relieve or gratify certain sensations, desires, etc., and whenever the same state of mind is induced, however feebly, there is a tendency through the force of habit and association for the same movements to be performed, though they may not then be of the least use [Darwin, 1872, p.28]." These reflexes are transmitted as inherited facial expressions characteristic of certain situations and represent the "last vestige of the total primitive reaction our forbears made to objects arousing the emotions [Allport, 1924, p.210]."

2. *The principle of antithesis.* "Certain states of the mind lead to certain habitual actions, which are of service. . . . Now when a directly opposite state of mind is induced, there is a strong and involuntary tendency to the performance of movements of a directly opposite nature, though these are of no use [Darwin, 1872, p.28]."

3. *The principle of actions due to the constitution of the nervous system, independently from the first of the will, and independently to a certain extent of habit.* This principle of the *direct action of the nervous system* argued that "When the sensorium is strongly excited, nerve-force is generated in excess, and is transmitted in certain definite directions, depending on the connection of the nerve-cells, and partly on habit. . . . Effects are thus produced which we recognize as expressive [Darwin, 1872, p.29]."

In developing the argument for the universality of these three principles, Darwin presented a broad range of what was mainly anecdotal evidence based on the behavior of lower animals. With his characteristic thoroughness, however, he used evidence from several other sources as well.

(1) He observed infants in order to observe "the pure and simple source from which (our expressions) spring in infancy [p.13]."

(2) He inquired into the expression of the insane, "since they are liable to the strongest passions, and give uncontrolled vent to them [p.13]."

(3) He photographed the face of an old man and showed the photographs to judges, asking them to identify the emotion or feeling that the old man was expressing.

(4) He looked at photographs and engravings of many well-known works by the great masters in painting and sculpture—with little profit, he concluded, since "in works of art, beauty is the chief object and strongly contracted facial muscles destroy beauty [p.14]."

(5) He inquired into the evidence bearing on whether or not the same expressions and gestures prevail with all the races of mankind, "especially with those who have associated but little with Europeans [p.15]."

(6) He inquired into the expressions of the congenitally blind who would, therefore, have had no opportunity to observe directly the facial expressions of others. This would be especially true for such things as blushing, since this expression would not involve movements of the facial muscles, and the blind could not have acquired the expression by feeling the faces of others.

The thoughtful attention to the various lines of evidence bearing on the particular argument is characteristic of all of Darwin's work, and constitutes one of the major strengths of his contributions to science.

Darwin has often been accused of engaging in an excessive amount of anthropomorphism in *The Expression*. I agree with Ghiselin (1969), who argues that the ill effects of such anthropomorphism are usually overplayed. A careful reading of *The Expression* supports the conclusion that Darwin was well aware of the difficulties of relying exclusively on the anecdotal method. Indeed, as mentioned above, he was open to all lines of evidence that had bearing on his hypotheses. He made heavy use of the anecdotal method to communicate without losing the richness of language—to take advantage of the surplus meaning that resides in our language. Evidence that this did not involve a fatal degree of anthropomorphism is offered by Ghiselin, who points out that Darwin used the same anthropomorphic language when describing the reactions of plants—and it is difficult to argue that Darwin was seriously intending to invest them with human-like qualities.

Darwin does employ some Lamarckian notions in both *The Descent* and *The Expression*. In *The Expression* (1872), he states that associated expressional movements might be acquired through habit and that "certain strange gestures or tricks" might have arisen in association with certain states of the mind, and are "undoubtedly inherited [p. 33]." In *The Descent* (1871), he states that whether modification of bodily structure would become hereditary or not if the same habits of life were followed for many generations "is not known, but it is probable [p. 418]." In another place he states, "some intelligent actions, after being performed during several generations, become converted into instincts and are inherited, as when birds on oceanic islands learn to avoid man [p. 447]."

In *The Descent*, he qualifies this Lamarckian position by pointing out that the greater number of the more complex instincts appear to have been gained through natural selection. For example, "It is, therefore, highly probable that with mankind the intellectual faculties have been mainly and gradually perfected through natural selection . . . [p. 497]." He accepted, then, a coexistence of natural selection and Lamarckian mechanisms, with natural selection being regarded as the more effective.

Darwin made many contributions to science other than those sketched above. Ghiselin, in his insightful and scholarly book, *The Triumph of the*

Darwinian Method (1969), discusses Darwin's major contributions in several areas: geology, biogeography, natural selection, evolution, sexual selection, psychology, taxonomy, the study of barnacles, and botany. Anyone seriously interested in understanding the scope and the significance of Darwin's contributions will find this book indispensible. At this juncture, I would like to acknowledge my own indebtedness to Professor Ghiselin's book; it has helped place many of my own thoughts in proper perspective and I have taken the liberty of adopting some of his points regarding methodology as a foundation for certain of the arguments which appear later in this paper.

DARWIN'S MAJOR CONTRIBUTIONS

Let us examine a bit more systematically the unique contributions that Darwin made to the history of ideas. After these contributions have been outlined, I will discuss their influence (or lack of it) on subsequent psychological and biological theories. Finally, I will attempt a more modern statement of the essential virtues of the Darwinian approach and then will illustrate these virtues through an examination of some current research on the expression of emotion.

Deductive Method

Darwin possessed a quality which is all too rare in science. He was a careful and thoughtful observer who took pains to gather all available evidence on whatever question was under consideration; witness the variety of methods used to evaluate the principles suggested in *The Expression of the Emotions*. Darwin did not, however, merely amass facts in an inductive manner. This misconception has been suggested by several detractors in view of the pains Darwin took to make and to present voluminous and detailed observations of the phenomena in which he was interested. Ghiselin (1969) has argued convincingly that Darwin used the hypothetico-deductive method extensively in all of his work—from that on the formation of coral reefs to his classic studies on worms. Darwin consistently applied the theory of evolution and natural selection to all of his endeavors, taking the trouble, however, to make numerous objective observations, to organize them, and to bring them to bear on his hypotheses. His own thoughts on the matter were expressed when he wrote "no one could be a good observer unless he was an active theoriser [Irvine, 1955]." In the finest spirit of the deductive method, Darwin speculated and formed hypotheses and then insisted upon verifying these hypotheses. His attitude toward the interplay of fact and theory is stated quite nicely in the last chapter of *The Descent of Man* (1871):

> False facts are highly injurious to the progress of science, for they often endure long; but false views, if supported by some evidence, do little harm, for every one takes a salutary pleasure in proving their falseness: and when this is done one path towards error is closed and the road to truth is often at the same time opened [p.909].

Ghiselin (1969) presents yet another quotation from Darwin's notebooks that reveals this same point of view: "The line of argument often pursued throughout my theory is to establish a point as a probability, by induction, and to apply it as hypothesis to other points and see whether it will solve them [1969, p.63]."

Probabilism

Not only did Darwin utilize deductive procedures, but these deductions also allowed for a probabilism that is essential if one is dealing with organism–environment interactions at the molar level on which Darwin operated. This probabilism, in evidence throughout his writings, is what lends such strength to his model. He makes a series of "if . . . if . . . if . . . then" conditional statements of the type characteristic of much of modern science. And this type of probabilism, it will be argued later, is indispensible in dealing with complex organism–environment interactions.

Darwin used probabilism both in terms of causative factors and in terms of vicariousness of evolutionary outcomes. In other words, he understood that a given end point could be the result of several classes of factors, such as natural selection, or sexual selection, and also that the same selection pressures could produce different outcomes, any of which might be satisfactory solutions to the demands of the environment. Ghiselin (1969) emphasizes this same point of view.

> Thus it is predicted that *if* there are variations, *if* these are inherited, *if* one variant is more suited to some task than another, and *if* the success in accomplishing that task affects the ability of the organisms to survive in whatever happens to be their environment, *then* natural selection will produce an evolutionary change. Such conditional statements are basic to the Darwinian theory . . . [p.65].[2]

I have attempted to illustrate the possible nature of this type of evolutionary process in the development of communication in birds and language in man (Petrinovich, 1972). It is argued that the behavioral processes involved

[2]From Ghiselin, M. T. *The triumph of the Darwinian method.* Berkeley: Univ. of California Press, 1969, reprinted by permission of The Regents of the University of California.

in each can be considered to be the product of analogous biological mechanisms produced by parallel evolution in response to similar environmental demands. Understanding the probabilistic nature of evolutionary processes makes it possible to understand why vocal communication does not follow any straight-line evolutionary development (Andrew, 1962), but seems to have occurred several times independently in response to similar environmental demands. Viewed in this manner, it is easy to understand why bird and man could have attained a behavioral mechanism that is more similar one to the other than is the case with monkey and man.

Dynamism

The complex interplay of variables which Darwin envisaged and for which he provided such abundant evidence resulted in a dynamic system that emphasized the flux of the evolutionary process. This was an essential aspect of his theorizing when viewed against the static nature of the doctrine of special creation or the artificial dynamics of the cataclysmic theories of evolution.

THE ESSENTIAL BREAKTHROUGH IN
"THE ORIGIN OF SPECIES"

The first step toward the development of the theory of evolution, with natural selection being the basic mechanism, was provided by the Malthusian notion of competition for survival in the face of limited natural resources (and, of course, a resultant extinction of some animals).

The idea of fundamental importance is that of a *population* as the basic unit of interaction in nature. This was a radically different way to conceive of species; prior to Darwin, species were considered to be static classes. The whole question of the importance of the distribution patterns Darwin noticed in the Galapagos Islands began to make sense when considered in the context of the existence of a population of animals coping with varying environmental pressures. This led him to consider the nature of the possible dispersal mechanisms that would distribute the members of a population. In order that separate species might evolve as a result of such dispersal, he also had to consider the nature of the barriers that might exist to maintain reproductive isolation. Darwin's manner of approaching this question embodied his usual deductive attitude: He considered how these particular forms on the Galapagos Islands might have been transported, decided on the basis of these considerations how they should now be distributed, and then looked at the actual pattern of distribution. This model for the mechanism of dispersal was quite successful as a synthesis, and led him to perform experiments to determine the effects of seawater on seeds, to determine whether or not it was possible for seeds to pass undamaged through the guts of birds, and to determine whether or not seeds would sprout from the mud taken from the bodies of decayed animals. These experiments provided direct empirical evidence for some of the proposed dispersal mechanisms. In addition, he found that the eggs of some amphibians cannot withstand the action of seawater, and then determined that these species were not present on the oceanic islands of the Pacific. The beautiful interplay of deduction, observation, and experimentation provided powerful support for Darwin's basic evolutionary ideas. The conception of populations and the manner in which these populations were formed and dispersed led him to the notion of speciation—the formation of permanently separated groups.

The next major development in Darwin's thinking involved the relationship between the environment and the organism's adaptation to it. The first step was extending the Malthusian notion to consider the extinction of less well-adapted organisms. This extension was not adequate, however, since it said nothing of the direction evolution might take. With the addition of the idea that the survival of an individual can affect the characteristics of the species by gradually altering the proportion of individuals with a given characteristic, the directions in which the population might evolve could be understood. In other words, the idea of population dynamics is at hand: the nature of individual interactions and the laws which govern these interactions. Regarded in this light natural selection is, basically, differential reproduction with all of its causes.

The major lack in the complete Darwinian model was the nature of the precise mechanism by which hereditary variations were effected. The inclusion of this mediating mechanism awaited the rediscovery of Mendel's laws of heredity in 1900. With the unification of Mendellian and Darwinian theory in the 1920s and 1930s, the modern synthetic theory of evolution was established and has held sway since that time.

Darwin's Immediate Influence on Animal Psychology

The argument up to now has been that Darwin has presented a complex system and a methodology adequate to understand the precise nature and interplay of the processes involved in the interaction of organisms with their environment. His use of the deductive method and his understanding of the value of probabilistic statements were two of his most important methodological contributions. It is appropriate, now, to inquire into his effect on the succeeding theories of behavior. I will begin by discussing theories of animal behavior and will then proceed to a concern with American structuralism, functionalism, learning theory, and social psychology.

Sir John Lubbock, an English naturalist whose primary work was published in 1882, observed ants in natural environments, and attempted to interpret the orientation and aggregation of invertebrates as an expression of conscious choice based on the pleasure–pain principle. His major influence was, however, a methodological one: he originated the Y-maze to study the sensory capacities of the ant. His rejection of the anecdotal method of Romanes in favor of controlled experimentation is one of the first steps taken from field-oriented research toward the laboratory problem method.

Such influential writers as Carl Warden (1927) consider Jacques Loeb and C. Lloyd Morgan to be the founders of the "new scientific order" in animal psychology, as contrasted to the old tendency by such Darwinians as Romanes to humanize the behavior of animals. The anthropomorphic tendency was considered by Warden to be a "serious menace to scientific developments within this field [p.151]."

Loeb's publication, in 1890, of his tropism theory helped to establish a mechanistic tradition in the study of animal behavior. The principle of forced movements as a result of sensory stimulation provided an alternative to concepts based on the anecdotal methods of studying the behavior of animals, and gave a strong impetus to the attempts to analyze the behavior of animals experimentally.

At about the same time C. Lloyd Morgan (1894) began to apply laboratory methods to the study of the behavior of the higher vertebrates. He investigated the instinctive behavior of ducks, chicks, and partridges, and emphasized the prime importance of trial and error in animal learning. He accepted the principle of Darwinian natural selection, but rejected all Lamarckian views. He also insisted that animal behavior should be investigated for its own sake and not merely to provide evidence for or against the doctrine of mental continuity and evolution.

Morgan (1894) is primarily remembered for his statement of the law of parsimony, known as Lloyd Morgan's canon. "In no case may we interpret an action as the outcome of the exercise of a higher psychical faculty, if it can be interpreted as the outcome of the exercise of one which stands lower in the psychological scale [p.59]."

Herbert Spencer Jennings worked with simple organisms such as protozoans and, while adding tremendously to the experimental literature Jennings, 1906), came to the conclusion that the behavior of even the simplest organisms was not as simple as Loeb's theory would suggest. He found that there was great deal of variability between different animals, and in the same animal on different occasions, in response to the same stimulating environment. He attributed these differences to variations in the inner physiological states of the animals at different times. This tended to make better explanatory sense and introduced a dynamic factor into the highly static and mechanistic hypotheses of Loeb (1890).

The tremendous interest in the application of experimental laboratory methods to the study of animal behavior is most evident in the enthusiastic reception accorded to the research of Thorndike, which began appearing in 1898. He employed the problem box to study learning in chicks, cats, dogs, and monkeys. The extent to which his laboratory approach was accepted was indicated by the fact that major laboratories were immediately established at Clark, Harvard, and Chicago; by 1927 there were some 19 laboratories in the United States devoted to the laboratory investigation of animal behavior (Warden & Warner, 1927). Thorndike's specific contributions will be discussed later when learning theories are considered.

This brief survey indicates that the initial impetus to the study of behavior was provided by Darwin's principle of mental continuity. Individuals such as Romanes continued the tradition of using the anecdotal method, which was so effectively used by Darwin. However, a skepticism developed regarding the degree of anthropomorphism inherent in the anecdotal method, and a more mechanistic position was accepted. More and more attention became centered on the experimental laboratory, especially within the discipline of psychology. With Thorndike, the field of psychology split from the Darwinian biological tradition, and the development of what have come to be known as "theories of learning" began.

Structuralism

The ready acceptance of laboratory methods into animal psychology was aided by the attitudes regarding psychology as a science that prevailed in other branches of the field. Wundt, in Germany, and his student, Titchener, in the United States were quite influential in the developing science of psychology, and are important in the present context in terms of their views on methodology. They represent the school that was known as structuralism, the aim of which was to discover the contents of the mind and, in this way, to delineate the structure of consciousness. Titchener defined psychology as "experience dependent on an experiencing person." He sought to reduce mind to its elements and discover the laws by which the elements combine. Titchener considered psychology to be an extension of the scientific method to a new field of inquiry and believed that the subject matter (and, ideally, the methods) of the two sciences, physics and psychology, were essentially the same: that physics studies the world without reference to man, while psychology studies the world with reference to the person who experiences it. This led to a descriptive and static view and represented the dominant influence of classical German psychophysics on psychology. This view of the organism helped to establish the use of systematic laboratory-based experimentation as the preferred method in psychology. The specific method of introspection was rejected subsequently, as was the insistence that the study of consciousness was the proper subject matter of psychology. Yet, one should not underestimate the strong methodological influence the Structuralists had on the developing science of psychology.

Functionalism

The functionalists were much more in the main line of Darwinian thought. They followed Darwin in their interest not only in description but in discovering the principles by which the mind developed. They were pragmatists, and were interested in the activities of the mind and the adaptation of organisms to their environment. Their interests made it inevitable that a more dynamic view would be championed by the functionalists than by the structuralists.

Perhaps the single most influential book on the developing science of psychology was *The Principles of Psychology,* published in 1890 by William James. James had a strong philosophical and pragmatic bent and did almost no experimental research. His breadth of interest and the far-reaching scope of his pragmatic outlook made him quite receptive to Darwinian principles. For example, he argued that mental facts cannot be properly studied apart from the physical environment in which these facts take place. He rejected the ideas of such people as Wundt and Titchener that one should start with the simplest basic units of consciousness and seek to understand the manner in which they are compounded. Rather, he emphasized the importance of impalpable functional *acts* as opposed to palpable structural *contents.* James suggested that consciousness evolved for a use and that it was "to the highest degree improbable *a priori*" that it should have no use. This molar functional view led Heidbreder (1933) to write "Whereas Titchener was intent chiefly on making the new psychology a science, James was more concerned that the new science be psychology [p.152]."

The theory of emotion which bears his name, The James-Lange theory of emotion, characteristically emphasized the total situation in which an organism finds itself. Throughout the development of the emotion theory in *The Principles,* James quotes Darwin with approval except for a rejection of the Lamarckian notions which run through both *The Descent* and *The Expression.*

The psychology of James became embodied in a modestly self-conscious school, functionalism. This school regarded mental processes as being useful to an organism in the act of adapting itself to its environment. James Angell, one of the dominant spokesman of the new University of Chicago based functionalism, argued that functionalists should study mental activity not in and by itself, as structuralists would have it, but that mental activity should be viewed as a part of the whole world of biological activity which is a result of organic evolution.

Harvey Carr, whose influential *Psychology: A Study of Mental Activity* (1925) represented functionalism at its most mature stage, emphasized the adaptive significance of mental acts and discussed adaptive responses in terms of organisms adapting to situations—a molar and dynamic view. For example, he states (1925) "Any adaptive response to an object must thus be influenced by and be dependent upon the entire sensory situation of the moment. We may then say that an organism reacts to the sensory situation as a whole while it adapts to or reacts toward but one aspect of that situation [p.76]." The functionalists did not reject introspection, but neither did they accept it as the only method for psychology as the structuralists insisted they should. They were more prone to accept observational data from naturalistic situations. Even in their animal experimental reports, they would tend to speculate regarding the nature of the animal's consciousness and then discuss how these processes function to adapt the animal to its environment. This emphasis on consciousness retarded the acceptance of the basic functionalist position in the objectivist climate of American psychology—a climate in which one of the primary interests was in establishing psychology as a legitimate scientific enterprise. It is unfortunate that the conceptualizations of the functionalists were essentially lost to the mainstream of psychological thought. Functionalism, with its emphasis on conscious processes, gave way to the onslaught of the behaviorist crusade, and many of those individuals considered to be in the functionalist tradition, such as John McGeoch, turned to the molecular and systematic study of human verbal learning.

Learning Theory

The study of animal behavior came to be identified within psychology with general theories of learning. These theories were concerned mainly with rat behavior, and the aim of the empirical research was to explicate and to evaluate tenets of theory rather than to inquire into the behavioral propensities of organisms. The strategies used to study animal behavior made use of laboratory tasks in the interest of achieving rigorous control of conditions and of making replication easier to accomplish. Variability in behavior came to be regarded as unwanted error variance that obscured the search for general laws, and any technique that tended to reduce variability, thereby being sensitive to the systematic manipulation of experimental variables, tended to be the preferred technique.

As mentioned earlier, Thorndike pioneered in the establishment of the laboratory problem method. His monograph, in 1898, is regarded as the first systematic report of the study of animal intelligence by means of laboratory experimentation. Thorndike accepted mental continuity in principle, but believed the essential continuity had been misunderstood because of reliance on the anecdotal method. He wrote of the field of animal psychology that "most of the books do not give us a psychology, but rather a *eulogy* of animals. They have all been about animal intelligence, never about animal *stupidity* [p.37]."

In his monograph (1898), he enumerated the problems inherent in the use of the anecdotal method and concluded that answers regarding the nature of animal behavior could only be achieved through the use of carefully designed crucial experiments. He wrote "experiments must be substituted for observation and the collection of anecdotes [p.6]." He believed that a science could be built only if conditions can be repeated at will, if a number of animals can be subjected to the same test, if the animals can be freed from the influence of the observer (thereby increasing inter-experimenter reliability), and if animals can be tested in "instructive" situations "which call into activity their mental functions and permit them to be carefully observed [p.7]."

Thorndike (1911) concluded that reason was lacking among all animals except man and that one should engage in the study of association in seeking the general psychological law. "When this is done, we shall . . . relieve human mentality from its isolation and see its real relationships with other forms . . . [p.240]."

Although he accepted the proposition (1911) that there is mental continuity—"The most important of all original abilities is the ability to learn. It, like other capacities, has evolved [p.278]"—he has focused on general principles of learning at the molecular associative level instead of at a molar functional level. This "reversed" doctrine of mental continuity (that the basic associative principles are the same for all organisms) was quickly accepted, and it helped to provide the rationale, for basing theories of learning on one representative of the animal series—the laboratory rat. (Lockard, 1968, should be consulted for an interesting discussion of some of the implications of this choice of the rat as a representative species.)

Thorndike not only provided a rationale for much of the succeeding research in animal learning, but also urged a method and argued its merits in a very convincing manner to a science having difficulty staying afloat in a sea of introspections and anecdotes.

While Thorndike provided the scientific and methodological impetus, it was Watson who popularized the idea that nothing of significance was to be learned about behavior from the study of instinctive biological processes—that all emphasis should be turned to a study of environmental events.

One of Watson's first influential books was *Behavior: An Introduction to Comparative Psychology*, published in 1914. In it he clearly stated the aims of behaviorism as being the prediction and control of behavior and insisted that any concern with consciousness and introspection was outside the scope of psychology. He outlined much of what was known at the time concerning biological systems and the instinctive mechanisms in behavior, including a discussion of Darwinian principles. However, he rejected the idea that there was any inheritance of continuous variation in behavior. Watson correctly characterized this type of inheritance as basic to the whole Darwinian theory. Since he concluded that heritable characteristics are constant, and since the total variation is due to responses of the organism to changes in its environment, such heritable characteristics play no significant role in behavior. He based this rejection on a study of the heritability of seed size in a population of bean plants (Watson, 1914, pp.160–161). In this study it was found "for the different races" that the variations in seed size within a race were *not* inherited. From this simple genetic expression determining the size of seeds, he extrapolated to the complex genetic expression that is involved in even the simplest molar behavioral characters. Watson accepted environmental effects as being the determinants of all individual differences. He accepted natural selection only as a negative factor, "killing off those organisms unfitted to live in the environment in which they are placed [p.169]"; and rejected its positive nature, since it "has no part in shaping . . . adaptations . . . [p.169]."

Watson's third book, *Behaviorism,* published in 1924, contained almost no reference to Darwin or to evolutionary processes. The only importance of complex inherited tendencies was considered to be in the realm of emotions: fear, rage, and love were held to be the basic unlearned responses to loss of support, hampering of bodily movement, and gentle tactile stimulation, respectively.

The *Zeitgeist* was ready for this extreme environmentalism. Warden (1927) expressed this readiness as follows: "The behavioristic postition represents the complete overthrow of metaphysical speculation in comparative psychology and the substitution therefore of biological conceptions and methods [p.163]." Warden goes on to enumerate the objective phenomena available to psychology as being the "organism, stimulus and response or behavior which can be reduced to the quantitative terminology of natural science." Thus he concludes that "Watson and the behaviorists [mark] the overthrow of metaphysical speculation and anthropomorphic interpretation in comparative psychology. A biological or organismic viewpoint has come to be the prevailing one with a proper insistence on objective, quantitative data [p.164]."

Watson (1924) did not accept the law of effect, since he believed that speaking in such a way that pleasure is thought to "stamp in responses" and displeasure to "stamp them out," after the manner of Thorndike, implied the existence of manikins in the brain "as though they were a group of tiny servants of Vulcan there who run through the nervous system with hammer and chisel digging new trenches and deepening old ones [p. 206]."

The new behaviorism has been accurately characterized by Boring (1950) as being experimental, elementistic (behavior is composed of reflexes), and associationistic (the task is to discover the laws of compounding).

The later theories of Hull (1943) and of Skinner (1938) embraced the methodological and systematic views outlined by Watson (albeit in quite different ways), and psychology moved into a phase in which the rat and pigeon were used to delineate the general laws of learning.

Tolman (1932) among the behaviorists remained unconvinced by the necessity for the elementistic and associationistic views of the others and sought to retain a functionalistic and probabilistic flavor to his theory—a theory that was, however, based almost entirely on laboratory studies of the rat. Tolman's contributions will not be discussed at this point, since many of his views which are salient to the present argument will be presented when the position of Brunswik (who was brought to the United States by Tolman) are discussed.

Thus the Darwinian influence moved out of the mainstream of the study of animal behavior as represented by the learning theories of the 1940s and 1950s. These theories accepted the environmentalism of Watson, used controlled laboratory methods, systematic research designs, and molecular definitions of response units to discover the nomothetic principles on which learning is based.

Social Psychology

It is ironic that the major influences of Darwinian biology should have been on that aspect of psychology—social psychology—which is the least involved in matters pertaining to the major aspects of Darwin's own research and theories. The study of emotional expression, of the communication of emotion, and of social interactions was assumed by social psychologists who attempted to grapple with the complex molar problems inherent in organism–environment interactions rather than define these complex matters as being outside their purview. Thus they were generally receptive to molar functional analyses such as those used by Darwin and tended to resist the temptation to concentrate on molecular detail.

William McDougall (1908) developed a functional purposive psychology which accepted Darwinian evolution. McDougall believed that much of man's behavior can be understood by looking into the instinctive bases of behavior, that these instincts have evolved by natural selection, and that there is a relationship between human and prehuman instincts. His

Social Psychology was immensely successful and, according to Murphy (1949), more than 100,000 copies were sold over the 20-year period following its publication. Building on mental continuity as a base, McDougall developed an elaborate social psychology using complex instincts as his "units" and assigning them a leading role in the determination of human conduct and mental process.

The associationistic and anti-instinct psychologists of the behaviorist tradition immediately rose to the challenge and attacked McDougall's system. The final result was that the behaviorists carried the day, and the major emphasis within social psychology turned to the role of environmental factors, in opposition to *any* consideration of the biology of the individual. Although this rejection of the instinct theory was quite generally accepted, vestiges of Darwinism remained alive within social psychology whenever emotional expression was considered.

Floyd Allport, in his *Social Psychology* (1924), outlined with approval Darwin's three principles of emotional expression and suggested that they be modified in such a way that facial movements be considered important in adapting to the social environment. He considered both the biologically useful reactions and the expressive vestiges of these reactions to be inherited and to have evolved through natural selection. Craig, 1921, had argued earlier that expressions are evolved adaptations "expressive movements are useful as a means of communication between organisms . . . and they must have evolved as adaptations to this end [p. 36]."

Solomon Asch, in his 1952 text, *Social Psychology,* argued that the evolutionary process must extend to psychological and social phenomena. He outlined Darwin's principles regarding emotional expression and recognized the importance of *The Descent of Man* in directing "interest to the biological basis of human sociability [p. 325]."

No purpose will be served by any further analysis of historical trends at this point. It will be more instructive, rather, to examine some contemporary trends in psychological research that embody the Darwinian principles emphasized in the preceding sections. Following this examination, some general methodological principles will be outlined, and it will be argued that these principles are essential whenever one wishes to study and understand organism–environment interactions.

PROBABILISTIC FUNCTIONALISM

The most consistent spokesman for the methodological point of view advocated in this paper is Egon Brunswik. Brunswik contributed many significant ideas to the historical analysis of conceptual trends in science (Brunswik, 1952) and to the development of methodologies adequate to the study of organism–environment interactions (Brunswik, 1956). Excellent summaries of Brunswik's point of view are available (Hammond, 1966; Postman & Tolman, 1959) and should be consulted along with the two monographs cited above to understand the scope of his thought. Only a few salient points will be developed which are germane to the methodological considerations of interest here.

"Brunswik's psychology is Darwinian; it is a form of functionalism because its main focus is on the adaptive interrelation of the organism with the environment [Hammond, 1966, p. 16]." Brunswik argues that one must deal with the nature of the environment as carefully as with the nature of the organisms, and that this environmental analysis must be done in terms of what he refers to as distal objects and events.

Brunswik (1956) has pointed out that the historical development of scientific systems can be characterized as a shift from dichotomies to gradations, from subjective speculation to objectivism, from classification to causation, from static existence to dynamic flow. These trends have been evident in the historical development of psychology and have been accompanied by an increasing degree of distal reference—an extension of description and analysis outward and away from peripheral terms such as the behaviorists' classical S-R unit. The emphasis on distal achievement brings with it a concept of vacariousness, both in terms of the cues supporting behavior (cue–family–hierarchy) and in terms of the behavioral responses themselves (habit–family–hierarchy).

Brunswik developed most of his ideas regarding research design within the field of the psychology of perception, including social perception. He was, as mentioned earlier, influenced by Tolman, who emphasized the purposiveness of behavior and argued for a molar behaviorism. Tolman believed that in order to attain a goal, an organism must manipulate the "means–objects" that enable it to gain access to the goal. He stressed the facts that there are many alternative means—objects providing access to a goal. It is this focus on the functional achievements of the organism as it deals with the distal features of the environment that struck a resonant chord with Brunswik's belief (1952) that "vicarious functioning is thus indeed of the essence of behavior [p.92]."

Brunswik's functionalism has a distinct Darwinian flavor, and focuses concern on the relationship between the oganism and the environment. He called the system probabilistic functionalism because of the intraenvironmental object–cue and means–end relationships that must be utilized by the organism [p.23]." Brunswik is in the Darwinian tradition with his emphasis on the fact that the organism is dealing with cues of limited trustworthiness and that we must, therefore, regard behavior in terms of biological adjustment rather than in terms of physiological mediation. This gives us a statistically based science that must deal with behavior in terms of conditional probabilities. The "probabilistic character of behavioral laws is not primarily due to limitations in the researcher and his means of approach, but rather to imperfection inherent in the potentialities of adjustment on the part of the behaving organism living in a semichaotic environmental medium [p.28]." This macrostatistical view of psychology is required because of the immense array of molar cues and behaviors that must be considered. Such vicariousness makes it necessary to link behavior and the environment statistically in contrast to the situation found in such microstatistical sciences as physics, in which the identity of the individual elements is lost at the lowest levels rather than at the more complex levels, as is true in behavioral science.

Brunswik has made a convincing case that when dealing with behavior at the molar functional level we must develop a probabilistic science, and that this lack of absolute predictability is not a sign of weakness in the science but is, rather, required by the complexity of the cue and response systems involved. (This point was debated by Brunswik, 1955, and Postman, 1955, and the argument will not be pursued any further here.)

Most psychological research has employed what Brunswik calls systematic design, in which a relatively small number of variables is chosen for study, and then these variables are systematically manipulated. The ideal of this method is to hold all variables constant but one, to vary it systematically then control it and to allow another to vary, and so forth. This manner of proceeding is regarded by most scientists as representing an optimal strategy. As Hammond (1966) has pointed out,

> Every psychologist, and every student of behavioral sciences has been taught that without the ability and intent to control variables, that is, without the ability and intent systematically to include and exclude, and systematically to vary as the experimenter deems appropriate, there could be no science of psychology [p. 64].

McGuire (1969) has noted this same tendency within the field of social psychology: "The past 20 years has witnessed a progressively closer identification in the minds of the establishment (and of the students we train) of good social psychological research with laboratory manipulational research [p.21]."

Brunswik (as does Hammond, incidentally) raises objections to the use of systematic designs in the study of behavior. He points out that systematic designs almost inevitably involve the use of atypical backgrounds for the behaviors in question and embed the behavior in atypical contexts. Variables are manipulated by the experimenter in an arbitrary manner according to such guiding principles as symmetry and regularity.

Several problems with this procedure have been carefully discussed by Brunswik. One such problem involves the artificial tying of variables. As an example, consider the classic apparatus used to study the ability of individuals to estimate length—the Galton Bar. With this apparatus, two lines of unequal length can be presented at the same distance from the observer. The apparatus consists of a horizontal metal bar divided at the middle. The task of the observer is to adjust the length of one-half of the bar, which is movable, so that it appears to be equal to the length of the other, stationary, side. With this arrangement, the physical length of the line and the size of the retinal image vary in a one-to-one relationship. In Brunswik's terms (1956), the distal and the proximal cue (the physical length of the line and the size of the projected retinal image, respectively) "are inseparably tied by arrangement of the experimenter. This holds true as long as the scope of the investigation is confined to the laboratory situation in question. The two variables then vary in perfect unison, their correlation is artificially made to be one [p.9]."

Another problem involves what he calls the *artificial interlocking* of variables. This occurs when two lines are presented at different distances from the observer, who is required to judge the lengths of the lines. In this case the retinal projections are unequal. Thus the correlation between the variables is arbitrarily set at lower than 1.0, and this can be considered a small step toward greater representativeness.

The meaning of individual differences within the framework of systematic design also deserves comment. Since external conditions are systematically controlled, any individual differences in responses are treated as random error variance and are treated "quasi-systematically by computational elimination." Individual differences are, thus, considered as unwanted error variance produced by a lack of control of relevant factors. Postman (1955) adopts this view explicitly: "Proponents of the nomothetic point of view see the difficulty in inadequate knowledge of antecedent conditions, while retaining their belief in the essential uniformity of the behavioral laws; proponents of the probability view believe that the laws themselves must be stated in probability terms [p.222]."

REPRESENTATIVE DESIGN

Systematic design must be replaced by representative design if we are to understand the normal interplay of environmental and organismic variables. In representative design, the probabilistic nature of environmental circumstances is accurately reflected, and the full measure of the organism's ability to cope with environmental circumstances is exhibited. These ends are attained by representative sampling of situations from the organism's

ecology—the natural cultural habitat of the organism. Variables remain correlated as they are in the environment with such representative designs.
Any control that is exerted is a passive control, and the experimenter proceeds
by actuarial registration of the values of the relevant variables. The use
of this design implies that the choice of the variables themselves should
be based on their biological relevance.

Experimenters must be concerned with "ecological" or "situational"
generality of research results, and will have to devote as much attention
to the structure of the environment and to take as much trouble to obtain
representative samples from that environment as they usually do with the
problem of obtaining representative samples of subjects.

Brunswik (1956) argues that "No matter how much the results of systematic
experiments may anticipate those of a representative survey, in a technical
sense only representative design can answer functional problems definitely
[p. 70]." He makes the interesting point that systematic design is useful
to demonstrate *possiblity,* whereas representative design is adequate to the
task of investigating *probability.*

> Quite often the demonstration of mere possibility . . . is all that is necessary and desired
> of a piece of research, and may be fully sufficient to establish tentatively a principle
> for purposes of further verification and thus to stimulate further research; in all cases
> of this kind the systematic experiment is in place and may save the burdens that would
> go with a proof of ecological generality. In other cases, a systematic experiment may
> serve to exclude certain trivial factors from the explanation of a phenomenon. On the
> other hand, the most striking shortcomings in the generalizability of results of systematically
> rather than representatively conducted experiments are given when it comes to a quantita-
> tive estimate of the relative contribution of competing factors in functional adjustment
> to the environment [p.55].[3]

This brings us to two basic concepts in representative design: ecological
validity and functional validity. *Ecological validity* is defined as the correlation between a proximal cue and a distal object. This means that if the
height of an individual's forehead (proximal cue) was perfectly correlated
with his intelligence (distal object), then the forehead cue would have complete ecological validity in regards to the trait in question, intelligence.
Intraecological correlation refers to the relationship between various cues
in the environment. If intraecological correlations between different cues,
say forehead height and length of nose, are high, then we would consider
the environment to be *redundant.*

---

[3]From Brunswik, E. *Perception and the representative design of psychological experiments.*
Berkeley: Univ. of California Press, 1956, reprinted by permission of The Regents of the
University of California.

Functional validity is defined as the correlation between the distal object and the perceptual response: the study of environmental cues *as used* by the observer to make the response. In a perceptually well-adjusted organism the rank order of utilization of environmental cues (functional validity) should be the same order as the order of their environmental significance (ecological validity).

Brunswik's statement of probabilistic functionalism is a sophisticated methodological point of view. It focuses on the functional adjustment of organisms to their environment and outlines the research strategies adequate to the task of understanding these adjustments. Brunswik's acceptance of a basic probabilistic texture underlying behavior was forced by the same reality as was Darwin's—the underlying probabilistic structure of the environment. Brunswik demonstrated the necessity of studying the ecology itself and of insuring that research be based on a representative sample from the ecology in order to derive conclusions having ecological generality.

There is, undoubtedly, a place for both systematic and representative design. Clearly, we need systematic research in order to identify the *possible* variables related to an outcome so that they might be sampled (or "registered") and so that we might proceed to the study of such things as intra-ecological correlation, ecological validity, and functional validity. In fact, the value of the combination of the two strategies is evident in one of Brunswik's own examples. Brunswik (1956, p.111) studied the impressions of observers to schematic faces. In this study he used 189 face stimuli and had them judged by 10 observers. Samuels (1939) selected 10 of the 189 faces that were at the extremes on the impression scale established by Brunswik and showed them to 247 observers. The final outcome of this research program was that there can be some confidence regarding both the ecological and the organismic generality in the conclusions arrived at as a result of using the two different research strategies.

It is interesting that Brunswik dealt with the same problem as did Darwin—the nature of facial expression in emotion—and that he adopted the same methodological strategies. It is also interesting that Brunswik indicated that his "functional theory takes on certain features of economic theory"—and that Darwin indicated that it was his reading of the economic theories of Malthus which led him to the keystone for the theory of evolution.

I would like to conclude this section on Brunswik with a quotation from Hammond (1966):

> We know, however, that the history of every scientific discipline provides an admonition that credence, wary though it may be, must be given to those who reexamine the fundamental concepts of the discipline in a responsible and particularistic way. For it is the relentless scrutiny of the least questioned, most apparent truths that

uncovers the greatest scientific gold. But such efforts are dangerous, for failure at this venture is complete failure—or what may be worse, one's work may be reduced to a curiosity and a warning to the timid. Moreover, history may be slow to provide its judgment. As a result, we must prejudge the issue. Because some of us who were Egon Brunswik's students caught a glimmer of gold, we believe that the fundamental changes he envisioned will occur. Even more important, perhaps, we were inspired to investigate thoughtful unorthodoxy, to admire the scholarly unconventional, and given courage to lend credence to the new idea—a result worthwhile in its own right [p. 77].[4]

I concur heartily with Hammond's view and suggest that as the study of behavior moves to more careful studies of organism—environment interactions, Brunswik's historical and methodological contributions will be ranked among the most important in the last few decades.

ETHOLOGY

The most direct line of Darwinian influence on the study of complex behavior has been through the branch of zoology called ethology. The ethologists believe that in order to understand the behavior of any species, it is necessary to study that behavior in the natural environment. They argue that one must begin such a study with careful observation of the behavior patterns of the organism in its ecology. They call this inventory of the behavioral patterns of a species an *ethogram* and believe that it must be the starting point for any investigation of behavior (Tinbergen, 1951). This emphasis on naturalistic observation places the ethologists in agreement with Darwin as far as what they consider to be the proper starting point for science.

Lorenz (1965) underscores the importance of developing such ethograms to understand the effects of any experimental manipulation on an animal's behavioral patterns. Instead of studying arbitrarily selected components of an animal's behavior repertoire, it is more meaningful to observe the effects of an experimental manipulation on the animal's whole system of actions.

Tinbergen (1951) points out that the usual strategy of the comparative psychologist, in which he places different species in exactly the same experimental arrangement and then studies some aspect of the organism's behavior in this environment, is an "anthropomorphic kind of standardization." He argues that "it might be useful to approach learning phenomena from a more naturalistic standpoint than is usually done and to ask, not what can

---

[4]From Hammond, K. R. Probabilistic functionalism: Egon Brunswik's integration of history, theory, and method in psychology. In K. R. Hammond (Ed.), *The psychology of Egon Brunswik.* New York: Holt, Rinehart and Winston, 1966.

an animal learn, but what does it actually learn under natural conditions? [p.142]." This statement is reminiscent of our earlier distinction between a science that is based on the study of behavioral *possibilities* rather than the more satisfactory study of behavioral *probabilities*. It is interesting that Tinbergen considers the laboratory strategies adopted by animal psychologists to embody the very anthropomorphism they were seeking to avoid in their rejection of the anecdotal method.

Furthermore, the ethologists have emphasized, as did Darwin, the necessity of carefully studying the instinctive bases of behavior—the bases on which all later modifications are built. The concept of instinct as defined by ethologists is one that lacks the stereotyped, mechanistic qualities of the earlier definitions. They emphasize, instead, the vicarious nature of instinctive expression and, indeed, embrace a strong functionalist point of view with an emphasis on a distal achievement orientation. Tinbergen (1951), for example, defines instinct as

> . . . a hierarchically organized nervous mechanism which is susceptible to certain priming, releasing and directing impulses of internal as well as of external origin, and which responds to these impulses by coordinated movements that contribute to the maintenance of the individual and the species [p.112].

Even the ethologists' most mechanistic entity, the fixed-action pattern, has been endowed with a degree of vicariousness and hierarchical organization. Tinbergen (1951) emphasizes the importance of such things as displacement activities—activities that result from a surplus of motivation whose discharge is prevented through normal channels. This surplus motivation triggers other fixed patterns that have a higher threshold and that may not be appropriate to the situation.

Barlow (1968) has suggested that the hierarchical conception of the structure of fixed-action patterns should be recognized more sharply and makes a convincing argument for considering fixed action patterns as *modal action patterns,* since there is usually a distribution of patterns around a central tendency. This distribution of patterns could well be both intra- and interindividual and could provide yet another expression of the probabilistic texture of behavior.

On the stimulus side, we find the ethologists expressing ideas that emphasize the probabilistic texture of cue systems:

> . . . an animal responds "blindly" to only part of the total environmental situation and neglects other parts, although its sense organs are perfectly able to receive them (and probably do receive them), and although they may seem to be no less important, to the human observer, than the stimuli to which it does react [Tinbergen, 1951, p.277].

The necessity of recognizing the importance of variables at the molar level is demanded by the existence of behavior systems in which innate reactions display a selective responsiveness to special stimulating situations. One reaction may be released by light of a certain wavelength, while another reaction is released only by intensity differences and is independent of wavelength. As Tinbergen indicates, anybody studying the first reaction would come to the conclusion that the animal sees colors, whereas somebody studying only the second reaction would judge the animal to be color blind. Thus we must have a thorough knowledge of the behavior patterns available to the organism in given situations, and we must recognize the inherent flexibility of organism–environment interaction systems.

I have argued elsewhere that to understand the phenomenon of habituation, it is necessary to consider the meaningfulness of particular habituation stimuli in terms of the ecology of the species. It is not possible to develop an understanding of the laws of habituation apart from such a "species-meaningful" analysis (Petrinovich, 1973).

The approach of the ethologists is toward the molar, functional, and dynamic view which characterizes Darwinism and which Brunswik has demonstrated to characterize a maturing science. This same tendency is expressed in a comparison of the ecologists' and physiologists' view of organism–environment interactions by Klopfer and Hailman (1967):

> The ecologist's explanation is a molar approach to behavioral control: how is a stimulus transformed (in the descriptive sense) into a response? The physiologists' approach is molecular: what are the series of transformations (and the structures that mediate them) that take place between stimulus and response? [p.196]

Klopfer and Kilham consider these two approaches to be complementary. I would argue that they are complementary only in the sense that they are legitimate scientific concerns and that only one, the molar view, is adequate to the specific task of delineating organism–environment interactions.

There is a great complementarity between the views of Darwin, Brunswik, and the ethologists. This complementary has been forced by the necessity of dealing with complex relationships both at the individual and at the species level. One further quotation from Tinbergen (1951) makes this point even more compelling—Darwin could have written the same passage; the last two sentences exemplify Brunswik's basic position:

> There is another way in which adaptiveness fails to tell the whole story. Each form of behaviour may be adaptive and yet have characteristics that can only be explained historically. For instance, pigeons and sand-grouse drink in a different way (viz. by sucking) from other birds, which scoop water. These two modes of behavior are both adaptive. The differences, however, are of historical origin; the two move-

ments are not homologous, but they are convergent solutions based on different foundations. *In this way all behaviour is at the same time adaptive and non-adaptive, and both aspects are found by comparative study. The study of convergences helps to show up adaptiveness; the study of differences in convergent behaviour types helps to reveal the basic historic background* [p. 153; italics added].[5]

Recently, the field of comparative psychology has become sensitive to many of the problems inherent in a strict reliance on laboratory experimentation that does not take into account species-specific actions to different environmental contexts. Bolles (1970) has made a convincing case that avoidance learning in the laboratory can only be understood if one considers the response requirements of a task in terms of species-specific defense reactions. Garcia (Garcia & Koelling, 1966; Garcia, McGowan, Erwin, & Koelling, (1968) has demonstrated that avoidance learning is not completely plastic, but that the biological appropriateness of the antecedent stimulus and response and the consequent effects on the animal must be understood to predict whether or not the animal is able to make the required association. There is a recognition that the lack of progress in understanding organism—environment interactions has been due to a faulty conceptual framework. Hodos and Campbell (1969), Lockard (1971), and Seligman (1970) have each outlined some of these problems, and a comparative psychology is appearing that is based on naturalistic observation and on the utilization of molar biological theory.

Another interest in naturalistic research has come about partly as a function of the recent concern with the environment and with the realization that we know little concerning the way individuals react in representative situations. This interest has been stimulated and maintained for many years by Barker (1968), and a sampling of the breadth of this interest can be found in the volume edited by Willems and Raush (1969). McGuire (1969) has developed the thesis that theory-oriented research in social psychology should be conducted in natural settings more than is now the case.

"THE EXPRESSION OF THE EMOTIONS"

It is time, now, to turn from our historical and methodological analyses and to conclude with a consideration of that research which is most directly related to the ideas contained in *The Expression of the Emotions in Man and Animals.* In research in this area, one is faced with a high degree of complexity in terms of cues, in terms of the judgmental processes involved, and in terms of the presumed underlying dispositions. Brunswik (1956) studied facial expression partly because of the realization that it represented

---

[5]From Tinbergen, N. *The study of instinct.* London: Oxford Univ. Press, 1951.

one of the areas of perceptual research, in which representative design was the most essential:

> ... human appearance, and especially the face, constitutes as tight a package of innumerable contributing variables as might be found anywhere in cognitive research. This is what makes the face the choice paradigm for illustration of problems in multidimensional representativeness [p.115].

Ekman (Ekman, Friesen, & Ellsworth, 1972) has approached the same problem with a similar recognition of the complexity:

> The *complexity* of the face is apparent when we consider its sending capacity, the information it may convey, and its role in social life ... The face can send messages about such transient and sometimes fleeting events as a feeling or emotion, or the moment-to-moment fluctuations of a conversation [p.1].

Recent investigators in this field, influenced by both Darwin and Brunswik, have approached the study of facial expression with an awareness of some of the underlying conceptual problems and a concern for the problem of the ecological generality of their results. This awareness and concern has led to a methodological sophistication that acknowledges the probabilistic textures involved and resists the temptation to retreat into controlled systematic experimentation. Tomkins (1962), for example, is quite sensitive to the broad-reaching evolutionary implications of the study of affect, and has chided American psychology for its refusal to face such issues. "Proud and aloof on the banks of the mainstream of human history, American psychology guards its virginity. It will give itself to the laboratory but not to man in real time [Tomkins, 1964, p.72]."

From the ethological perspective, Eibl-Eibesfeldt (1970) has been concerned with the expression of emotion and has followed the Darwinian tradition of seeking observational evidence wherever it may be found. In his recent book (1970), he has summarized a broad range of evidence based on animals, on deaf and blind infants, on cross-cultural studies, and on posed emotion. In addition, he has developed a system making it possible to photograph facial expression in the field without the subject's awareness. This technique should make it possible to obtain objective records which do not have as many shortcomings as do the typical anthropological field data on which many cross-cultural studies depend.

The most comprehensive and compelling experimental evidence regarding facial expression has been obtained by Paul Ekman and his collaborators (Ekman et al., 1972). Ekman's program has been successful because of his recognition of the methodological difficulties inherent in the study of facial expression and because of his concern with the problems in achieving representativeness and generality. He has faced the problem of ecological generality by using representative object sampling as well as representative subject sampling; he has faced the issues of the comparability, the advantages and disadvantages of using posed as compared to spontaneous facial expressions; he has taken cognizance of the fact that in attempting to decide whether or not there is any universality in facial expression among humans it will be necessary to understand the contribution of what he calls display rules: cultural overlays on whatever innate foundation there might be. Ekman believes this interference system influences emotional behavior in three ways: "by determining which situations evoke which emotions, by conditioning the amount of overt emotional behavior which is culturally acceptable in a situation, and by directing the manner in which the emotions manifest themselves [Ekman et al., 1972, p.154]."

Ekman has summarized eight studies (Ekman et al., 1972) of facial behavior in different cultures: Six of them indicate that the same facial behaviors are judged as representing the same emotions by observers from different cultures; one indicates that emotions posed by members of a preliterate culture (New Guinea native) are accurately judged by members of a literate culture (United States college students); and one indicates that the same facial components are elicited in emotion-provoking situations in two different cultures.

Ekman et al. (1972) conclude on the basis of these data that there is "very strong evidence that facial expressions are universally associated with the same specific emotions [p.45]." "There is one fundamental aspect of the relationship between facial behavior and emotion which is universal for man: the association between the movements of specific facial muscles and specific emotions [Ekman et al., 1972, p. 177]." They conclude:

> We believe, then, that we have isolated and demonstrated the basic set of universal facial expressions of emotion. They are not a language which varies from one place to another. . . . While facial expressions of emotion will often be culture specific because of differences in elicitors, display rules, and consequences, there is also a pan-cultural set of facial expression of emotion [p.51].

Thus when we return to the Darwinian tradition of broad-ranging naturalistic observation at an adequate level of functional analysis, many of the most complex problems begin to yield—problems that have been unyielding for many years to both the pressures of laboratory investigation and to those of unbridled reliance on anecdotal report. An awareness of the inherent strengths of the Darwinian method combined with the strength of the Brunswikian strategies will lead us in the direction of finding many answers to long-standing problems and will, in addition, open new avenues of inquiry that will help us understand the mutual impact of organism and environment.

I will close with an eloquent statement by Ghiselin:

The explorer's virtues must not be confounded with those of the prophet. Darwin was a great scientist because he asked great questions. He was an influential scientist because he seized upon those problems which, at the time, could be exploited in futher research. His works retain their interest for the working biologist because they continue to generate new and useful theories. His thoughts have been historically important because they illuminated the path of investigation, regardless of where that path may lead [1969, p.241].

REFERENCES

Allport, F. H. *Social psychology*. New York: Houghton Mifflin, 1924.

Andrew, R. J. Evolution of intelligence and vocal mimicking. *Science,* 1962, **137**, 585–589.

Asch, S. *Social psychology*. Englewood Cliffs, New Jersey: Prentice-Hall, 1952.

Barker, R. G. *Ecological psychology*. Standford: Stanford Univ. Press, 1968.

Barlow, G. Ethological units of behavior. In D. Ingle (Ed.), *The central nervous system and fish behavior*. Chicago: Univ. of Chicago Press, 1968. Pp.217–232.

Bolles, R. C. Species-specific defense reactions and avoidance learning. *Psychological Review,* 1970, **77**, 32–48.

Boring, E. G. *A history of experimental psychology*. New York: Appleton-Century-Crofts, 1950.

Brunswik, E. *The conceptual framework of psychology*. In *International encyclopedia of united science*, Vol. 1, No. 10. Chicago: Univ. of Chicago Press, 1952.

Brunswik, E. *Perception and the representative design of psychological experiments*. Berkeley: Univ. of California Press, 1956.

Brunswik, E. Representative design and probabilistic theory in a functional psychology. *Psychological Review,* 1955, **62**, 193–217.

Carr, H. A. *Psychology: A study of mental activity*. New York: Longmans, Green, 1925.

Craig, W. A note on Darwin's work on the expression of the emotions in man and animals. *Journal of Abnormal & Social Psychology,* 1921, **16**, 356–366.

Darwin, C. *The voyage of the Beagle*. London: Henry Colburn, 1839. (Reprinted, New York: Doubleday and Co., 1962.)

Darwin, C. *On the origin of species by means of natural selection*. New York: D. Appleton and Company, 1859. (Reprinted New York: Modern Library, 6th ed., 1872.)

Darwin, C. *The Descent of Man*. New w York: D. Appleton and Company, 1871. (Reprinted New York: Modern Library.)

Darwin, C. (1872) *The expression of the emotions in man and in animals*. New York: D. Appleton and Company, 1872. (Reprinted Chicago: Univ. of Chicago Press, 1965.)

Darwin, C. *The Autobiography of Charles Darwin*. London: John Murrary, 1887. (Reprinted New York: W. W. Norton and Company, 1969.)

Eibl-Eibesfeldt, I. *Ethology: The biology of behavior*. New York: Holt, Rinehart and Winston, 1970.

Ekman, P. Universals and cultural differences in facial expressions of emotion. In J. K. Cole (Ed.), *Nebraska Symposium on Motivation, 1971*. Lincoln, Nebraska: Univ. of Nebraska Press, 1972.

Ekman, P., Friesen, W. V., & Ellsworth, P. *Emotion in the human face: Guidelines for research and a review of findings*. New York: Pergamon Press, 1972.

Garcia, J., & Koelling, R. A. Relation of cue to consequence in avoidance learning. *Psychonomic Science,* 1966, **4,** 123–124.

Garcia, J., McGowan, B. K., Ervin, F. R., & Koelling, R. A. Cues: Their relative effectiveness as a function of the reinforcer. *Science,* 1968, 160, 794–795.

Ghiselin, M. *The triumph of the Darwinian method.* Berkeley: University of California Press, 1969.

Hammond, K. R. Probabilistic functionalism: Egon Brunswik's integration of the history, theory, and method of psychology. In K. R. Hammond (Ed.) *The psychology of Egon Brunswik.* New York: Holt, 1966.

Heidbreder, E. *Seven psychologies.* New York: Appleton-Century-Crofts, 1933.

Hodos, W., & Campbell, C. B. G. *Scala naturae:* Why there is no theory in comparative psychology. *Psychological Review,* 1969, **76**, 337–350.

Hull, C. L. *Principles of behavior.* New York: Appleton-Century-Crofts, 1943.

Irvine, W. *Apes, angels and victorians.* New York: McGraw-Hill, 1955.

James, W. *Principles of psychology.* New York: Holt, 1890.

Jennings, H. S. *Behavior of the lower organisms.* New York: Columbia Univ. Press, 1906.

Klopfer, P. H., & Hailman, J. P. *An introduction to animal behavior.* Englewood Cliffs, New Jersey: Prentice-Hall, 1967.

Lockard, R. B. The albino Rat: A defensible choice or a bad habit? *American Psychologist,* 1968, **23**, 734–742.

Lockard, R. B. Reflections on the fall of comparative psychology. *American Psychologist,* 1971, **26**, 168–179.

Loeb, J. *Der Heliotropismus der Thiere und seine Uebereinstimmung mit dem Heliotropismus der Pflanzen.* Wurzburg: Hertz, 1890.

Lorenz, K. *Evolution and modification of behavior.* Chicago: Univ. of Chicago Press, 1965.

Lubbock, J. *Ants, wasps, and bees.* New York: Appleton, 1882.

Malthus, T. R. *Population: The first essay (1798).* Ann Arbor: Univ. of Michigan Press, 1959.

McDougall, W. *An Introduction to social psychology.* London: Methuen, 1908.

McGuire, W. J. Theory-oriented research in natural settings: The best of both worlds for social psychology. In M. Sherif, and C. W. Sherif (Eds.), *Interdisciplinary relationships in the social sciences.* Chicago: Aldine, 1969.Pp.21–51.

Morgan, C. L. *Introduction to comparative psychology.* London: Walter Scott, 1894.

Murphy, G. *Historical introduction to modern psychology.* New York: Harcourt, 1949.

Petrinovich, L. Psychobiological mechanisms in language development. in G. Newton & A. H. Riesen (Eds.) *Advances in Psychobiology,* Vol. 1. New York: Wiley, 1972.

Petrinovich, L. A species-meaningful analysis of habituation. In H. V. S. Peeke & M. J. Herz (Eds.) *Habituation: Behavioral studies and physiological substrates,* Academic Press,1973.

Postman, L. The probability approach and nomothetic theory. *Psychological Review,* 1955, **62**, 218–226.

Postman, L., & Tolman, E. C. Brunswik's probabilistic functionalism. In S. Koch (Ed.) *Psychology: A study of a science,* Vol. 1. New York: McGraw-Hill, 1959. Pp. 502–564.

Samuels, M. Judgments of faces. *Character & Personality,* 1939, **8**, 18–27.

Seligman, M. E. P. On the generality of the laws of learning. *Psychological Review,* 1970, **77**, 406–418.

Skinner, B. F. (1938) *The behavior of organisms.* New York: Appleton, 1938.

Spencer, H. *Principles of psychology.* New York: Appleton, 1855.

Thorndike, E. L. Animal intelligence: An experimental study of the associative processes in animals. *Psychological Review Monograph Supplement,* 1898 (Whole No. 8).

Thorndike, E. L. *Animal intelligence.* New York: Macmillan, 1911.

Tinbergen, N. *The study of instinct.* London: Oxford Univ. Press, 1951.

Tolman, E. C. *Purposive behavior in animals and men.* New York: Appleton, 1932.

Tomkins, S. S. *Affect–Imagery–Consciousness.* Vol. 1. New York: Springer, 1962.

Tomkins, S. S. Affect and the psychology of knowledge. In S. S. Tomkins and C. E. Izard (Eds.) *Affect, Cognition, and Personality.* New York: Springer, 1964. Pp.72–97.

Warden, C. J. (1927) The historical development of comparative psychology. *Psychological Review*, **34**, 196–205.

Warden, C. J., & Warnen, L. H. The development of animal psychology in the United States during the past three decades. *Psychological Review*, 1927, **34,** 196–205.

Watson, J. B. *Behavior: An introduction to comparative psychology.* New York: Henry Holt, 1914.

Watson, J. B. *Behaviorism.* New York: People's Institute Publishing Company, 1924.

Willems, E. P., & Raush, H. L. *Naturalistic viewpoints in psychological research.* New York: Holt, 1969.

6

Conclusion

Paul Ekman
University of California, San Francisco

Considering the separate chapters on facial expression in infants and children, in nonhuman primates, and on members of different cultures, we can now ask how well Darwin's central thesis fared. Chevalier-Skolnikoff tells us that Darwin's interpretation of facial expressions in nonhuman primates as *emotional* is, in light of present evidence, considered correct. Furthermore, many of the facial expressions of primates appear to have evolved, as Darwin suggested, from intention movements, the incomplete or preparatory phases of initially noncommunicative activities. And, what Darwin thought was most crucial, the evidence does indeed suggest that human facial expression has evolved from nonhuman primate facial expressions.

Darwin's view is also supported by Charlesworth and Kreutzer's review of the research on infants and children. They show Darwin to have been correct in claiming that facial expressions of emotion appear early in life, and that therefore extensive learning is apparently not required for their appearance. Furthermore, they interpret the research on the blind as favoring Darwin's hypothesis that facial expressions do not require visual learning for their appearance, and thus facial expressions are at least partially the result of innate factors.

My own review of facial expressions shown by members of different cultures also supports Darwin's claims. In studies of 13 literate and two visually isolated preliterate cultures, the same facial expressions were found to be associated with the same emotions. Thus there is definitive evidence that some facial expressions of emotion are universally characteristic of the human species.

The convergence of evidence in support of Darwin, across species, across cultures, in infants and children, and in the blind, is remarkable especially in view of the fact that Darwin's work on emotional expression was so long uninfluential (see Chapter 1). Together these various sources of information strongly argue for an innate contribution to facial expression. Each of the authors of this book takes that view, although each is careful to point out that facial expressions of emotion are the result of the complex interplay between innate and environmental factors. There is agreement about the aspect of facial expression where there is a major genetic contribution: it is the morphology of facial expression, the particular patterning of the appearance of the face for each particular emotion that is said to be constant. Different ways in which learning or other environmental influences may determine facial expression are considered by the different authors, although there is no logical inconsistency in what they each mention. Such environmental factors determine or condition the time at which a facial expression is first shown, how often it will reappear, the extent to which and the manner in which it is controlled according to socially learned rules about facial appearance, some of the events that elicit it, and many of the other behavioral consequences which coincide with it or immediately follow it. Our knowledge of just how these factors operate in children, across cultures, and across species is still quite deficient.

*

In the last few pages of Darwin's own concluding chapter, he discussed the importance for our welfare of expressive movements of the face and body, whatever their origin might be. He first mentions that they serve as the initial means of communication between the mother and her infant. This is a topic that is now receiving considerable research attention (Rosenfeld, 1971). Next Darwin mentions that we can perceive sympathy from others by their facial expression, and this creates good feelings. I know of no current research on this topic. The third way this phenomenon is relevant to human welfare is that "The movements of expression give vividness and energy to our spoken words [Darwin, 1965, p.364]." The relationship between body movement, facial expression, and speech is one of the most active areas of current research (see for example Dittmann & Llewellyn, 1969; Efron, 1972; and Freedman, Blass, Rifkin, & Quitkin, 1972). Next Darwin writes, "They reveal the thoughts and intentions of others more truly than do words, which may be falsified [1965, p.364]." The study of the differences between facial expression and body movement in the way each may reveal or conceal information when a person is attempting to deceive another has been a major area of investigation in the last four years (Ekman & Friesen 1969; 1972, in press). Darwin also proposed that it the physiognomy of the face—the permanent appearance of the face—contains any truthful information, it does so because the frequent use of particular facial movements, presumably in connection with repeated emotional experiences or simulations, leads to the development of permanent facial wrinkling. Other writers have commented on such a possibility, but no one has taken a systematic approach to investigating this aspect of static facial appearance. Finally, Darwin mentioned that the free expression of an emotion intensifies it, while the repression of outward signs softens it. This is another area in which little research has yet been done, although a number of investigators have been considering studying what happens, for example, to psychophysiological measures of arousal, such as heart rate, when a person attempts to control facial expressions.

This brief summary should indicate that Darwin was cognizant of many of the uses of emotional expression as well as many of the intriguing questions which could be asked about it. Actually, Darwin mentioned but did not fully develop other fascinating ideas about emotional expression, many of which remain significant but unanswered questions today. For the reader whose interest in emotional expression has been sparked by this book, it might be well to indicate that a new field of study, nonverbal communication, is continuing aspects of Darwin's work and has become an increasingly popular subject for scientific study. Some of the books published in the last two years on nonverbal communication are: *Emotion in the Human Face* by Ekman, Friesen, and Ellsworth (1972); *Nonverbal Communication,* edited by Hinde (1972); *The Face of Emotion* by Izard (1971); *Nonverbal Communication in Human Interaction* by Knapp (1972); and *Nonverbal Communication* by Mehrabian (1972).

*

In the last sentences of his book on emotional expression Darwin said,

> We have also seen that expression in itself, or the language of the emotions, as it has sometimes been called, is certainly of importance for the welfare of mankind. To understand, as far as possible, the source or origin of the various expressions which may be hourly seen on the faces of the men around us, not to mention our domesticated animals, ought to possess much interest for us. From these several causes, we may conclude that the philosophy of our subject has well deserved the attention which it has already received from several excellent observers, and that it deserves still further attention, especially from any able physiologist [1965, p.366].

One hundred years later these words endure.

REFERENCES

Darwin, C. *The expression of the emotions in man and animals.* London: John Murray, 1872. Reprinted Chicago: Univ. of Chicago Press, 1965.

Dittmann, A. T., & Llewllyn, L. G. Body movement and speech rhythm in social conversation. *Journal of Personality and Social Psychology,* 1969, **11**(2), 98–106.

Efron, D. *Gesture and environment.* New York: King's Crown, 1941. Reprinted as *Gesture, race, and culture.* The Hague: Mouton, 1972.

Ekman, P., & Friesen, W. V. Nonverbal leakage and clues to deception. *Psychiatry,* 1969, **32**, 88–105.

Ekman, P., & Friesen, W. V. Detecting deception from the body or face. *Journal of Personality and Social Psychology,* 1972, in press.

Ekman, P., Friesen, W. V., & Ellsworth, P. *Emotion in the human face: Guidelines for research and an integration of findings.* New York: Pergamon, 1972.

Freedman, N., Blass, T., Rifkin, A., & Quitkin, F. Body movements and verbal encoding of aggressive affect. *Journal of Personality and Social Psychology,* 1972, in press.

Hinde, R. A. (Ed.), *Nonverbal communication.* London: Cambridge Univ. Press, 1972.

Izard, C. E. *The face of emotion.* New York: Appleton, 1971.

Knapp, M. L. *Nonverbal communication in human interaction.* New York: Holt, 1972.

Mehrabian, A. *Nonverbal communication.* Chicago: Aldine, 1972.

Rosenfeld, H. Time-series analysis of mother infant interaction. Project K-1A, Progress Report, Kansas Center for Research in Early Childhood Education. November, 1971, Univ. of Kansas.

EPILOGUE

Paul Ekman
University of California, San Francisco

In December 1972, after the completion of the writing of this book, I had the good fortune to visit the Library at Cambridge University, where I examined materials in the Darwin archives. I looked through Darwin's own copy of his expression book. Darwin had noted typographical errors in the printing, and had jotted minor changes in wording for an anticipated but unrealized second edition. The archival materials contained a number of notes for and partial early drafts of the expression book. There were also copies of some of the reviews of the expression book and Darwin's answers to his reviewers.

The materials did not shed much new light on Darwin's thinking, but they did give an intimate impression of Darwin's curiosity and carefulness. An example:

> Baboons seem to act consciously when they threaten by opening their mouths and showing their great canine teeth; for Mr. Bartlett has had species with their canine teeth sawn off, and these never acted in this manner; they would not show their comrades that they were powerless [November 12, 1873, Vol. 53.1, Darwin Archives, Cambridge Library].

Chevalier-Skolnikoff told me that Washburn and DeVore, who have studied baboons in natural settings in Kenya, have made similar observations; older baboons who have lost their teeth try not to reveal their lack of teeth when they yawn.

The archives also contain hundreds of photographs which Darwin had collected in preparing the expression book. Most are of mental patients, are rather gloomy to inspect, and are not very informative about more than the clothing of that time. Looking at the other pictures in the collection, I was impressed that Darwin had most sensibly published in the expression book the best and most interesting of his photographs. I have included a few of the photographs not previously published to give the reader a flavor of the archival material and the notes Darwin made about the pictures.[1]

Figure 1 is a previously unpublished drawing of a dog; on it are Darwin's notes to the artist about what was wrong in the drawing. Figure 2 is a reproduction of the drawing Darwin actually used in his expression book (as Figure 5).

FIGURE 1

[1] I am grateful to the Cambridge University Library for permission to publish these photographs, and to Mr. P. J. Gautrey for his aid in my inspection of the archives.

FIGURE 2

Figure 3 shows an example of shrugging the shoulders, a gesture Darwin wrote about in Chapter XI of the expression book. Darwin rejected this photograph, noting next to the picture that "the head is too much on one side—shoulders more raised—mouth a little open." Figure 4 shows the figure Darwin published in its place (as part of Plate VI).

FIGURE 3

FIGURE 4

FIGURE 5

Figure 5 shows photographs of an actor attempting to reproduce the facial expression of an infant. On these photographs, not before published, Darwin noted, "Fun only—[and presumably giving the actor's comment] There I laughed! violently, ha, ha, ha—in the other I cried eee yet how similar in expression."

Author Index

Numbers in italics refer to the pages on which the complete references are listed.

A

Ahrens, R., 107, 120, 121, *162*
Allport, F. H., 229, 242, *254*
Allport, G., 127, *162*
Altmann, S. A., 12, 17, 18, 20, 21, 22, 29, 36, 39, 41, *83*, *84*
Ambrose, J. A., 106, 108, 151, *162*
Amen, E. W., 146, *162*
Andrew, R. J., 20, 21, 30, 41, 59, 60, 61, 62, *84*, 233, *254*
Aronson, L., 52, *84*
Asch, S., 242, *254*

B

Banham, K. M., 115, *162*
Bard, P., 44, *84*
Barker, R. G., 251, *254*
Barlow, G., 249, *254*
Bassett, J., 143, 145, 146, *167*
Bastian, J. R., 28, *84*
Bates, E., 135, *166*
Beach, F. A., 29, *84*, 171, *220*,
Berlyne, D. E., 117, *162*
Berne, E. V. C., 133, *162*
Bernstein, I. S., 43, *88*

Bertrand, M., 17, *84*
Birdwhistell, R. L., 5, 8, 9, 127, *162*, 185, 186, 198, 210, *220*
Blass, T., 258, *260*
Blatz, W. E., 103, 105, 106, *162*
Blurton-Jones, N. G., 9, 9, 111, 128, 129, *162*, *163*, 198, *220*
Bolles, R. C., 251, *254*
Boring, E. G., 3, *9*, 241, *254*
Bowlby, J., 108, *163*
Brackett, C. W., 128, 129, 130, *163*
Brain, C. K., 33, *85*
Bridges, K. M. B., 112, 113, 114, 115, 118, 128, 130, 131, 132, 133, 158, *163*
Bronson, G. W., 116, *163*
Bruner, J. S., 147, *163*
Brunswik, E., 223, 242, 243, 245, 246, 247, 251, *254*
Buettner-Janusch, J., 60, *84*
Bühler, C., 106, 109, 121, 122, 158, *163*
Burrell, H., 59, *84*
Busnel, R. G., 32, *84*
Buzby, D., 146, *163*

C

Campbell, C. B. G., 251, *255*
Carpenter, C. R., 12, 15, *84*

Carr, H. A., 238, *254*
Caul, W. F., 37, 40, *87*
Charlesworth, W. R., 117, 122, 123, 131,
    153, 154, 155, 157, *163, 166*
Chevalier-Skolnikoff, S., 16, 18, 24, 26,
    31, 37, 64, 66, 67, *84, 163*
Clark, W. E., 51, 52, 53, 61, *84*
Clayton, F., 122, 126, *167*
Coleman, J., 146, *163*
Collias, N. E., 32, *84*
Conaway, C. H., 43, *84*
Craig, W., 242, *254*
Crile, G. W., 128, 142, *163*
Cüceloglu, D. M., 197, *220*

D

Damarin, F., 145, *166*
Darling, F. F., 151, *84*
Darwin, C., 1, 2, 6, 7, 8, 10, 11, 12, 18, 19,
    20, 30, 31, 32, 43, 49, 83, *84*, 95, 98,
    105, 106, 108, 109, 112, 115, 117, 118,
    119, 122, 128, 129, 130, 132, 140, *163*,
    171, 172, 173, *220*, 223, 224, 225, 226,
    227, 228, 229, 230, 232, *254*, 258, 259,
    260
Dashiell, J. F., 141, 147, *163*, 210, *220*
Davis, K., 150, *163*
Delgado, J. M. R., 56, 57, *84, 85*, 87
Dennis, M. G., 105, 106, 108, 109, 151, *164*
Dennis, W., 102, 105, 106, 108, 109, 150,
    151, *163, 164*
Desai, M. H., 131, *164*
Dethier, V. G., 52, *85*
DeVore, I., 12, 18, *85, 89*
Dickey, E. C., 200, *220*
Ding, G., 130, *164*
Dittmann, A. T., 186, *220*, 258, *260*
Dodsworth, R. O., 37, *85*
Duchenne, B., 8, *10*
Dumas, G., 155, 157, *164*
Dunlap, K., 146, *164*
Dusenbury, D., 145, 146, *164*
Dyk, R. B., 145, *167*
Dymond, R., 146, *164*

E

Efron, D., 258, *260*

Eibl-Eibesfeldt, I., 100, 108, 129, 153, 154,
    164, 252, *254*
Eisele, S. G., 42, *85*
Ekman, P., 9, *10*, 21, 38, 54, 77, 79, *85*,
    141, 147, 162, *164*, 171, 176, 181, 184,
    188, 190, 195, 198, 201, 202, 204, 205,
    206, 210, 211, 212, 214, 215, 216, 219,
    220, *221*, 252, 253, *254*, 259, *260*
Ellsworth, P., 162, *164*, 176, 195, 201, 202,
    206, 215, *221*, 252, 253, *254*, 259, *260*
Enders, A., *164*
Engen, T., 205, *221*
England, A. O., 134, *164*
Ervin, F. R., 251, *254*
Exline, R. V., 201, 215, *222*

F

Farris, D., 135, *166*
Fattuson, H. F., 145, *167*
Fenton, J. C., 109, *164*
Foley, J. P., Jr., 177, *221*
Fong, R. W., 203, *222*
Fraiberg, S., 154, *164*
Freedman, D. G., 125, 152, *164*
Freedman, N., 258, *260*
Friesen, W. V., 9, *10*, 21, 77, *85*, 141, 147,
    162, *164*, 176, 181, 184, 190, 195, 198,
    201, 202, 204, 205, 206, 210, 211, 212,
    214, 215, 216, 217, *221*, 252, 253, *254*,
    259, *260*
Frijda, N. H., 162, *164*, 206, *221*
Frois-Wittmann, J., 205, *221*
Fulcher, J. S., 156, 159, *164*

G

Galanter, E., 17, *87*
Garcia, J., 251, *254*
Gardner, B. T., 28, *85*
Gardner, H., 158, *164*
Gardner, J., 158, *164*
Gardner, R. A., 28, *85*
Gartlan, J. S., 33, *85*
Gates, G. S., 140, 143, 144, 145, 146, 147,
    164
Gesell, A., 107, *164*
Gewirtz, J., 151, *165*

Ghiselin, M. T., 2, 4, 6, *10*, 14, 15, *85*, 223,
	230, 231, 232, 254, *255*
Gilbert, D., 146, *165*
Gombrich, E. H., 8, *10*
Goodenough, D. R., 145, *167*
Goodenough, F. L., 123, 132, 146, 153,
	154, *165*
Gorer, G., 179, *221*
Gottheil, E., 201, 215, *222*
Goy, R. W., 42, 43, *85*, *89*
Grant, N. G., 9, *10*, 198, *221*
Gray, H., 75, *85*
Gregg, A., 130, *165*
Gregory, W. K., 58, 59, *85*
Guernsey, M., 158, *165*

H

Hailman, J. P., 250, *255*
Haith, M. M., 120, *166*
Hall, K. R. L., 21, 29, 33, *85*
Hamburg, D. A., 29, *89*
Hamilton III, W. J., 15, *87*
Hammond, K. R., 243, 244, 247, 248, *255*
Hansen, E. W., 37, *86*
Harlow, H. F., 29, 37, *85*, *86*
Harlow, M. K., 37, *85*, *86*
Hearn, L., 175, *221*
Hebb, D. O., 146, *165*
Heidbreder, E., 237, *255*
Heider, E., 214, *221*
Herbert, J., 42, *87*
Herzka, H. S., 97, 106, 110, *165*
Hilgard, E. R., 92, *165*
Hill, W. C. O., 60, 61, *86*
Hinde, R. A., 12, 18, 21, 24, 30, 33, *86*,
	88, 259, *260*
Hjortsjo, C. H., 9, *10*, 198, *221*
Hodos, W., 251, *254*
Holaday, J. W., 43, *88*
Holmes, F. B., 134, *165*
Honkavaara, S., 113, 123, 139, 141, *165*
Huber, E., 9, *10*, 30, 58, 59, 60, 61, 63, 64,
	68, 74, 75, 77, *86*
Hughes, R., 146, *164*
Hulin, W., 140, *165*
Hull, C. L., *255*
Hunt, W. A., 215, *221*
Hutt, Corinne, 161, *165*
Hutt, S. J., 161, *165*

I

Imanishi, K., 39, *86*
Irvine, W., 231, *255*
Itard, J., 149, *165*
Izard, C. E., 20, 77, *86*, 143, 144, 146,
	162, *165*, *166*, 208, 209, *221*, 259, *260*

J

James, W., 134, *165*, 237, *255*
Jay, P. C., 21, *86*
Jenness, A., 141, *165*
Jennings, H. S., 235, *255*
Jersild, A. T., 130, 132, 134, *164*, *165*
Jersild, C. L., 134, *165*
Jones, H. E., 134, *165*
Jones, M. C., 106, 117, 134, *165*

K

Kashinsky, M., 145, *165*
Katz, D., 140, *165*
Kaufman, I. C., 21, 39, *86*
Kawai, M., 39, *86*
Kawamura, S., 39, *86*
Kenderdine, M., 130, *166*
Kessen, W., 120, *166*
Klineberg, O., 175, 176, 177, *221*, *222*
Klopfer, P. H., 250, *255*
Knapp, M. L., 259, *260*
Knapp, P. H., 1, *10*
Knower, F. H., 145, 146, *164*, 200, *220*
Kodama, M., 216, *222*
Koelling, R. A., 251, *254*
Kohts, N., 18, *86*
Kreutzer, M. A., 122, *166*
Kwint, L., 159, *166*

L

La Barre, W., 5, *10*, 179, 180, *222*
Lambert, W. W., 193, 194, *222*
Lancaster, J. B., 28, *86*
Landis, C., 215, *222*
Latta, J., 22, *89*
Lazarus, R. S., 216, *222*

Lehrman, D. S., 29, *86*, 171, *222*
Lemond, C. M., 143, *166*
Leuba, C., 109, *166*
Leventhal, H., 9, *10*
Levy, N., 205, *221*
Levy-Schoen, A., 146, *166*
Leyhousen, P., 26, *87*
Lind, J., 105, *166*, *167*
Linton, E., 130, *165*
Llewllyn, L. G., 258, *260*
Lockard, R. B., 239, 251, *255*
Loeb, J., 235, *255*
Lorenz, K., 171, *222*, 248, *255*
Lubbock, J., 235, *255*

M

MacLean, P. D., 45, 46, 56, 57, *87*
Malthus, T. R., 226, *255*
Markey, F. V., 132, 134, *165*
Marler, P., 15, 20, 21, 28, 31, 32, 33, 71, *87*, *89*
Mason, W. A., 37, 38, 40, *87*
Marvin, R., 135, *166*
McCarter, R., 77, *89*, 205, 206, *222*
McDougall, W., 241, *255*
McFarland, M., 132, 133, *166*
McGowan, B. K., 251, *254*
McGuire, W. J., 244, 251, *255*
Mehrabian, A., 259, *260*
Meltzer, L., 146, *167*
Mendel, G. J., 35, *87*
Messick, S., 145, *166*
Michael, R. P., 42, *87*
Miller, G. A., 17, *87*
Miller, M., 130, *165*
Miller, R. E., 19, 37, 39, 40, *87*
Millichamp, D. A., 103, 105, 106, *162*
Mirsky, A. F., 56, *88*
Mirsky, I. A., 37, 39, 40, *87*
Mistschenka, M. N., 156, *166*
Moore, K. C., 119, *166*
Morgan, C. L., 235, *255*
Moskowitz, N., 52, *87*
Moynihan, M., 33, 36, 42, *87*
Murphy, G., 127, 129, 136, *166*, 242, *255*
Murphy, J. V., 39, *87*
Murphy, L. B., 127, 129, 136, *166*

N

Napier, J. R., 61, *87*
Nappier, P. H., 61, *87*
Netter, F. H., 45, *87*
Newcomb, T. M., 127, 129, 136, *166*
Nissen, H. W., 12, *87*
Noback, C. R., 52, *87*

O

Odom, R. D., 143, *166*
Opton, E., Jr., 216, *222*
Osgood, C. E., 206, *222*

P

Papez, J. W., 44, 45, 46, *87*,
Paredes, A., 201, 215, *222*
Parke, R. D., 158, *167*
Partanan, T. J., 105, *166*, *167*
Peiper, A., 105, 112, 116, 117, 127, 128, 142, 160, *166*
Petrinovich, L., 232, 250, *255*
Phoenix, C. H., 43, *89*
Piaget, J., 107, 158, *166*
Ploog, D., 22, *89*
Plutchik, R., 206, *222*
Postman, L., 243, 244, 245, *255*
Premack, D., 28, *87*, *88*
Preyer, W., 93, 108, 109, 117, *166*
Pribram, K. H., 17, 44, 56, *87*, *88*

Q

Quitkin, F., 258, *260*

R

Raabe, V., 146, *164*
Raush, H. L., 251, *256*
Reynolds, F., 72, *88*
Reynolds, V., 72, *88*
Rheingold, H. L., 106, 107, *166*
Ricketts, A. F., 132, 133, *166*
Rifkin, A., 258, *260*
Robinson, B. W., 56, *88*

Romer, A. S., 50, 51, 52, 53, *88*
Rosberg, G., 105, *166*
Rose, J. E., 51, *88*
Rose, R. M., 43, *88*
Rosenblum, L. A., 21, 39, 43, *86*, *88*
Rosenfeld, H., 258, *260*
Rosvold, H. E., 56, *88*
Rowell, T. E., 12, 18, 21, 24, 33, 41, *86*, *88*
Ruckmick, C. A., 146, *166*

S

Sackett, G. P., 37, 40, *88*
Sade, D. S., 39, 43, *84*, *88*
Salapatek, P. H., 116, 120, *166*
Samuels, M., 247, *255*
Savitsky, J. C., 146, *166*
Scarr, S., 116, *166*
Schaffer, H. R., 117, *166*
Schaller, G. B., 72, *88*
Schlosberg, H., 205, *221*
Schnierla, T. C., 15, 16, *88*
Seligman, M. E. P., 251, *255*
Sharp, E., 9, *10*
Sherman, M., 112, 123, *167*
Shinn, M. W., 93, *167*
Shirek-Ellefson, J., 18, 21, 22, 24, 25, 28, *88*
Simonds, P., 21, 24, *88*
Singh, J. A., 149, *167*
Skinner, B. F., 241, *255*
Sobotta, J., 75, *88*
Sorenson, E. R., 77, *85*, 204, 210, *221*
Spencer, H., 225, *255*
Spitz, R. A., 106, 107, 121, *167*
Sroufe, L. A., 109, *167*
Staffieri, R., 143, 145, 146, *167*
Stellar, E., 52, *85*
Stirnimann, F., 112, 114, 116, *167*
Stone, L. J., 151, *167*
Storer, T. I., 50, *88*
Struhsaker, T. T., 28, *88*
Szebenyi, E. S., 58, 63, *88*

T

Tagiuri, R., 147, *163*
Thompson, D., 146, *167*

Thompson, J., 152, 153, *167*
Thorndike, E. L., 236, 238, 239, *255*
Tiedemann, O., 109, *167*
Tinbergen, N., 30, *89*, 248, 249, 250, 251, *255*
Tinker, M. A., 146, *165*
Tolman, E. C., 241, 243, *255*
Tomita, M., 216, *222*
Tomkins, S. S., 9, *10*, 77, *89*, 162, *167*, 178, 182, 184, 198, 204, 205, 206, 208, 216, *221*, *222*, 252, *255*
Triandis, H. C., 193, 194, *222*

U

Usinger, R. L., 50, *88*

V

Valentine, C. W., 116, 134, *167*
Vallane, E., 105, *167*
Vandenbergh, J. G., 43, *89*
Van Hooff, J. A. R. A. M., 18, 20, 21, 22, 23, 24, 36, 39, 42, 59, 60, 64, 66, 67, 69, 70, 71, 72, 79, 80, *89*
VanLawick, H., 71, *89*
Van Lawick-Goodall, J., 69, 70, 71, 72, 74, *89*, 178, *222*
Vinacke, W. E., 203, 215, *222*
Vuorenkoski, V., 105, *166*, *167*

W

Walters, R. H., 158, *167*
Warden, C. J., 224, 235, 236, 240, *256*
Warnen, L. H., 236, *256*
Washburn, R. W., 106, 107, 109, 110, *167*
Washburn, S. L., 12, 29, 77, *89*
Wasz-Hockert, O., 105, *166*, *167*
Watson, J. B., 107, 112, 113, 114, 116, 117, 118, 129, 134, 135, *167*, 239, 240, *256*
Weiner, M., 145, *165*
Wilcox, B., 122, 126, *167*
Willems, E. P., 251, *256*

Williams, F. E., 175, *222*
Wilson, A. P., 43, *89*
Winkelmayer, R., 201, 215, *222*
Winter, P., 22, *89*
Witkin, H. A., 145, *167*
Wolf, K. M., 106, 107, 121, *167*
Wolff, P. H., 105, 106, 107, 108, 116, 129
    167, 168
Woodworth, R. S., 146, *168*, 206, *222*
Woolsey, C. N., 51, *88, 89*

Y

Young, W. C., 43, *89*

Z

Zahn, C., 131, *163*
Zazzo, R., 158, *168*
Zimmerman, R. R., 37, *86*
Zingg, R. M., 149, *167, 168*

Subject Index

A

Affection
  in animals, 48, 62, 67, 69, 70, 72
  in infants and children, 97, 115, 133
Anger
  across cultures, 194-195, 202, 205,
    206-207, 209, 211, 212
  in animals, 26-27, 48, 62, 64-66, 69, 72,
    82
  in humans, 77-78, 184, 201
  in infants and children, 95-96, 114-115,
    132-133, 153-157
Anthropomorphism, 2-3, 15, 230, 235
Antithesis, principle of, 13-14, 30-31, 229

B

Behavioral units in primate research, 17
Blends of facial expression
  in animals, 26-28
  in humans, 77, 182, 196, 198-199,
    204-205
Brunswik and Darwin, 243-248, 250-251

C

Communication, definition in animal
  studies, 21

Contempt, *see* Disgust
Context and facial expression
  in animals, 28
  in infants, 123
  in judgment studies, 191-192
Cortical control of facial expression, 54,
  56-57
Crying, 80, 97-98, 104-106, 128-129, 150,
  153
Cultural relativism, 174-175, 179

D

Delight, 113-114, 130-131
Determinants of facial expression, 30-48
  evolutionary adaptation, 30-34
  experience, 36-41
  external stimuli, 41-42
  genetic potential, 35-36
  hormones, 42-43
  muscular anatomy, 46-48
  nervous system, 43-46
Development of facial expression
  in humans, 91-162
  in primates, 37
Direct action of nervous system,
  principle of, 13, 14, 229
Disgust, 79, 82, 183, 201
  across cultures, 205-207, 209, 212

Displacement activities, 30-31
Display rules, 54, 176-177, 186-187, 195,
   215-217, 253
Distress, 113-114, 209
Dominance status and facial expression, 24,
   39

E

Ecological validity, 246-247, 252-253
Embarrassment, 100, 118, 135-136, 180
Emblematic expressions, 183-184, 205, 215
Emblems, 181-182
Enjoyment, *see* Happiness
Ethology, 6, 15, 100, 248-251, 252
Excitement
   across cultures, 209
   in animals, 67, 71-72, 178
Expression versus recognition, 104, 139, 188

F

Fear
   across cultures, 205-207, 211-212
   in animals, 26-27, 48, 62, 64-66, 69, 72,
      78
   in humans, 183, 199, 201
   in infants and children, 97, 115-117, 133,
      134, 155-157

G

Gestures, *see* Emblems
Grief, 101

H

Happiness, 77, 79, 155-157, 176, 183, 201
   across cultures, 202, 205-207, 209,
      211-212
Humiliation, *see* Shame

I

Innate versus learned basis of facial
   expression, 4, 29-30, 49, 93, 102, 111,

   125, 148, 157, 160, 170-171, 179, 219,
      258
Instinct, *see* Innate versus learned basis of
   facial expression
Intention movements, 30, 257
Intentionality, 21, 23, 39
Interest, *see* Excitement

J

Jealousy, 98-99, 118, 134-135
Joy, *see* Happiness
Judgment of chimpanzee facial expression
   by humans, 177-179
Judgment of faces as a research method,
   174, 188-189, 191-192, 195-197

K

Kinesics, 185-186

L

Lamarck's theory, 5, 31-32, 36, 225, 230,
   235
Laughing, 80-81, 108-110, 129-130,
   153-154, 180
Learned basis of facial expression, *see*
   Innate versus learned basis of facial
   expression
Limbic system, 52-54, 56-57

M

Measuring facial expression, 111, 188
Mental continuity, doctrine of, 227-228,
   236, 239
Methodological problems
   cross-cultural studies, 173
   infant's recognition of facial expression,
      119-120
   number of stimulus persons, 191, 195
   posing facial expression, 190-191, 215
   selecting faces for a judgment study,
      190-191, 204-205
   studying children's expressions, 137

studying infant expressions, 96-97, 123-124, 126
visual isolation of observers of facial expressions, 195, 197, 203-204, 209-210
Muscular anatomy of facial expression, 46-48, 58-82

N

Natural selection, principle of, 5, 31-32, 36, 227, 234-235
Nervous system, evolution of, 50-58

P

Papez's theory of emotion, 44-47, 56
Photographs versus films, 147, 201
Posed facial expressions, 189-191, 203, 214-215

R

Rage, see Anger
Representative design, 245-248
Ritualization, 30

S

Sadness
across cultures, 202, 205-207
in animals, 71-72, 81-82
in humans, 77, 79, 81, 153, 155-157, 201, 212
Serviceable associated habits, principle of, 13, 30, 229

Sexual selection, principle of, 228
Shame, 100, 118, 135-136, 209
Shyness, 99, 118, 135-136
Similarities in facial expression
across cultures, 169-220
in apes and humans, 80-82
in blind and sighted children, 152-157
Simulated facial expressions, 183-184, 215
Smiling, 80, 98, 106-108, 113, 129-130, 151-154, 175-177, 183-186
Startle, see Surprise
Submission, 22, 66, 69-70, see also Fear
Surprise, 79, 82, 117-118, 131-132, 153-155, 183, 192, 199, 201
across cultures, 205-207, 209, 212
Systematic design, criticism of, 244-245, 247

T

Terror, see Fear
Threat, 22, 24-27, 62, 64, 66, 69

V

Variability in facial expression
between species, 26, 36
within species, 36, 38
Vocalization and facial expression
in animals, 32, 61-62
in infants, 105, 144
Voluntary control of facial expression
in animals, 38, 58
in contrast to spontaneous expressions in the blind, 155-157
in relation to cultural rules about control of facial expression, 176, 185-186
in relation to emblematic and simulated expressions, 182-183